CHRISTFORMATION IN YOU

FROM GENESIS TO REVELATION: THE BIG PICTURE

RONALD
AND
CHRISTINAL PILLAI

WestBow
PRESS
A DIVISION OF THOMAS NELSON

WestBow Press books may be ordered through booksellers or by contacting:
WestBow Press
A Division of Thomas Nelson
1663 Liberty Drive
Bloomington, IN 47403
www.westbowpress.com
1-(866) 928-1240

ISBN: 978-1-4497-3577-7 (sc)
ISBN: 978-1-4497-3578-4 (hc)
ISBN: 978-1-4497-3576-0 (e)
Library of Congress Control Number: 2011963391

Printed in the United States of America
WestBow Press rev. date: 3/2/2012

DEDICATION

To all of God's beloved children, born and yet to be born again of the Holy Spirit in Christ our Lord for the eternal glory of the heavenly Father; who resides in every nation, city, tribe, and village of all the languages of this world.

"My dear children, for whom I am again in the pains of childbirth until Christ is formed in you." **Galatians 4:19 (NIV)**

CONTENTS

Preface xi

Acknowledgments xiii

Introduction xv

Chapter One: What Is Christformation in You? 1

    A) There Are Only Two Kinds of Formations with God (Trees). 1

    B) There are Only Two Kinds of Wisdom (Seeds) 6

    C) God's Secret Wisdom 13

    D) God's Garden in Christ Our Lord 15

    E) Christformation Seed 22

    F) Christformation Growth 24

    G) Christformation Fruit. 26

        Summary: Chapter One. 35

Chapter Two: Why Is Christformation in You Necessary? 38

    A) Predestination of Christformation in You 38

    B) Christformation was Promised in the Garden of Eden 41

    C) God's Promise of Christformation to Abraham 45

    D) The Old Testament Type of Christformation Journey 48

    E) Christformation in the Seven Appointed Feasts of the Lord 53

    F) Milk and Honey: "Bread and Wine" for Full Christformation
       in You 61

    G) Christformation in the Tabernacle of Moses 63

        Summary: Chapter Two. 71

Chapter Three: Where Else Is Christformation Mentioned in the Bible? **74**

   A) The Four Gospels of the Lord Jesus Christ. 74

   B) In the Books of the Old Testament 77

   C) The Old Testament Prophets of God 78

   D) The New Testament Apostles of Christ 79

   E) The Book of Acts 79

   F) Pauline Epistles. 80

   G) The Book of Revelation 80

       Summary: Chapter Three. 81

Chapter Four: How Does Christformation Occur in You? **84**

   A) Christformation is the Demonstration of the Power of God—the Holy Spirit—in You 84

   B) An Explanation from the Parable of the Sower 90

   C) An Explanation from the Parable of the Hidden Treasure or Pearl 93

   D) An Explanation from the Parable of the Growing Seed, Mustard Seed, and Yeast. 98

   E) The Cost of Being a Disciple 102

   F) Christformation as the Armor of God 106

   G) Running the Race of Christformation in You with Perseverance to the End 110

       Summary: Chapter Four. 115

Chapter Five: Who Will Have Christformation? **118**

   A) There are Only Two Kinds of Objects 118

   B) An Explanation from the Parables of the Lost Sheep, Coin, and Son. 122

   C) An Explanation from the Parable of the Wise and Foolish Builders and Virgins. 129

   D) The Seven Churches in Revelation. 137

E) The New Jerusalem. 141

F) Those Fully Obedient to God the Holy Spirit (Led by the Spirit) 146

G) The Called, Chosen, and Faithful of Christ 151

Summary: Chapter Five 156

Chapter Six: Who Is Involved with Your Christformation? . . . 159

A) God the Father 159

B) God the Son 163

C) God the Holy Spirit 168

D) The Five-fold Ministry Led by God the Holy Spirit. 174

E) The Angels of God 180

F) The Old Testament Witnesses 185

G) You and Your Decision. 190

Summary: Chapter Six 195

Chapter Seven: Full Christformation in You: When Does it Occur? 198

A) An Explanation from the Parable of the True Vine 198

B) Through the Act of Sowing and Reaping. 199

C) Circumcision of the Sinful Nature by Christ through His Spirit. 205

D) The Race of Christformation toward Full Christformation in You 209

E) An Explanation from the Parable of the Talents. 213

F) Word became Flesh; Obedient Flesh becomes Word. 218

G) We will become the Dwelling of the Father, Son, and Holy Spirit. 221

Summary: Chapter Seven. 227

Conclusion: The Big Picture of Christformation in You 229

A Personal Testimony of Christformation in You. 234

PREFACE

This book, *Christformation in You*, was written over a span of thirty-four years, beginning October 9, 1977. When we first started out, we could not envision the outcome of this book. However, we were seriously searching and recording as the Word of God became real through our daily experiences in the Lord. The Holy Bible, the written Word of God, has always been the main guide and light to our path. Of course, there were many days when we struggled to accept God's word as the unchanging truth. But, in the end, we had to because it has been proven in our lives, time and again, that there is no other resounding truth that could bring us nearer to God the heavenly Father.

We need to affirmatively state here that the word of God has always been revealed to us as Jesus Christ our Lord Himself. Christ our Lord is revealed throughout the whole Bible, and it is the will of the heavenly Father for our eyes to be opened to this remarkable truth. That is exactly what this book, *Christformation in You*, is all about; a book revealing Jesus Christ our Lord from the books of Genesis to Revelation, the big picture of Christformation in you. Also, we will be delving further into God's promises and the certainty of Christformation through our total obedience to Him.

God the Holy Spirit inspired the writing of these precious truths, so we must mention that God the heavenly Father, the Lord Jesus Christ, and God the Holy Spirit are the three most important persons in our lives. We would not be where we are today if not for them. In fact, we are nothing without them. Of course, as brothers and sisters, we need each other for encouragement, for that's how God works. He makes us interdependent on one another and works through those upon whom we are dependent and vice-versa. It could be a pastor, a teacher, an evangelist, a spouse, a relative, a friend, or anyone who has the right counsel of God at the time of your need. So do not despair. He is there for you at all times.

God the heavenly Father planned that Christ should be formed in those who love Him way before the garden of Eden even existed. His plan had been revealed through the patriarchs, prophets, priests, kings, judges, and all His other servants of the Old and the New Testaments. God's eternal plan is the full formation of Christ in you. That was, is, and will be His ultimate plan. He does not shift or change. He did not have a separate plan before He created the garden of Eden and another after He had created it. He had one plan from the beginning and that is formation of Christ in you, which is being introduced through this book.

We will be delving deeply into God's plan of Christformation in you in the initial chapters of this book. Everything was created by Him and for Him. Everything was created to be like Christ our Lord, for that pleased God the heavenly Father. Everything of God was hidden in Him, and that's why He was called the Word of God. This Word was made flesh by the power of the Holy Spirit to reveal what was hidden in Him, the secret wisdom of God.

Today, God the Holy Spirit still reveals Christ our Lord to us by taking what is His and making them known to us only when we love and obey Him. He leads us to all truth about Christ our Lord, for He is the truth that leads us to the heavenly Father, to whom we cannot go except by Him. However, the Lord Jesus Christ was first revealed in the book of Genesis, and it is wise that we start this discourse from this very informative book. Follow along with us as we seek to take you from Genesis to Revelation, the big picture of Christformation in you. There will also be ample Bible references from various translations accompanying you on your journey toward a sound understanding of Christformation in you.

The writing of this book was a trying and challenging experience for us. There were many times when it seemed impossible to obey Him with this immense task. Nonetheless, we persevered with the help of God the Holy Spirit. Here we are, by His grace, provision, and strength, to deliver this message to you. God's greatest promise to His people is "I am with you." The most important thing in our lives is the assurance that God is with us in all our pursuits for Him. We felt this throughout the countless days of prayer and intercession while writing this book.

Acknowledgments

We would like to express our appreciation toward all of God's beloved people worldwide who have encouraged us during the writing, publishing, and distribution of this precious book. We would like to thank the many Christian bloggers and believers who have followed our web and blog sites since *Christformation in You* was first introduced in January 2006.

Special thanks to our editorial and publishing team, Joshua Jayam Pillai (editing) and Jeremy Pillai (illustration), for their excellent support and effort rendered toward the success of this book.

Introduction

The Lord Jesus Christ invites you to come and rest from struggling in your own strength so that you can attain full Christformation with the help and power of God the Holy Spirit. Christformation can only occur when you are born again of the Spirit of God after you have believed in and accepted the Lord Jesus Christ. This personal decision is the first step towards freedom from the grip of sin that originated from Satan, who seeks to control you through his sinful nature sown in you. To show you how you can be freed from the Devil's sinful nature, the Gospels of Matthew, Mark, Luke, and John were written under the anointing of God the Holy Spirit to guide you toward it.

Upon believing and accepting Jesus Christ as the Lord of your life, you may ask yourself, "What is happening inside of me?" You will experience the Holy Spirit's conviction of all your sins that you have and are still committing. At this point, you should confess all your sins to God. He is faithful and just to forgive you all your sins, constantly cleansing you by the precious blood of Christ. This is the most powerful and everlasting cleansing of your conscience. Thereafter, you will innately refrain from sinning.

Once you have experienced the perfect peace of God from the forgiveness of all your sins, you will be guided by the Holy Spirit to live a life of obedience to God and His Christ. The Word of God continues to be the guide to your path and the indispensable Holy Spirit helps you understand it. At this point, the leading of God the Holy Spirit becomes very real. "What happens next?" is a question that keeps you constantly listening to God the Holy Spirit for answers. Then, He leads you to Christ every step of the way towards full Christformation for the heavenly Father's pleasure and fulfillment of His eternal will in you.

But, you may ask, "Why don't all these experiences occur in my life?" In the past, we had written and posted on our blog about "The Temptations of Christ" and how it relates to Christformation in you. In that article, we pointed out how Jesus Christ was tempted by the Devil to give up obeying God's word. The Devil also attempted to deter Christ from doing God's will, which would have hindered God's work. God's Word, will, and work in a born-again child of God in Christ will always be targeted by the Devil so that he or she will give up on God completely. However, Christ victoriously showed how you can overcome the temptations of the Devil in these three areas of your life: doing as the Word says, submitting to God's will, and doing the works of God on earth.

You should listen to Christ our Lord, for He is God's appointed faithful shepherd and overseer of your life. He sacrificed himself on the cross. Why risk plodding along aimlessly, not knowing where you are heading, simply because you aren't listening to God? Instead, invite Christ to perfect your ways so that you live a life that pleases the heavenly Father.

Of course, along the way, you may stray, but through the gentle convictions of God the Holy Spirit, you can repent and turn away from your sins. You may have felt the heavy load of sin that was causing enormous guilt and discouragement as you committed them knowingly or unknowingly. Now that you are convicted of your sins, you should seek forgiveness from the Lord and make every effort to turn completely away from these sins. . This struggle may repeat itself time and again until you overcome sinful living. Overcoming a life of sin is a tumultuous but rewarding battle that occurs within you. So don't give up!

In our thirty-four years of walking by faith in the Lord, "What happens next?" was the question that lingered in our minds. In the past, the answers came as puzzle pieces rather than the big picture. We struggled with trying to understand what was happening within us and others who profess to follow the Lord Jesus Christ. We found that there were serious battles within us that left many unanswered questions. We sought the Lord with all our hearts, knowing deep inside that only He had all the answers.

We were not seeking theories because we had lots of them, but rather the practical leading of the shepherd was visibly lacking. We looked for shortcuts, but there were none. There are no shortcuts. We learned that the hard way. During that point in time, we made a lot of unnecessary mistakes in life. But, God the Holy Spirit was always there to help pick up the pieces. He is truly "The Helper" that Christ our Lord promised before He ascended to the heavenly Father's right hand. He is the One who is interceding for us to the heavenly Father. Each time we act foolishly out of our own ignorance or even in plain disobedience, He stands in the gap as our merciful High Priest.

We learned that ignorance and disobedience has limits and boundaries that straying sheep should avoid. Crossing these boundaries can result in injury or even death. During our pastoral days, some believers asked us why such drastic chastisements had come their way. The only answer we could think of was the crossing of limits and boundaries. However, we are sure that if we walk faithfully on the pathway toward full Christformation, we can avoid taking the destructive path that hurts unnecessarily and even kills. Christformation is an eternal journey under the trustworthy shepherding and oversight of the Lord Jesus Christ Himself.

In both the Old and New Testament, God's servants were commanded to seal the message to His children until His appointed time. Nevertheless, the word of God always comes with a timely message for His people. God prepares the hearts of man for hidden secrets of His kingdom, turning many toward Him when they are finally revealed. *Christformation in You* is one such message from God to you.

CHAPTER ONE:
WHAT IS CHRISTFORMATION IN YOU?

-Part One-

A) THERE ARE ONLY TWO KINDS OF FORMATIONS WITH GOD (TREES)

Christformation occurs in those who choose to "eat" from the tree of life. The sinful nature of the Devil is formed in those who choose to "eat" from the tree of death. As the divine nature of Christ matures in a believer, there will be the equal, but opposing, maturity of the sinful nature of the Devil in his children. We will learn about this more in the next chapter in the "Parable of the Weeds."

The tree of death is the tree of knowledge of good and evil that brings death if you choose to eat from it. The secret of a tree is in its formation or growth. Similarly, the formation or growth of a fetus in a womb is not certain until its safe delivery. May it be the fruit of a tree or the fruit of a womb; both of these go through rapid changes and a painful process in their formation and growth until you can see their fruit. The Lord Jesus Christ spoke about this formation through the parable of the growing seed in the Gospel according to Mark. However, in this first chapter, we will discuss truths about the "Parable of the Growing Seed" and how they relate to only two distinct formations that can occur. Let's observe how these tree formations explain Christformation in us in the parable below.

Mark 4:26–29 (NIV):
"He also said, 'This is what the kingdom of God is like. A man scatters seed on the ground. Night and day, whether he sleeps or gets up, the seed sprouts and grows, though he does not know how. All by itself, the soil produces grain—first the stalk, then the head, then the full kernel in the head. As soon as the grain is ripe, he puts the sickle to it, because the harvest has come.' "

This parable is about formation or growth that occurs in a tree by stages. The first few chapters of Genesis show God's eternal plan of formation, using the parable of a tree. We can see these two distinct formations since the garden of Eden to this very day. These formations occurred and continue to occur today although one of the formations was kept hidden as a secret because of the disobedience that took place in the garden of Eden. God revealed it when the time was right. There was a formation that was sowed through the personal choice of Adam and Eve, and it was not forced against their will. The command was given as to which formation they should choose or avoid. The consequence of choosing the bad formation was laid out clearly before them, but the choice was still theirs. The decision they made was theirs alone.

Now let's discuss the actual situation in that garden, using this parable of the growing tree. Human beings were created different from the rest of God's creation, as they were created with the free will to choose between good and bad. In God's Word, the secret of the formation in human beings was always spoken in parables, whether in the Old or New Testament. Comparably, it becomes clearer in the New Testament, which is why we are able to discuss them here.

Most of the incidents in the garden of Eden were parabolic or spoken in parables; for that matter, the whole Bible is full of parables from the books of Genesis to Revelation. We call it "parabolic" because the Lord Jesus Christ repeatedly spoke about this formation through parables.

What stood out and remains till this day about the garden of Eden is the wrong choice made for the formation. Let's carefully compare these verses below and understand what the Lord Jesus Christ said because He, too, was in that garden of Eden when that sinful formation began with the partakers' choice. However, this parable was not the only one that referred to this formation in the garden of Eden. There were many more parables, and we will be looking into them in the following chapters thoroughly so that we will soundly understand truths about Christformation in you.

Matthew 7:17–20:
"Likewise, every good tree bears good fruit, but a bad tree bears bad fruit. A good tree cannot bear bad fruit, and a bad tree cannot bear good fruit. Every tree that does not bear good fruit is cut down and thrown into the fire. Thus, by their fruit you will recognize them."

The Lord Jesus Christ reveals Himself as the "good tree" while the Devil is referred to as the "bad tree." He said that no "bad fruit" would come out of Him nor would "good fruit" come out of the Devil. The "fruit" here refers to two different "natures" that come from them. No evil will be found in the divine nature of Christ and nothing good will be found from the sinful nature of the Devil. Jesus said we could recognize who is behind the formation in each person by looking at their nature. The formation of the tree will show by its fruit.

He acknowledged that there was a "bad tree" in God's garden while the "good tree" will be revealed that you can choose to eat from. Everything in God's garden is decided by which tree you ate or are still choosing to eat from.

The Lord Jesus Christ brings us back to the incident that happened in the garden of Eden through this parable. He said that everything had originated from there, even how we behave toward one another today. Again, He said that "by their fruit (natures produced in them) you will recognize" which "tree" they had eaten from or are still eating from. The formation of the sinful nature of the Devil in mankind was first seen in the garden of Eden. Let's look carefully into these verses in the book of Genesis below.

Genesis 3:8–13:
"Then the man and his wife heard the sound of the LORD God as he was walking in the garden in the cool of the day, and they hid from the LORD God among the trees of the garden. But the LORD God called to the man, "Where are you?" He answered, "I heard you in the garden, and I was afraid because I was naked; so I hid." And he said, "Who told you that you were naked? Have you eaten from the tree that I commanded you not to eat from?" The man said, "The woman you

put here with me—she gave me some fruit from the tree, and I ate it."
Then the LORD God said to the woman, "What is this you have done?"
The woman said, "The serpent deceived me, and I ate." "

When God walked into the garden of Eden, Adam and Eve, who
were the first created couple in the previous passage, started behaving
strangely toward Him. At once, God knew which tree they had eaten
from. He asked them, "Have you eaten from the tree that I commanded
you not to eat from?" Matthew 7:17–20 was only a reminder of what
God the heavenly Father said to Adam and Eve here.

Your behavior on earth will show which "tree" you have eaten from—
the "good" or "bad" tree. Here, God the heavenly Father knew that
they had eaten from the "bad" Tree. What exactly was bad about that
tree? First, you know that it was a "tree of death." For God the Heavenly
Father had earlier commanded Adam and Eve not to eat from it because
they would die if they did so. Let's look at these verses below.

Genesis 2:16–17:
"And the LORD God commanded the man, 'You are free to eat from
any tree in the garden; but you must not eat from the Tree of Knowledge
of Good and Evil, for when you eat from it you will certainly die.' "

We see clearly here that this "bad tree" that the Lord Jesus Christ had
reminded us about in Matthew 7:17–20, was a "tree of death" because
if Adam and Eve were to eat from it, "they would surely die." God the
Heavenly Father had warned them so. But the choice was still theirs to
obey God's commandment or not, as this choice still remains the same
for you and me today. Remember, our behavior will show to God from
which "tree" we have chosen to eat from. We cannot deceive Him. He
is the best person to judge us. We will not be able to judge between
the two natures of the "good" and the "bad" trees, but the "good" and
the "bad" trees have now been revealed to us through Christ our Lord.
Which tree would we choose to eat from? Will it be the tree of life or
the tree of death? The tree of death is also known as the tree of the
knowledge of good and evil.

Genesis 2:8–9:
"Now the LORD God had planted a garden in the east, in Eden; and there he put the man he had formed. The LORD God made all kinds of trees grow out of the ground—trees that were pleasing to the eye and good for food. In the middle of the garden were the tree of life and the tree of the knowledge of good and evil."

Visibly, there were two eternal choices they could choose from, just as the Lord Jesus Christ had reminded us in Matthew 7:17–20. They could either eat fruit from the "good" tree or "bad" tree. Please note that He did not say they could choose good *and* bad but rather good *or* bad. They could only choose one tree to eat from, not both. This is the deception that had taken place in the garden of Eden. Adam and Eve were deceived by the serpent, or the Devil, who is also referred to as Satan. The deception with a capital D was, "Eve saw that the fruit of the tree was good for food and pleasing to the eye and also desirable for *gaining wisdom*" (emphasis added). Let's look at this verse very carefully below:

Genesis 3:6:
"When the woman saw that the fruit of the tree was good for food and pleasing to the eye, and also desirable for gaining wisdom, she took some and ate it. She also gave some to her husband, who was with her, and he ate it."

She saw that it was "desirable for gaining wisdom." Isn't this a parable? What we mean is this: Is there literal fruit from a literal tree in this world that will give you wisdom to know good and evil when you eat it? Has there been ever since this world was created? No, definitely not! So, what was this parable about, precisely? This parable was about the two kinds of wisdom from the two kinds of trees that brings about two different kinds of formations in you when you choose to eat from their two different fruits.

What are the two kinds of trees and the two kinds of wisdom that bring about two different kinds of formations? We shall go into this in depth.

The two trees—the good and the bad—involved two different persons in the garden of Eden. We will see this clearer as we progress into the next section of this chapter on the two kinds of wisdom (or seeds). The fruits of the two trees are the two natures of the two persons that are chosen by the partaker. The consequences of each fruit are laid down before the partaker. The choice has always been ours, as it was for Adam and Eve, and so it remains for us today. This truth had become clearer to us after the Lord Jesus Christ revealed it through the many parables He spoke which explained the consequences of choosing the wrong tree to eat from.

B) There are Only Two Kinds of Wisdom (Seeds)

Adam and Eve had found it necessary to "gain wisdom," but they chose to eat from the wrong tree. There are explicitly only two kinds of wisdom to choose between, just as there were only two kinds of fruit from the two kinds of trees to choose from.

As we said earlier, all these parables were referring to two specific persons—one good and the other bad—whose natures (fruit) we can choose between and have their "formations" in us for eternity. Remember, the food we choose to eat is what will form our physical body. Spiritual formation also occurs from the nature we choose.

One of the two natures that brought and still brings eternal death to anyone who eats from it today is the sinful nature of the Devil. The Devil, or Satan, is the author of deception and has devised or disguised himself with many other names similar to the good but is actually good confused with bad—a counterfeit of the good, which is the cause for much of our confusion about who God actually is. Even the very elect will be deceived by this if not forewarned thoroughly.

So how do we differentiate between the two wisdoms? Let's read these verses below in the book of James:

James 3:13–18:

"Who is wise and understanding among you? Let them show it by their good life, by deeds done in the humility that comes from wisdom. But if you harbor bitter envy and selfish ambition in your hearts, do not boast about it or deny the truth. Such "wisdom" does not come down from heaven but is earthly, unspiritual, and demonic. For where you have envy and selfish ambition, there you find disorder and every evil practice. But the wisdom that comes from heaven is first of all pure; then peace-loving, considerate, submissive, full of mercy and good fruit, impartial, and sincere. Peacemakers who sow in peace reap a harvest of righteousness."

There are only two kinds of wisdom in this world. We can fill ourselves with either of them, which come in the form of seeds. Seeds need to be sown and, when properly sown, will grow into a tree that will bear fruit accordingly. If a tree only produces bad fruit, there is something terribly wrong with that original seed.

Seeds are found in the fruit, but are grown in the ground to be turned into a tree again. James 3:13–18 refers to the two different kinds of wisdom as seed needed to grow into a tree. These two wisdoms originate from two different sources. The first mentioned in this passage is one that comes from the Devil, which is "earthly wisdom," the wisdom of this world, the one that Adam and Eve had desired. This wisdom does not last. It is unspiritual wisdom and demonic. This is the wisdom that Eve found attractive and desired to gain, as recorded in Genesis 3:6. Apostle Paul refers to this wisdom as the "wisdom of this world," one that is self-destructive because it is driven by selfish ambition and bitter envy, as stated in James 3:14–15. Let us compare these two wisdoms with the Bible passage below.

1 Corinthians 1:17–20:

"For Christ did not send me to baptize, but to preach the gospel—not with wisdom and eloquence, lest the cross of Christ be emptied of its power. For the message of the cross is foolishness to those who are perishing, but to us who are being saved it is the power of God. For it is written: "I will destroy the wisdom of the wise; the intelligence of the intelligent I will frustrate." Where is the wise person? Where is the teacher of the law? Where is the philosopher of this age? Has not God made foolish the wisdom of the world? "

God will Himself destroy this earthly wisdom because it's of no good or eternal use to anyone. Those who don't know or refuse the wisdom that comes from heaven, considering it foolishness, are of the Devil, who disguises his devilish or demonic wisdom as the "wisdom of the world." How do we know that this devilish wisdom is self-destructive?

Wisdom that is driven by bitter envy and selfish ambition brings every kind of disorder and evil practice on this earth. Doesn't that sound very familiar to you? Haven't you thought of all the disorder that comes from corrupt envy and selfish ambition of men that translates into greed, jealousy, strife, covetousness, factions, cheating, lying, stealing, swindling, divisions, killings, murder, war, rioting, violence, physical abuse, and many other forms of evil practice and disorder on earth? This was the same wisdom that Adam and Eve desired. Of course, envy and selfish ambition seemed more attractive to Adam and Eve because it promised more pleasures and the pleasurable feeling that centers on self; it doesn't care how it hurts others. The end result of living such a life boomerangs too, bringing self-destruction, as we have witnessed.

As we have said from the start, wisdom is a seed that brings about a formation in you. What was the seed that was sown into Adam and Eve by the Devil through deception that resulted in their self-destruction? Adam and Eve willingly invited the embedding of the sinful nature of the Devil, and mankind has lived to obey the sinful nature ever since rather than obey God, with the exception of the few godly men and women who saw the truth of Christformation in them even during the Old Testament times. This truth will be thoroughly explained in the following chapters.

Mankind had found it more attractive to obey the sinful nature of the Devil, more pleasurable than to obey God, very much like Adam and Eve. Both formations start from two different types of seed. The wisdom that fills you brings its formation into you. But can you imagine your confusion if you claim that both wisdoms are being formed at the same time in you? Apostle Paul says in his epistles that this is not possible. One of them has to be put to death, while the other thrives.

Romans 8:12–14:
"Therefore, brothers, we have an obligation—but it is not to the sinful nature, to live according to it. For if you live according to the sinful nature, you will die; but if by the Spirit you put to death the misdeeds of the body, you will live, because those who are led by the Spirit of God are sons of God."

The Devil seeks to control your thoughts to cause your body to sin and hold you in its grip so that you continue sinning till the end. "Who is wise and understanding among you? Let them show it by their good life, by deeds done in the humility that comes from wisdom," says James 3:13. Now God is asking in this verse, "What is true wisdom and understanding?" True wisdom and understanding is the fruit you produce with your good life with deeds done in humility from the nature of the tree you have eaten from. So that tree must be wisdom, right? Let's look at these verses from the book of Proverbs. Who is this wisdom who produces a good life in us?

Proverbs 3:13–18:
"Blessed are those who find wisdom, those who gain understanding, for she is more profitable than silver and yields better returns than gold. She is more precious than rubies; nothing you desire can compare with her. Long life is in her right hand; in her left hand are riches and honor. Her ways are pleasant ways, and all her paths are peace. She is a tree of life to those who take hold of her; those who hold her fast will be blessed."

The verses above fit the description of the Tree of Life in the garden of Eden. The gender pronoun *she* is used to describe the formation that heavenly wisdom promises through reproduction, as if from the womb. Where is the Tree of Life now? He is in heaven at the right hand of the heavenly Father. Job the great, persevering, and righteous man in the Old Testament had searched for this wisdom during his days on earth. He was overjoyed when he had found Him. This is how he describes the wisdom he found:

9

Job 28:20–28 (NLT):

"But do people know where to find wisdom? Where can they find understanding? It is hidden from the eyes of all humanity. Even the sharp-eyed birds in the sky cannot discover it. Destruction and Death say "We've heard only rumors of where wisdom can be found." God alone understands the way to wisdom; he knows where it can be found, for he looks throughout the whole earth and sees everything under the heavens. He decided how hard the winds should blow and how much rain should fall. He made the laws for the rain and laid out a path for the lightning. Then he saw wisdom and evaluated it. He set it in place and examined it thoroughly. And this is what he says to all humanity: "The fear of the Lord is true wisdom; to forsake evil is real understanding." "

The passage above perfectly fits the Lord Jesus Christ, for who had obeyed God, the heavenly Father, like He did? Absolutely no one on earth! Who was and is fervent for the fear of the Lord if not Him! Wasn't the Tree of Life hidden from Adam and Eve the moment they disobeyed God, the Heavenly Father? Let us search what had happened in the garden of Eden the moment Adam and Eve sinned against God:

Genesis 3:21–24:

"The LORD God made garments of skin for Adam and his wife and clothed them. And the LORD God said, "The man has now become like one of us, knowing good and evil. He must not be allowed to reach out his hand and take also from the tree of life and eat, and live forever." So the LORD God banished him from the Garden of Eden to work the ground from which he had been taken. After he drove the man out, he placed on the east side of the Garden of Eden cherubim and a flaming sword flashing back and forth to guard the way to the tree of life."

God the heavenly Father sent Adam and Eve out of the garden of Eden because they knew good and evil now, but something else was lacking in them, and they might put their hands on the Tree of Life and live forever. That would mean both formations would grow in them together, which cannot occur simultaneously. One will live while the other will die. What was still lacking in them that even though they knew good and evil, God had to send them out of the garden? Let us compare these two verses again.

Genesis 3:22:
"And the LORD God said, 'The man has now become like one of us, knowing good and evil. He must not be allowed to reach out his hand and take also from the tree of life and eat, and live forever.' "

Hebrews 5:13–14:
"Anyone who lives on milk, being still an infant, is not acquainted with the teaching about righteousness. But solid food is for the mature, who by constant use have trained themselves to distinguish good from evil."

Knowing good and evil and distinguishing good from evil derive from two different natures. One has its origin in the sinful nature of the Devil, and the other is from the divine nature of Jesus Christ our Lord. One nature can distinguish good from evil, and the other cannot. When you are in the habit of obeying the sinful nature of the Devil, you'll *know* good and evil, but you won't know how to *distinguish* between the two.

Right will seem wrong, and bad will appear good to you. That's how the Devil or the evil demons operate. At one time, they had existed in God's presence but were later "thrown to this earth like lightning", as mentioned in the verses below. This is because sin was found in them, although they knew the truth. If you have heard the truth but do not obey it, your behavior will translate as rebellion to the Lord our God. The Devil and his minions' fall and judgment, for all their rebellion toward the Lord our God, was pronounced. We urge you to look carefully into these verses and understand what has happened to these fallen angels and where we stand with Christ, who is God's heavenly wisdom filling us.

Luke 10:17–19:
"The seventy-two returned with joy and said, 'Lord, even the demons submit to us in your name.' He replied, 'I saw Satan fall like lightning from heaven. I have given you authority to trample on snakes and scorpions and to overcome all the power of the enemy; nothing will harm you.' "

Jude 1:6:

"And the angels who did not keep their positions of authority but abandoned their proper dwelling—these he has kept in darkness, bound with everlasting chains for judgment on the great Day."

Only heavenly wisdom can give us the ability to distinguish good from evil. This heavenly wisdom fills us with the pure and divine nature of Christ, which is formed in us as we obey God's commandments. We will produce a harvest of righteousness through the divine nature of Christ like being peace–loving, considerate, submissive, full of mercy and good fruit, impartial and sincere. God the Holy Spirit is the true helper that God the Heavenly Father had sent to us for full Christformation in us. His help results in the fruit mentioned in the following Scriptures:

Galatians 5:22–25 (NLT):

"But the Holy Spirit produces this kind of fruit in our lives: love, joy, peace, patience, kindness, goodness, faithfulness, gentleness, and self-control. There is no law against these things! Those who belong to Christ Jesus have nailed the passions and desires of their sinful nature to his cross and crucified them there. Since we are living by the Spirit, let us follow the Spirit's leading in every part of our lives."

We must obey the leading of God the Holy Spirit to have the divine nature of Christ formed in us eternally. This will please our heavenly Father. The Lord Jesus Christ is the perfect example of obedience to the heavenly Father. When we obey the leading of God the Holy Spirit, Christ's divine nature will be formed in us. Before that, we must actively submit to the leading of God the Holy Spirit to put to death the misdeeds of the flesh or the sinful nature of the Devil, which will defile us with rebellion toward the Lord. The Lord Jesus had warned us about this. Let us look at more verses below.

Mark 7:20–23 (NLT):

"And then he added, 'It is what comes from inside that defiles you. For from within, out of a person's heart, come evil thoughts, sexual immorality, theft, murder, adultery, greed, wickedness, deceit, lustful desires, envy, slander, pride, and foolishness. All these vile things come from within; they are what defile you.' "

All these vile sins come from the sinful nature of the Devil sown through Adam and Eve. They have their origin from the bad tree, who is the Devil, or Satan. "Those who belong to Christ Jesus have nailed the passions and desires of the sinful nature to the cross and crucified them there," the apostle Paul reminded the believers in Galatia. Have we done this in obedience to the leading of God the Holy Spirit in every part of our lives yet? "Since we are living by the Spirit, let us follow the Spirit's leading in every area of our lives," Paul exhorts us in Galatians 5:25. If you don't actively put these vile sins to death on the cross of Christ, they will become active with the temptations that the Devil attacks with and defile you completely if you live according to these passions. God's Word is hidden in our hearts to fight temptations from the Evil One, who prowls around seeking weaklings who doubt God's promises.

C) GOD'S SECRET WISDOM

The Lord Jesus Christ is the secret wisdom of God because He was the Tree of Life in the garden of Eden that God the heavenly Father had hidden from Adam and Eve until it was God's appointed time to reveal Him to the world. As He was the hidden Word of God, he had to become flesh first. Galatians 4:4 has a record of the right time He appeared:

Galatians 4:4 (NKJV):
"But when the fullness of the time had come, God sent forth His Son, born of a woman, born under the law."

The Lord Jesus Christ was hidden from mankind since the time Adam and Eve had deliberately disobeyed God. In the Old Testament times, only the representations of Christ such as the patriarchs, prophets, priests and places of worship were revealed, but Christ Himself was hidden from man's eyes. It was not easy for ordinary men, filled with the wisdom of this world, to see Him or understand the time of His coming to this earth. Everything of God the heavenly Father was bestowed upon Christ our Lord. All secrets of God were placed on Him; you could not go to God except by Him. Let's study what these verses tell us about Him:

1 Corinthians 2:6–10:
"We do, however, speak a message of wisdom among the mature, but not the wisdom of this age or of the rulers of this age, who are coming to nothing. No, we declare God's wisdom, a mystery that has been hidden and that God destined for our glory before time began. None of the rulers of this age understood it, for if they had, they would not have crucified the Lord of glory. However, as it is written: "What no eye has seen, what no ear has heard, and what no human mind has conceived" the things God has prepared for those who love him—these are the things God has revealed to us by his Spirit. The Spirit searches all things, even the deep things of God."

Christ our Lord has been the secret wisdom of God—a mystery from the garden of Eden, a mystery of the Tree of Life. There are records heralding His coming throughout the pages of the Old Testament, yet mere men filled with the wisdom of this world did not understand it. If they had understood, they wouldn't have been evil toward Him. They had no fear for God's own Son whom He had sent to be the Redeemer and Savior of the world.

This secret wisdom of God came to be formed in all those who would believe in and love Him. He is revealed to all those who are born-again, as God the Holy Spirit assists them towards full Christformation. This secret wisdom of God is to be formed in all those who obey Him. If you love Him, you will obey Him because He is the perfect example of love and obedience to the heavenly Father.

Christ our Lord is the secret of God who is revealed as the heavenly wisdom. His divine nature is formed in you as a result of your believing and accepting Him as Lord of your life. Job, who had never cursed God for any of the testings of his faith, said in Job 28:28, "The fear of the Lord is true wisdom; to forsake evil is understanding." This is the true wisdom and understanding that will be formed in you, where you will forsake all evil and be filled with Him. If the forsaking of evil doesn't follow, it isn't the true wisdom filling you. If you are still grappling with selfish ambition and bitter envy within yourself, you are far away from the true heavenly wisdom of God, the Lord Jesus Christ. You have only the devilish formation of worldly wisdom in you. Some of us are so confused, not knowing whom we belong to. We should be convicted of our sins, repent and return to the wisdom of God, if we truly belong to Him. The world will not know Him, but we have known Him. The verses below testify that He is the wisdom of God who should fill us.

1 Corinthians 1:22–24:
"Jews demand signs and Greeks look for wisdom, but we preach Christ crucified: a stumbling block to Jews and foolishness to Gentiles, but to those whom God has called, both Jews and Greeks, Christ the power of God and the wisdom of God."

Christformation begins in you when the wisdom of God is invited to fill you through the power of God the Holy Spirit. A new garden of the Lord in Christ appears here on earth through this promise.

D) God's Garden in Christ Our Lord

God the heavenly Father has a new garden in Christ our Lord that needs to be sown again with seed for trees of righteousness in Him. Through Christformation in you, this new garden of God in Christ is being built. This is a garden that will please the Lord, built on the land He desires and had set apart.

The following verses speak of the type of land that God has prepared for His new garden. The other land with "thorns and thistles" is the Devil's garden that will be burnt up in the end by God.

Hebrews 6:7–8:
"Land that drinks in the rain often falling on it and that produces a crop useful to those for whom it is farmed receives the blessing of God. But land that produces thorns and thistles is worthless and is in danger of being cursed. In the end it will be burned."

Do you see here that there are only two types of land—one that will have the eternal blessing of God while the other will be cursed and burned? These lands refer to those in whom Christformation occurs in one and in the other in whom there is no Christformation. The latter is of no eternal use to God, so it's cursed and burned. The following verses from the book of Isaiah say what kind of garden God is preparing with Christformation in you and me.

Isaiah 61:1–3:
"The Spirit of the Sovereign LORD is on me, because the LORD has anointed me to proclaim good news to the poor. He has sent me to bind up the broken-hearted, to proclaim freedom for the captives and release from darkness for the prisoners, to proclaim the year of the LORD's favor and the day of vengeance of our God, to comfort all who mourn, and provide for those who grieve in Zion—to bestow on them a crown of beauty instead of ashes, the oil of joy instead of mourning and a garment of praise, instead of a spirit of despair. They will be called oaks of righteousness, a planting of the LORD for the display of his splendor."

These oaks of righteousness will be a planting of our heavenly Father through the power of God the Holy Spirit with eternal Christformation in all those who would believe that Christ is their Lord and Savior. Christformation in you will be the eternal beauty and splendor of the Lord. Christformation in you will be the crown of beauty; you will have no more ashes of the sinful nature in you that bring enormous guilt and shame. No more bondage to the sinful nature of the Devil that weighs you down. No more despair from not being able to overcome sinful living. Instead, you will be clothed with full Christformation that will bring praise unto God the heavenly Father for eternity through His beloved Son successfully formed in you. You will not be bound to the "thorns and thistles" that are signified as the sinful nature of the Devil. Isn't this what God the Holy Spirit is helping to set you free from—the sinful nature of the Devil?

Romans 8:26–27:
"In the same way, the Spirit helps us in our weakness. We do not know what we ought to pray for, but the Spirit himself intercedes for us through wordless groans. And he who searches our hearts knows the mind of the Spirit, because the Spirit intercedes for God's people in accordance with the will of God."

The Lord Jesus Christ intercedes to the heavenly Father for full Christformation in us. But before that occurs, God the Holy Spirit brings our inexpressible groans from our spirits to God. An example of such a groan would be the apostle Paul's lament in Romans 7:15, "For what I want to do I do not do, but what I hate I do." Let us look at this promise of God and learn to trust Him more. The Word of God is there to encourage us, especially when we feel downtrodden, brokenhearted, or discouraged.

Romans 8:34–35:
"Who then is the one who condemns? No one can. Christ Jesus who died—more than that, who was raised to life—is at the right hand of God and is also interceding for us. Who shall separate us from the love of Christ? Shall trouble or hardship or persecution or famine or nakedness or danger or sword?"

The trees of righteousness in the garden of God will go through all kinds of trials and tribulations. But who can separate them from God once Christformation has occurred in them? No one can remove them from God's garden this time, not even the Devil. The Devil may grow his weeds side by side amongst the wheat, seeking to cause confusion in God's new garden just as in the garden of Eden, but this time it won't work because Christ has been revealed and formed in these trees of righteousness. The distinction will be made clear to the world through Christformation in them because Christformation occurs deep in their born-again spirits with the help of God the Holy Spirit, who will continually form the divine nature of Christ our Lord till the end. The Parable of the Sower in Matthew 13:18–23 best describes Christformation from the start to the end. Let's examine what this very important parable reveals about Christformation in you.

Matthew 13:18–23:
"Listen then to what the parable of the sower means: when anyone hears the message about the kingdom and does not understand it, the evil one comes and snatches away what was sown in their heart. This is the seed sown along the path. The seed falling on rocky ground refers to someone who hears the word and at once receives it with joy. But since they have

no root, they last only a short time. When trouble or persecution comes because of the word, they quickly fall away. The seed falling among the thorns refers to someone who hears the word, but the worries of this life and the deceitfulness of wealth choke the word, making it unfruitful. But the seed falling on good soil refers to someone who hears the word and understands it. This is the one who produces a crop, yielding a hundred, sixty or thirty times what was sown."

Christformation in you produces the likeness of Christ our Lord in you. Your obedience to God the Holy Spirit is vital for this to occur. He reminds you about the words of Christ and convicts you of your sins so that you obey Christ. Salvation is free through the redemptive work of Christ our Lord on the cross when we believe in Him, but Christformation only occurs in your born-again spirit when you obey every word that Christ had commanded you. The Lord Jesus Christ is the Word of God. He is also the heavenly wisdom of God. This wisdom of God is tested wisdom. He Himself was tested with obedience to God the heavenly Father. Take special note of this verse below:

Hebrews 5:8–10 (NLT):
"Even though Jesus was God's Son, he learned obedience from the things he suffered. In this way, God qualified him as a perfect High Priest, and he became the source of eternal salvation for all those who obey him. And God designated him to be a High Priest in the order of Melchizedek."

Our personal obedience to God plays a very important part to the partaking of the divine nature of Christ our Lord. There are four specific steps toward Christformation in you according to the Parable of the Sower in Matthew 13:18–23. Let us see how it applies to Christformation:

1) **Hear it**

   i) You must be able to hear God's voice. God speaks, but you should be able to hear Him first. Many hear but do not listen to what He says.

ii) If you hear Him but do not understand what is exactly required of you by God, you already are defeated by the Devil. You should make every effort to understand what you hear.

2) Understand it

i) After you have heard Him, you should seek to understand what you have heard from Him because, most of the time, God speaks with parables. The Holy Spirit is there to help you.

ii) After you have heard Him and understand what He has commanded, but don't seek to act beyond that, you will remain a half-deceived person.

3) Accept it

i) After you have heard Him and understand clearly what He has commanded, you should go a step further by humbly accepting the planting of God's eternal word in you. You should be humble before God to admit that you need that word in you.

ii) If you have heard from God, understand His word, and have humbly accepted His word planted in you, yet still do not obey it, you are a fully deceived person. You should seriously check why you can't bring yourself to obey Him. Could it be rebellion?

4) Obey it

i) If after you have heard from God, understand everything He has commanded you to do, and humbly accept the planting of God's word in you, you should do as it says.

ii) Christformation in you will be determined by how much you obey all that Christ has commanded. You should fully obey God's word for full Christformation in you.

Are you able to see the truth that God's word is all about Christformation in you? If you obey only a third of God's word, there will only be a third of Christformation in you. So there is no place for carelessness or complacency in your walk with the Lord.

Of course, we do get discouraged sometimes, but God the Holy Spirit, who is the greatest comforter, will comfort and bring us back to God. This happens if we truly belong to Christ our Lord. The discouragements we go through may come in many ways, such as those mentioned in the Parable of the Sower. Check if these discouragements and temptations are truly the factors that hinder you from obeying God. Sometimes they could hinder, abort, or just stunt the growth of Christformation in you. These are tools deployed by the Devil to stop us from obeying our God.

The lack of seriousness in sowing God's word in your life, an unrepentant and hardened heart in sin, personal negligence toward preparation for trouble or persecution because of the Word, the worries of this life, the deceitfulness of wealth, or the lack of self-control in seeking the things of this world could be some of the reasons for the stunted or non-occurrence of Christformation in you. The Devil may capitalize on your weaknesses in these areas of your life if you are not watchful and prepared for the attacks with much prayer and obedience to the Lord. Like a careless soldier, we shouldn't blame anyone but ourselves for the consequential casualties. The Good Shepherd always seeks to lead us through God the Holy Spirit; speaking and convicting us of our sins and waywardness. But are we listening to Him? Consider these verses below.

John 16:7–11:
"But I tell you the truth: It is for your good that I am going away. Unless I go away, the Counselor will not come to you; but if I go, I will send him to you. When he comes, he will convict the world of guilt in regard to sin and righteousness and judgment: in regard to sin, because men do not believe in me; in regard to righteousness, because I am going to the Father, where you can see me no longer; and in regard to judgment, because the prince of this world now stands condemned."

Always remember that the Lord Jesus Christ warned us of the very important role of God the Holy Spirit toward full Christformation in us. He helps us to remember the words of Christ our Lord and God the heavenly Father at all times. Christformation is the testimony of Jesus Christ our Lord in you and is spread about as a witness by God the Holy Spirit as in the book of Acts which states:

Acts 1:8:
"But you will receive power when the Holy Spirit comes on you; and you will be my witnesses in Jerusalem, and in all Judea and Samaria, and to the ends of the earth." "

When you have Christformation increasing in you, it may not mean that you will no longer have trials and testing of your faith and that you will be strong all the time because the power of God the Holy Spirit is in you. There will be times when you will be tested to see if you will remain obedient to Him in all the circumstances of your life. Many times, because of your personal struggles and weaknesses, you may step out of line with God's Word. You may profess one thing, but your actions may show otherwise. This will be the moment when God the Holy Spirit will step in to correct your ways if you will allow Him some room for correction. If you do not respond to His gentle counsel, discipline might be necessary in order for Christformation to continue in you. Take special note of how God's discipline works for our own good in this passage below. Ample warning follows those who are careless about Christformation in them.

John 15:1–8 (NLT):
"I am the true grapevine, and my Father is the gardener. He cuts off every branch of mine that doesn't produce fruit, and he prunes the branches that do bear fruit so they will produce even more. You have already been pruned and purified by the message I have given you. Remain in me, and I will remain in you. For a branch cannot produce fruit if it is severed from the vine, and you cannot be fruitful unless you remain in me. Yes, I am the vine; you are the branches. Those who remain in me, and I in them, will produce much fruit. For apart from me you can do nothing. Anyone who does not remain in me is thrown

away like a useless branch and withers. Such branches are gathered into a pile to be burned. But if you remain in me and my words remain in you, you may ask for anything you want, and it will be granted! When you produce much fruit, you are my true disciples. This brings great glory to my Father."

When Christformation increases within you through your obedience to God's Word, the testimony of Jesus grows along with you. The measure of Christformation in you will determine how much glory is raised to the heavenly Father through you. Christ is the heavenly Father's glory, and the more He fills you, the higher will be God's approval upon your life. Christformation in you increases (or bears more fruit) only by you remaining in God's Word, which is Christ our Lord. Remaining in Him means continually obeying Him without giving up for any reason.

What happens to those who claim that they belong to the vine but are void of Christformation in them because they had refused to obey Christ our Lord? They will be "thrown away like a useless branch, gathered into a pile to be burned." But those who have remained in Christ our Lord by obeying Him and His words will have the approval of God the heavenly Father. When they ask anything in Christ's name, in accordance to God's will, it shall be answered. Discipline through hardships to prove your faithfulness at all costs will come your way to ensure continual Christformation in you. God's approval with an increasing Christformation in you through your obedience to Christ our Lord will become Christformation-seed to others. God will sow this seed through the powerful witness of God the Holy Spirit in "Jerusalem, Judea, Samaria, and the uttermost parts of this earth." as mentioned in Acts 1:8.

E) CHRISTFORMATION SEED

Matthew 13:36–43:
"Then he left the crowd and went into the house. His disciples came to him and said, "Explain to us the parable of the weeds in the field." He answered, "The one who sowed the good seed is the Son of Man, the field is the world, and the good seed stands for the people of the kingdom. The weeds are the people of the evil one, and the enemy

who sows them is the devil. The harvest is the end of the age, and the harvesters are angels. As the weeds are pulled up and burned in the fire, so it will be at the end of the age. The Son of Man will send out his angels, and they will weed out of his kingdom everything that causes sin and all who do evil. They will throw them into the blazing furnace, where there will be weeping and gnashing of teeth. [43] Then the righteous will shine like the sun in the kingdom of their Father. Whoever has ears, let them hear."

What is Christformation Seed? The Parable of the Weeds above best describes it. Christformation Seed stands for the people of the kingdom of God who have Christformation in them. They are the "good seed" who have chosen to eat the "good fruit" (His divine nature) through their believing and obedience to Christ our Lord in the heavenly Father's new garden. In the Garden of Eden, there wasn't a garden that belonged to the Lord Jesus Christ because of the presence of sin, but now, after His work on the cross at Calvary, He owns a garden through you and me who love Him. He cares for this new garden through His completed work on the cross. He places this new garden in the middle of this world as a living testimony for His glorious name to be lifted up among mankind.

The Enemy is jealous of Christ's new garden and seeks to create confusion by secretly sowing bad seed in it. The good seed grows into wheat while the bad seed grows into weeds. They are intended to confuse the world so that the weeds will be confused for the wheat and vice versa. Light will be darkness, and darkness will appear as light through the masquerading of the Devil, the demons, and his children who obey the sinful nature. The 'weeds' are those who live obeying the sinful nature. They will be seated alongside the 'wheat' who obey Christ. This may affect Christformation in those who are the 'wheat' as they may be influenced by the sinful actions of the 'weeds'. Sin can be contagious. Both will claim their right to be seated in God's garden. At one point, the servants will ask if they should pull the weeds, but the Master will say "no." For now, let them be seated together, for you will not be able to judge between the weeds and the wheat and may displace them unfairly. There is a fair judge coming soon, and He will command the angels to separate them accordingly. Each will then be placed where they rightfully belong. In Mathew 13:30, the owner of the garden, who is God Himself, allowed the weeds and the wheat to grow side by side in order that His servants do not pull up the wheat accidentally before the harvest.

This confusion will go on until the end of the age, as God the heavenly Father has willed from the beginning. He will send in the angels when the time arrives to put an end to the weeds forever. Then, those who have Christformation in them "will shine like the sun" in the kingdom of the heavenly Father through Christ their Redeemer. The weeds will be thrown into the furnace of "weeping and the gnashing of teeth" because of the distress they had caused with their sins in God's garden.

F) Christformation Growth

Matthew 13:31–35:
"He told them another parable: "The kingdom of heaven is like a mustard seed, which a man took and planted in his field. Though it is the smallest of all seeds, yet when it grows, it is the largest of garden plants and becomes a tree, so that the birds come and perch in its branches." He told them still another parable: "The kingdom of heaven is like yeast that a woman took and mixed into about sixty pounds of flour until it worked all through the dough." Jesus spoke all these things to the crowd in parables; he did not say anything to them without using a parable. So was fulfilled what was spoken through the prophet: "I will open my mouth in parables, I will utter things hidden since the creation of the world." "

Christformation growth is visible in the passage above. Christformation in you will be the greatest growth ever. Nothing can be compared with it. Although it starts with one insignificant seed, it will grow into the largest tree ever. This seed appeared as the most foolish thing in the eyes of this world, as does a mustard seed, being the smallest seed among all seeds. The one that appears the weakest will become the strongest; the meekest will become "more than a conqueror", as mentioned in Romans 8: 37-39.

What had appeared "marred and bruised" temporarily as in Isaiah 53, will become God's splendor for eternity. Seen as the poorest, most barren, and forsaken tree, it will be turned into the most fruitful tree God had ever created through full Christformation in you and me. This will bring great glory to God the heavenly Father, forever and ever. Consider what Christ our Lord had gone through for us, as Isaiah the prophet prophesied, which came to pass about His sufferings for us:

Isaiah 53:1–6 (NLT):
"Who has believed our message? To whom has the Lord revealed his powerful arm? My servant grew up in the Lord's presence like a tender green shoot, like a root in dry ground. There was nothing beautiful or majestic about his appearance, nothing to attract us to him. He was despised and rejected—a man of sorrows, acquainted with deepest grief. We turned our backs on him and looked the other way. He was despised, and we did not care. Yet it was our weaknesses he carried; it was our sorrows that weighed him down. And we thought his troubles were a punishment from God, a punishment for his own sins! But he was pierced for our rebellion, crushed for our sins. He was beaten so we could be whole. He was whipped so we could be healed. All of us, like sheep, have strayed away. We have left God's paths to follow our own. Yet the Lord laid on him the sins of us all."

Christformation in you works through your whole being just like the yeast does to the dough. The born-again spirit, the whole soul that is your mind, is fully transformed into the mind of Christ, and your new, immortal body is being prepared in heaven, which will clothe and fit you according to the Christformation in you. It will come out of your personal obedience to the leading of God the Holy Spirit. In the end, what we have sowed with our lives, we will reap individually for eternity, as we have helped to contribute to the growth of this greatest tree (creation) of God ever. All of God's children who have believed and accepted Christ our Lord to be their Redeemer and Savior will be as one, and together will be the biggest tree with God the heavenly Father, God the Son, and God the Holy Spirit dwelling with them for eternity.

G) CHRISTFORMATION FRUIT

Revelation 22:1–5:
"Then the angel showed me the river of the water of life, as clear as crystal, flowing from the throne of God and of the Lamb down the middle of the great street of the city. On each side of the river stood the tree of life, bearing twelve crops of fruit, yielding its fruit every month. And the leaves of the tree are for the healing of the nations. No longer will there be any curse. The throne of God and of the Lamb will be in the city, and his servants will serve him. They will see his face, and his name will be on their foreheads. There will be no more night. They will not need the light of a lamp or the light of the sun, for the Lord God will give them light. And they will reign for ever and ever."

Most parts of the book of Revelation contain parables. The restoration of the garden of Eden is in the passage above. The Tree of Life in this garden is Jesus Christ our Lord, and He bore twelve crops of fruit, meaning the twelve tribes of Israel in the Old Testament and His twelve disciples in the New Testament, representing God's people chosen through Christ our Lord by the washing of His blood shed for us on the cross. The River of God is God the Holy Spirit in whom we are born again. The Tree of Life yielded its "fruit every month," meaning there was full Christformation in those who obeyed God and His Christ, which pleases Him. Healing comes through Christ our Lord to all His people, and all the curses of the garden of Eden earned by Adam and Eve are removed because they have believed in Him whom God the heavenly Father sent to bring full redemption and restoration through full Christformation in them. Let us consider again what the apostle Paul encouraged and promised to the Corinthian church:

1 Corinthians 15:45–49 (NLT):
"The Scriptures tell us, "The first man, Adam, became a living person." But the last Adam—that is, Christ—is a life-giving Spirit. What comes first is the natural body, then the spiritual body comes later. Adam, the first man, was made from the dust of the earth, while Christ, the second man, came from heaven. Earthly people are like the earthly man, and heavenly people are like the heavenly man. Just as we are now like the earthly man, we will someday be like the heavenly man."

What we sow is what we will reap. Adam sowed the sinful nature of the Devil in him and all mankind earned eternal death as a result when he disobeyed God's commandment not to eat from the tree of death. The Tree of Life was sealed off after Adam had eaten from the tree of death. Adam was the first man, and he failed all humankind. He didn't live up to the honor bestowed upon him as the first Adam. He shifted his allegiance and obedience to the Devil to rule him and all mankind after him. Adam was made out of the dust of the earth and died to become dust of this earth again. Jesus Christ our Lord, the second Adam, came from heaven through the virgin birth to redeem and save all those who were predestined to have Christformation in them by God the Heavenly Father. Christ our Lord came to give all those who believe in Him eternal life as the Tree of Life.

Let us begin by answering another very important question briefly, which we will be discussing in detail in later chapters:

-Part Two-

Where does Christformation occur in you?

Christformation occurs in your whole being when you obey God fully. Your new creation in Christ consists of:

1) The born-again spirit (where Christformation begins and continually occurs).

2) The soul (the renewed mind that is transformed into the mind of Christ).

3) The new body (will clothe the born-again spirit and renewed mind or soul at the rapture or otherwise at the first or second resurrection which is explained below in this section).

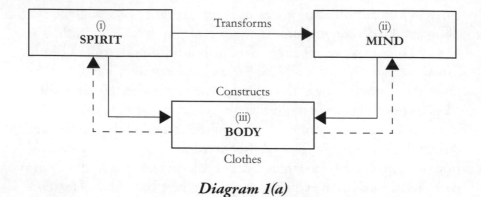

Diagram 1(a)

1) The born-again spirit

Diagram 1 above shows where God sows into you, but how can He sow if the land is not ready? Who makes the land ready for God to sow? God the Holy Spirit is sent into you, convicting you of your sins and your need for the full righteousness of Christ by creating hunger and thirst for full Christformation in you. When you obey Him, you will become the temple of the Holy Spirit for God to sow Christ fully into you, as Christformation cannot be sown in the temple of the Devil. From here on, God the Holy Spirit will help you by watering whatever God sows into you so that full Christformation occurs in you without being hindered or stunted, but this will require your total obedience to His leading. If along the way you do not listen to Him, the route to Christformation in you takes longer, just like the people of God who wandered aimlessly for forty years in the wilderness from Egypt to Canaan.

Once you are born again, you must cooperate with God the Holy Spirit for full Christformation in you or else you will be like a house swept clean and put in order but unoccupied by Christ our Lord. The more you actively fill yourself with Christformation in you, the less you will have any room left for evil spirits to occupy you. In fact, both can never live in the same house together. So the choice is still yours, but think of the consequences of living a careless life without Christformation in you, such as the person in the parable below.

Matthew 12:43–45:
"When an impure spirit comes out of a person, it goes through arid places seeking rest and does not find it. Then it says, 'I will return to the house I left.' When it arrives, it finds the house unoccupied, swept clean and put in order. Then it goes and takes with it seven other spirits more wicked than itself, and they go in and live there. And the final condition of that person is worse than the first. That is how it will be with this wicked generation."

Evil spirits seek rest too. They seek a house to rest in comfortably. The most comfortable house for them will be the house they are familiar with, one in which they once inhabited. This is the reason why Christformation in you is needed. You may want to be clean from any defilement of evil spirits, seeking to be washed by the precious blood of the Lamb offered to you freely on the cross of Christ our Lord. But do you seek to be filled with Him after He has made you clean? After you have been washed by the precious blood of Christ our Lord and made clean in your conscience, do you make every effort to obey all His commandments and seek to be an overcomer of the sinful nature of the Devil in you permanently? Are Christ's divine attributes formed in you? Unless you do exactly that, you will be inviting the old spirits to make their home in you once again, but this time to destroy you completely. In short, believing in Christ is actively followed by obedience to all that Christ commands. If you obey His commandments more, there will be an increase of Christformation in you. You can never deceive God. The obedience you sow to God the Holy Spirit will be the Christformation you will reap in you for eternity.

2) The soul (the renewed mind)

The soul, or the mind of a saved soul needs the eternal life of Christ our Lord. How will this eternal life transform the soul or the mind if it is still hostile toward God the Holy Spirit? Isn't He helping you with Christformation in you? Your soul or mind will only respond to transformation into the mind of Christ according to the measure of Christformation in your born-again spirit. If you obey the leading of God the Holy Spirit less than you should, there will then be less Christformation in you than what God requires of you. Wouldn't that amount to disobedience towards God's will for you?

We must watch our lives closely. We cannot afford to be careless in this world. The Enemy is on the prowl to abort or delay Christformation in you. Are you alert to his evil schemes through the temptations he brings your way? Do you succumb easily to his evil tactics to trap you with the pleasures of the sinful nature in you? If you are strong when temptations come and do not yield to its evil desires and pleasures, do you also prepare yourself well ahead of time for any subsequent testing of your faith, since the Devil may challenge God to test your true faith in Him? You should prepare yourself with Christformation in you so that your mind will be transformed into the mind of Christ. You should obey the leading of God the Holy Spirit, who reminds you that Christ our Lord overcame the Evil One. Christ is the perfect example of obedience to God the heavenly Father in every aspect of human life. You should follow God's Good Shepherd for a successful full Christformation in you. He who had suffered for obedience will lead you to the heavenly Father successfully with full Christformation in you if you obey Him. Meditate upon and apply this portion of the Word of God below to your life.

Romans 8:1–14:
"Therefore, there is now no condemnation for those who are in Christ Jesus because, through Christ Jesus, the law of the Spirit who gives life has set you free from the law of sin and death. For what the law was powerless to do because it was weakened by the flesh, God did by sending his own Son in the likeness of sinful flesh to be a sin offering. And so he condemned sin in the flesh, in order that the righteous requirement of the law might be fully met in us, who do not live according to the flesh but according to the Spirit. Those that live according to the flesh have their minds set on what the flesh desires; but those who live in accordance with the Spirit have their minds set on what the Spirit

desires. The mind governed by the flesh is death, but the mind governed by the Spirit is life and peace. The mind governed by the flesh is hostile to God; it does not submit to God's law, nor can it do so. Those that are in the realm of the flesh cannot please God. You, however, are not in the realm of the flesh but are in the realm of the Spirit, if indeed the Spirit of God lives in you. And if anyone does not have the Spirit of Christ, they do not belong to Christ. But if Christ is in you, then even though your body is subject to death because of sin, the Spirit gives life because of righteousness. And if the Spirit of him who raised Jesus from the dead is living in you, he who raised Christ from the dead will also give life to your mortal bodies because of his Spirit who lives in you. Therefore, brothers and sisters, we have an obligation—but it is not to the flesh, to live according to it. For if you live according to the flesh, you will die; but if by the Spirit you put to death the misdeeds of the body, you will live. For those who are led by the Spirit of God are the children of God."

The mind that has been transformed into the mind of Christ our Lord according to the measure of Christformation in the born-again spirit through obedience to God the Holy Spirit will be filled with life and peace of Christ our Lord. He or she will be alert and ready for the attacks of the Devil. The righteousness of Christ in you keeps you obeying the leading of God the Holy Spirit toward full Christformation. You can only please God the Father with Christformation, for that is His perfect will for you. You should read the verses below carefully to be able to apply them to your life.

Romans 12:1–2:
"Therefore, I urge you, brothers and sisters, in view of God's mercy, to offer your bodies as a living sacrifice, holy and pleasing to God—this is your true and proper worship. Do not conform to the pattern of this world, but be transformed by the renewing of your mind. Then you will be able to test and approve what God's will is—his good, pleasing, and perfect will."

The renewing of the mind is transformation into the mind of Christ our Lord according to the measure of Christformation in our born-again spirit. You worship God the heavenly Father when there is

31

Christformation in you. When you offer your body, soul (mind), and born-again spirit for full Christformation in you, God is pleased and worshipped through that living sacrifice to Him. Nothing is more pleasing to God than when Christ His beloved Son is formed in you.

3) The new body (that will clothe the born-again spirit and our renewed mind, or soul.)

When you offer your present body as a living sacrifice, and every act that proceeds from that body is holy and pleasing to the Lord as worship unto Him through Christ our Lord, you are sowing to your new, eternal, incorruptible, and immortal body like Christ's. This new body will clothe your born-again spirit, which now has full Christformation in it, and the soul, which is your renewed mind of Christ in you, so that you do not appear shamefully or partially naked of Christ's divine nature before the heavenly Father. Your new, Christ-conformed body will live forever, and God will dwell within you. You will become the eternal tabernacle of God where He will dwell within you forever. Read on to find out for yourself.

1 Corinthians 15:50–56:

"I declare to you, brothers and sisters, that flesh and blood cannot inherit the kingdom of God, nor does the perishable inherit the imperishable. Listen, I tell you a mystery: We will not all sleep, but we will all be changed, in a flash, in the twinkling of an eye, at the last trumpet. For the trumpet will sound as the dead will be raised imperishable, and we will be changed. For the perishable must clothe itself with the imperishable and the mortal with immortality. When the perishable has been clothed with the imperishable, and the mortal with immortality, then the saying that is written will come true: "Death has been swallowed up in victory. Where, O death is your victory? Where, O death, is your sting?" The sting of death is sin, and the power of sin is the law."

When the Word of God says that "flesh and blood will not inherit the kingdom of God and nor does the perishable inherit the imperishable," we are reminded of the Old Testament people of God. What happens to them who are dead now? Does it mean that they will not inherit eternal life because eternal life is only found in Jesus Christ our Lord? The Lord Jesus Christ wasn't revealed to them in the flesh, so how could they have known who had eternal life?

In the Old Testament, the Lord Jesus Christ was revealed as the Tree of Life, the Rock, the Manna, the Tabernacle of Moses, the Temple of (David) Solomon, Melchizedek the High Priest, Commander of the Lord's Army, the Lily of the Valley, the Rose of Sharon, Kinsman-Redeemer, Israel's Messiah, Immanuel, the Sun of Righteousness, the Law, the Wisdom, and the Servant of God. But He was only revealed in the flesh as the Lord Jesus Christ, the Son of Man, or the Son of God in the New Testament. How then could the Old Testament faithful have inherited eternal life? Can the perishable inherit the imperishable? Well, let us look into the book of Daniel and learn what happened there:

Daniel 12:13:
"As for you, go your way till the end. You will rest, and then at the end of the days, you will rise to receive your allotted inheritance."

The faithful people of the Old Testament will also be raised to life from death and will be crowned with Christformation in them as their allotted inheritance for eternity. Their obedience in faithfully observing all the ceremonial laws that showed the coming of Christ and the celebration of the festivals that heralded the coming and act of feasting on Christ, allotted to them an eternal inheritance.

But what about the New Testament believers in Christ? What have they been promised? This same inheritance in Christ, which is Christformation in you, as allotted according to their obedience to Him. Let's compare these verses in the New Testament:

Ephesians 1:13–14:
"And you also were included in Christ when you heard the message of truth, the gospel of your salvation. When you believed, you were marked in him with a seal, the promised Holy Spirit, who is a deposit, guaranteeing our inheritance, until the redemption of those who are God's possession—to the praise of his glory."

You do not need to keep or observe the ceremonial laws as the Old Testament people of God did, but you are guaranteed your inheritance of Christformation if you obey the leading of God the Holy Spirit, who is the seal of obedience to God and the deposit of Christ's obedience in you. He constantly reminds you about everything Christ our Lord had done on earth through His reverent submission to the will of the heavenly Father. He offered up His body on the cross so that you could inherit His imperishable body through your obedience to Him. God the Holy Spirit helps you with this. Look into the passage below that shows how He helps you with Christformation.

1 Thessalonians 5:23–24:
"May God himself, the God of peace, sanctify you through and through. May your whole spirit, soul, and body be kept blameless at the coming of our Lord Jesus Christ. The one who calls you is faithful, and he will do it."

God, who called you to full Christformation in you, will complete this good work in you. Your new body will clothe your fully Christ-formed, born-again spirit and transformed mind. The misdeeds of the sinful nature of the Devil in you will surely be put to death in you successfully when you fully obey God's Spirit in you. When you no longer obey the sinful nature of the Devil in you, you will be led to obey all that Christ commands through God the Holy Spirit in you for full Christformation in you.

SUMMARY: CHAPTER ONE

In the garden of Eden, only two choices were revealed:

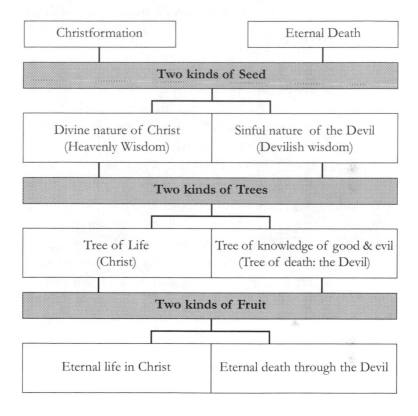

Diagram 1(b)

1) There are only two seeds that you can choose from in God's garden to be sown into you, and only one seed can grow in you. It's either the divine nature of Christ or the sinful nature of the Devil. The divine nature of Christ is heavenly wisdom, whereas the sinful nature of the Devil is devilish wisdom that Adam and Eve desired. James 3:13–18 details these two kinds of wisdom.

The seed you choose to be sown in you will grow into the tree of its kind. The divine nature of Christ will grow into the Tree of Life, who is Jesus Christ our Lord. The sinful nature of the Devil will grow into the tree of death, who is the Devil. If you obey the sinful nature of the Devil in you, you will mature into the nature of the Devil. If you obey Christ, you will have Christformation in you.

2) Seed will grow into a tree that will bear fruit of its kind. The fruit of the seed of the divine nature of Christ formed in you will be your growth into eternal life. However, the choice of obeying the sinful nature of the Devil will result in eternal death. The key word here is *obedience*. Adam and Eve, through their disobedience, chose to eat from the tree of death and earned death by sowing the sinful nature in themselves and in all mankind. But those who choose to eat from the Tree of Life will have eternal life through the formation of Christ's divine nature in them. We must eat from the Tree of Life to be filled with fruit of that tree.

CHRISTFORMATION
IS GOLD REFINED IN FIRE
1 PETER 1: 7

CHAPTER TWO:
WHY IS CHRISTFORMATION
IN YOU NECESSARY?

A) PREDESTINATION OF CHRISTFORMATION IN YOU

Romans 8:29–30 (NASB):
"For those whom He foreknew, He also predestined to become conformed to the image of His Son, so that He would be the firstborn among many brethren; and these whom He predestined, He also called; and these whom He called, He also justified; and these whom He justified, He also glorified."

Way before the earth and everything in it was created; God had predestined Christformation in you so that the Lord Jesus Christ would be the firstborn of God the heavenly Father. Christ our Lord was revealed as the exact representation of the heavenly Father on earth. So, having the divine nature of Christ formed in you is the same as having the divine nature of God the heavenly Father.

May the truth about Christformation in you be made clearer in the following verse:

Hebrews 1:3 (NASB):
"And He is the radiance of His glory and the exact representation of His nature, and upholds all things by the word of His power. When He had made purification of sins; He sat down at the right hand of the Majesty on high."

Even now, Christformation in you is upheld by the promises and power of His Word. He is interceding for you as the Great High Priest after the order of Melchizedek so that full Christformation occurs in you. Christ our Lord is the radiance of God's glory, and once He is fully formed in you, the radiance of Christ's glory will shine through you. This will please the heavenly Father because only Christ, the firstborn of God, can fully please Him.

The passage below is rather long. If you take time to meditate carefully on these words, you will understand how Christ our Lord pleased the heavenly Father and how you can please Him with Christformation in you.

Hebrews 10:1–14 (NLT):
"The old system under the Law of Moses was only a shadow, a dim preview of the good things to come, not the good things themselves. The sacrifices under that system were repeated again and again, year after year, but they were never able to provide perfect cleansing for those who came to worship. If they could have provided perfect cleansing, the sacrifices would have stopped, for the worshipers would have been purified once for all time, and their feelings of guilt would have disappeared. But instead, those sacrifices actually reminded them of their sins year after year. For it is not possible for the blood of bulls and goats to take away sins. That is why, when Christ came into the world, he said to God, "You did not want animal sacrifices or sin offerings. But you have given me a body to offer. You were not pleased with burnt offerings or other offerings for sin. Then I said, 'Look, I have come to do your will, O God—as is written about me in the Scriptures.' " First, Christ said, "You did not want animal sacrifices or sin offerings or burnt offerings or other offerings for sin, nor were you pleased with them" (though they are required by the law of Moses). Then he said, "Look, I have come to do your will." He cancels the first covenant in order to put the second into effect. For God's will was for us to be made holy by the sacrifice of the body of Jesus Christ, once for all time. Under the old covenant, the priest stands and ministers before the altar day after day, offering the same sacrifices again and again, this can never take away sins. But our High Priest offered himself to God as a single sacrifice for sins, good for all time. Then he sat down in the place of honor at God's right hand. There he waits until his enemies are humbled and made a footstool under his feet. For by that one offering he forever made perfect those who are being made holy."

How do you think God's enemies will be humbled and made a footstool under His feet? Yes, by Christformation in you and me. By His one perfect sacrifice, where He willingly offered His body for us on the cross at Calvary, you and I are being made holy and acceptable to God the heavenly Father through Christformation for eternity with the indispensible help of God the Holy Spirit. The Devil, who is the author of sin and death since the day Adam and Eve fell into his trap, desires that all remain in bondage to the sinful nature.

Christ's triumph over His enemies began at His resurrection from death on the third day and will continue until He brings all creation subjected to the heavenly Father through Christformation in you. Eternal judgment will follow those who continued with their allegiance to the Devil by obeying the lusts of the sinful nature, though they had been strictly warned of the consequences of living in sin. God has decided that Christformation will occur in those who respond to His call, and Christ's completed work on the cross justifies those who respond to His call. Furthermore, He will glorify them with full Christformation through the power of God the Holy Spirit when their obedience to God is perfected. It seems that the apostle Paul had this on his mind for the believers in Galatians 4:19, "My dear children, for whom I am again in the pains of childbirth until Christ is formed in you."

Most of the parables of the Lord Jesus Christ repeat God's Christformation plan in every believer through their personal obedience to the leading of God the Holy Spirit on earth. Apostle Paul said that he was very burdened for each believer in Christ our Lord to receive what God had already planned for them in advance. They would only need to obey God till the end to allow Christformation to increase in them. Christformation should be the goal of salvation for all who believe in Him.

He also says that the most painful and challenging part of Christian discipleship is bearing the responsibility of ensuring Christformation in those whom the Lord had placed under his leadership. Take note here that he wasn't worried about his own Christformation because he had surrendered his life with complete obedience to God the Holy Spirit. Rather, he was concerned about the obedience of the believers in Galatia to God's Christformation plan for them. They could hinder Christformation in themselves through disobedience to the leading of God the Holy Spirit. This was the "pains of childbirth" in him. The whole book of Galatians was about the battle that Christians go through within themselves, trying to overcome the sinful nature of the Devil so that full Christformation is unhindered within them. More will be written about this in the upcoming chapters.

B) Christformation was Promised in the Garden of Eden

Genesis 3:15:
"And I will put enmity between you and the woman, and between your offspring and hers; he will crush your head, and you will strike his heel."

It is not easy to crush the head of the Devil unless it is Christ Himself doing it. In fact, that is exactly what He did. He rendered the Devil powerless over man. He gave us the authority to trample and overcome all the power of the Enemy and assures us that nothing will harm us, even though the Enemy will strike the heel of those who oppose him. There are some obedient people of God whom the Devil cannot harm because he has been rendered powerless over them. This results from their victory over the power of the Enemy in their lives. As such, the children of God who have Christ's divine nature fully formed within them will be in constant enmity with the Devil and his minions, who only obey the sinful nature.

John 8:42–47:
"Jesus said to them, "If God were your Father, you would love me, for I have come here from God. I have not come on my own; God sent me. Why is my language not clear to you? It is because you are unable to hear what I say. You belong to your father, the devil, and you want to carry out your father's desires. He was a murderer from the beginning, not holding to the truth, for there is no truth in him. When he lies, he speaks his native language, for he is a liar and the father of lies. Yet because I tell the truth, you do not believe me! Can any of you prove me guilty of sin? If I am telling the truth, why don't you believe me? Whoever belongs to God hears what God says. The reason you do not hear is that you do not belong to God." "

The woman referred to in Genesis 3:15 is the same woman mentioned about in Revelation 12:1–6. She is the second Eve, who experienced the "pains of childbirth" that the apostle Paul spoke of. The first Adam and Eve faced eternal death, but the second Adam, who is the Lord Jesus Christ, gives eternal life to His body, of which He is the head. The second Eve is the body of Christ. This message is conveyed clearly through Ephesians 5:25–30. Let's cross-refer these passages and learn deeper truths of Christformation in you.

Revelation 12:1–6:

"A great sign appeared in heaven: a woman clothed with the sun, with the moon under her feet and a crown of twelve stars on her head. She was pregnant and cried out in pain as she was about to give birth. Then another sign appeared in heaven: an enormous red dragon with seven heads and ten horns and seven crowns on its heads. Its tail swept a third of the stars out of the sky and flung them to the earth. The dragon stood in front of the woman who was about to give birth, so that it might devour her child the moment he was born. She gave birth to a son, a male child, who will rule all the nations with an iron sceptre. And her child was snatched up to God and to his throne. The woman fled into the wilderness to a place prepared for her by God, where she might be taken care of for 1,260 days."

Ephesians 5:25–30:

"Husbands, love your wives, just as Christ loved the church and gave himself up for her to make her holy, cleansing her by the washing with water through the word, and to present her to himself as a radiant church, without stain or wrinkle or any other blemish, but holy and blameless. In this same way, husbands ought to love their wives as their own bodies. He who loves his wife loves himself. After all, no one ever hated their own body, but they feed and care for their body, just as Christ does the church—for we are members of his body."

Referring to the verses above, the church is the last Eve that Christ, the last Adam as stated in 1 Corinthians 15:45, is preparing as His eternal bride. The caring, feeding, and the pains of pregnancy and childbirth are all for full Christformation in you. We are His body that He personally cares for and feeds till there is full Christformation in us. But do you notice that the Devil, who is referred to as an "enormous red dragon," furiously tried to devour all those with full Christformation in them but couldn't? The One who will rule the world with an iron scepter was formed in them. How could the Devil devour them if Christ Himself is formed in them? This takes us to another portion of Scripture where this point is clearer.

Ephesians 6:10–18:
"Finally, be strong in the Lord and in his mighty power. Put on the full armor of God, so that you can take your stand against the devil's schemes. For our struggle is not against flesh and blood, but against the rulers, against the authorities, against the powers of this dark world and against the spiritual forces of evil in the heavenly realms. Therefore put on the full armor of God, so that when the day of evil comes, you may be able to stand your ground, and after you have done everything, to stand. Stand firm then, with the belt of truth buckled around your waist, with the breastplate of righteousness in place, and with your feet fitted with the readiness that comes from the gospel of peace. In addition to all this, take up the shield of faith, with which you can extinguish all the flaming arrows of the evil one. Take the helmet of salvation and the sword of the Spirit, which is the word of God. And pray in the Spirit on all occasions with all kinds of prayers and requests. With this in mind, be alert and always keep on praying for all of the Lord's people."

The "armor of God" refers to Christformation in you, the forming of the divine nature of Christ in you. Truth, righteousness, peace, faith, salvation, the word of God, and a prayerful, interceding nature can only come from the divine nature of Christ our Lord. In this passage, this divine nature is allegorized as armor needed during war. The Devil won't be able to touch you if Christ our Lord is fully formed in you.

All of us who belong to Jesus Christ our Lord should desire full Christformation in us, which becomes God's full armor. Those of us who do not have Christformation in us will be vulnerable to the Devil's vicious attacks and may not be able to stand through them. Imagine: If you do not have the full armor of God in you, won't some parts of your life be opened to the attacks of the Devil? The only way you can be alert is to be actively seeking Christformation in you all the time.

God promised Christformation in you on the same day the Devil declared war with God. The heavenly Father prepared the way for His only begotten Son to come to earth, revealed as the Son of Man, to defeat the Devil as the last Adam. Through Christformation in you, you too can defeat the Devil by not obeying the sinful nature anymore. Putting to death the misdeeds that originate from the sinful nature of the Devil enables you to obey Christ's commandments fully. The Great Commission of Christ in Matthew 28:17–20 stresses the importance of obedience to God's commandments so that the Devil will be defeated. You may not have noted the importance of obedience in this commission of Christ our Lord, so let's look at it here:

Matthew 28:18–20:
"Then Jesus came to them and said, 'All authority in heaven and on earth has been given to me. Therefore go and make disciples of all nations, baptizing them in the name of the Father and of the Son and of the Holy Spirit, and teaching them to obey everything I have commanded you. And surely I am with you always, to the very end of the age.' "

The part of the commission that we want to highlight is "teaching them to obey everything I have commanded you." We have to teach all those who believe in the Lord Jesus Christ and are baptized in the name of our heavenly Father, His only Son, and God the Holy Spirit, how to obey everything that the Lord Jesus Christ has commanded us. How can we teach others who need to hear this if we have not obeyed His commandments? Remember, the very reason Adam and Eve suffered eternal death was their disobedience to God. Now, Christ came to be an example of obedience to God the Father and commissioned us to teach them to obey everything He had commanded us. But, we ourselves must be an example of obedience to Christ our Lord first.

Many of us have missed out on this very important part of the Great Commission of the Lord. It's very important to teach them to obey everything He had commanded because it's only through obedience that Christformation can occur in them. In Genesis 3:15, God's promise in the garden of Eden was that we will defeat the Devil by obeying Christ our Lord as His children. Also in the book of Genesis, God promised the patriarch Abraham Christformation.

C) GOD'S PROMISE OF CHRISTFORMATION TO ABRAHAM

When you reflect upon the life of the patriarch Abraham in the Old Testament, you might think about God's great promises to him that remain to this day. God promised Abraham that He would make the people of God into a great nation through him. How was this promise fulfilled, except by the coming of Christ our Lord through Abraham's lineage? In Christ our Lord, this nation will be the greatest nation of God through Christformation in all those who have believed in God as Abraham did all his life.

Abraham was given a promise from God that will stand through eternity. We learn the truth that "God does not shift or change" from the promises He gave Abraham as mentioned in James 1: 17.

Genesis 12:1–3:
"The LORD said to Abram, 'Go from your country, your people and your father's household to the land I will show you. I will make you into a great nation, and I will bless you; I will make your name great, and you will be a blessing. I will bless those who bless you, and whoever curses you I will curse; and all peoples on earth will be blessed through you.' "

Faith pleases God. The Lord Jesus Christ left heaven and humbled Himself to be made equal to man on earth, even though He was the only begotten Son of God. He did this so that we could come to the heavenly Father through His redemptive work on the cross for all our sins. In this passage, God is inviting Abraham to live by faith, which means trusting in Him in all circumstances with no easy way to return to his old, comfortable life. God's specific promise was that Abraham would be blessed by God and would be a blessing to all peoples on earth. We ask, why would God need a channel of His blessing to His chosen ones? He could bless them directly if He wanted to. God was speaking these words in preparation for the coming of His own Son, the Lord Jesus Christ, to redeem mankind from the Evil One, which Abraham wouldn't be able to do even if he wanted to.

The greatest blessing of God to anyone who believes in Him is the deliverance from the Evil One. Many have and are still seeking for this desperately. Abraham was one of them. He loved God and sought deliverance himself. So, he was tested many times to see if his love for God was genuine. Why were these testings necessary?

The Word of God tells us that faith without actions is dead, just as a body without a spirit is dead. If you have a strong faith in the Lord, God will be pleased only if you prove it through your actions. Abraham did many things that proved his love for and faith in God that were spontaneous; God did not have to remind him repeatedly about what He required of him. In fact, Abraham was willing to be an example of obedience to God for others. Faith requires obedience, and when we do as God says, God is always pleased.

Abraham was a well-remembered patriarch for his faith and righteous acts by his obedience to God. Think about the tithe Abraham offered to Melchizedek, whom he had never seen or met before, as soon as he had returned from war. Through this particular act, we know that the Lord Jesus Christ was made the Great High Priest after the order of Melchizedek and not Aaron as the word of God confirms this in the whole of Hebrews chapter 7. We would have never heard of Melchizedek if Abraham didn't respect him with his tithes.

Christformation in you is the result of your obedience to God out of your faith in Him and Christ's completed work on the cross. Faith without actions is dead. Your faith alone without Christformation in you does not mean anything to God. Obedience to God follows the faith we have in Him. God assured Abraham about the blessing of

Christformation in him that would come through Christ our Lord and bless many. The faith that Abraham had in God was to be an example of obedience for many during the Old Testament times. God gave Abraham other promises too, such as the one in the passage from God's word below:

Genesis 18:17–19:
"Then the LORD said, 'Shall I hide from Abraham what I am about to do? Abraham will surely become a great and powerful nation, and all nations on earth will be blessed through him. For I have chosen him so that he will direct his children and his household after him to keep the way of the LORD by doing what is right and just, so that the LORD will bring about for Abraham what he has promised him.' "

Abraham's deeds proved that He loved and obeyed God at all costs. God was pleased with his obedience, but still this wasn't enough to deliver the whole world from the Evil One. If God was to overturn the curses from the garden of Eden, it could only happen through the obedient eating of the fruit from the Tree of Life, which He would reveal at the appropriate time to those whom He had chosen to receive His mercies by faith. His only begotten Son is that Tree of Life. God's eternal promise is that many will eat from this Tree of Life and live forever through Christformation in them. Let's consider this promise below too.

Genesis 15:5–6:
"He took him outside and said, 'Look up at the sky and count the stars—if indeed you can count them.' Then he said to him, 'So shall your offspring be.' Abram believed the LORD, and he credited it to him as righteousness."

The Lord Jesus Christ came as a promise to this world, just as Isaac was born to Abraham and Sarah in their old age through a promise from God that their offspring would be as many as the stars in the sky. This was a prophecy referring to the time of the Lord Jesus Christ, where many will believe in Him and be saved. This promise could have only been fulfilled through Christ our Lord.

As we have said earlier, Christformation in you happens in your born-again spirit after you believe that the Lord Jesus Christ is the Savior and Lord of your life as you are being delivered from the sinful nature of the Devil in you. Christformation in you is the greatest blessing one could receive from the Lord. God's promise to Abraham about his offspring meant that the children of God born in Christ our Lord would be as many as the stars in the sky, beginning with Isaac. We will learn more about this promise in the following chapters.

D) The Old Testament Type of Christformation Journey

Although there were many others, such as Noah, Lot, Jacob, and Joseph, whom we relate to as Old Testament types of Christformation in you, Moses and Joshua stand out clearly with their leadership of the two separate (broken) journeys from Egypt to Canaan. Every stage of their journeys had similarities to Christformation in you, starting with the calling of Moses to the settling down of God's victorious people through Joshua in Canaan, or the Promised Land. We will study the whole journey and the Scriptures to see how the times of Moses and Joshua relate to Christformation in you today. Let us start with these relevant verses below.

Hebrews 3:1–6:
"Therefore, holy brothers and sisters, who share in the heavenly calling, fix your thoughts on Jesus, whom we acknowledge as our apostle and high priest. He was faithful to the one who appointed him, just as Moses was faithful in all God's house. Jesus has been found worthy of greater honor than Moses, just as the builder of a house has greater honor than the house itself. For every house is built by someone, but God is the builder of everything. "Moses was faithful as a servant in all God's house," bearing witness to what would be spoken by God in the future. But Christ is faithful as the Son over God's house. And we are his house, if indeed we hold firmly to our confidence and the hope in which we glory."

The birth of Moses was important for the Old Testament journey of God's people from Egypt into the wilderness. If Moses was not born, there would have been no escape for God's people from slavery to the Egyptians. We could not imagine another person as brave and humble as Moses to lead them out from the evil grip of Pharaoh and his government. God made Pharaoh's daughter care for Moses from childhood into adulthood. When he grew up, he was not afraid of standing up for God against the same Pharaoh and his evil rule.

Similarly, the birth of Jesus Christ our Lord was important for our deliverance from the Devil and our Christformation journey into eternity. He was born and placed in a manger because there was no room for Him in the inn. The evil rule of Herod created this situation. When Jesus grew up, filled with heavenly wisdom and in full stature as the Son of Man, He sought to do the will of the heavenly Father and His work on earth. Like Moses, Jesus was offered a luxurious life by the Devil after His forty days and nights of fasting and prayer in the wilderness, but he shunned that evil life firmly. He was never distracted from what He was sent to do.

Moses represented Christ our Lord, from his birth experience to the coming as the Deliverer of God's people. His successor, Joshua, also represented Christ in bringing peace and ultimate salvation to God's people from their enemies in Canaan. There were two separate leaderships. Moses was a leader cum deliverer, but Joshua was a leader cum warrior. We have witnessed in the past the leader cum deliverer through Christ's completed work on the cross and are still witnessing the leader cum warrior in Him through Christformation in you and me.

The Lord Jesus Christ is a combination of both leaderships. One brought deliverance for God's chosen people from the Devil, and the other brings a successful Christformation in you. At this stage, Christ our Lord is the leader cum warrior at God's right hand, interceding, building, and bringing victory through full Christformation in you. You must cooperate with Him through complete obedience to God the Holy Spirit, working together towards full Christformation in you. That's what the apostle Paul meant by saying, "work out your salvation in you with fear and trembling." In other words, work out Christformation in you with all the reverence and the fear of the Lord.

Here are the seven important stages of the journey out of Egypt into Canaan and how it corresponds to Christformation in you today:

Old Testament Christformation	New Testament Christformation
a. Journey out of Egypt	The calling out of God's people in Christ our Lord.
b. Crossing of the Red Sea	The start of the salvation experience through the acknowledgment of Christ our Lord's work on the cross at Calvary. The only qualification for Christformation in you is revealed to you here.
c. Entering the Wilderness	The born again experience with the indispensable help of God the Holy Spirit. Christformation in you begins here.
d. Crossing the Jordan River	The provision of empowerment through God the Holy Spirit for full Christformation in you.
e. Entering Canaan Land	Life of daily warfare with the Devil's sinful nature in and around you for full Christformation in you.
f. Conquering Canaan Land	Successful overcoming of the Devil's sinful nature in you.
g. "Milk and Honey"	"Bread and Wine"- obediently feeding on Christ our Lord for full Christformation in you. It is the ultimate purpose of God the Heavenly Father that we be filled with Christ fully.

Diagram 2(a)

Let us read the passage below to understand why this journey was necessary.

Exodus 3:4–10:

"When the LORD saw that he had gone over to look, God called to him from within the bush, "Moses! Moses!" And Moses said, "Here I am." "Do not come any closer," God said. "Take off your sandals, for the place where you are standing is holy ground." Then he said, "I am the God of your father, the God of Abraham, the God of Isaac, and the God of Jacob." At this, Moses hid his face because he was afraid to look at God. The LORD said, "I have indeed seen the misery of my people in Egypt. I have heard them crying out because of their slave drivers, and I am concerned about their suffering. So I have come down to rescue them from the hand of the Egyptians and to bring them up out of that land into a good and spacious land, a land flowing with milk and honey—the home of the Canaanites, Hittites, Amorites, Perizzites, Hivites, and Jebusites. And now the cry of the Israelites has reached me, and I have seen the way the Egyptians are oppressing them. So now, go. I am sending you to Pharaoh to bring my people the Israelites out of Egypt." "

The calling of Moses occurred at the burning bush. He was chosen by God to deliver His people from bondage and slavery to the Egyptians. God had seen the misery and heard the cries of His people who were suffering under the cruelty of the slave drivers and their masters. God commanded Moses to do as He told him so that Moses could lead His enslaved people out of Egypt safely.

Similarly, the Lord Jesus Christ was sent into this world by the heavenly Father to deliver us from the grip of the sinful nature of the Devil and to lead us to full Christformation from the land that was "home to the Canaanites, Hittites, Amorites, Perizzites, Hivites and Jebusites," which symbolizes the sinful nature of the Devil that rules the hearts of God's people before Christformation occurs.

Christ our Lord is the commander of the Lord's army to defeat the demons through daily warfare. We will put to death the sinful nature of the Devil in us with the help of God the Holy Spirit through our obedience to Him. This is where Joshua took over from Moses. Joshua miraculously led the chosen people of God through the Jordan River into Canaan. The crossing of the Jordan River represents the baptism of the Holy Spirit experience today. The crossing of the river required total dependence and obedience to Him for this miracle to occur. Likewise, the baptism of the Holy Spirit will not occur unless we cease depending on ourselves and allow His full power to be demonstrated in and through us before the true battle to overthrow and overcome all the power of the Enemy within us begins. Zechariah, the Minor Prophet later announced how this war would be in us. Let's read what it says about Christformation in us.

Zechariah 4:5–7:
"He answered, 'Do you not know what these are?' 'No, my lord,' I replied. So he said to me, 'This is the word of the LORD to Zerubbabel: "Not by might nor by power, but by my Spirit," says the LORD Almighty.'

51

"What are you, mighty mountain? Before Zerubbabel you will become level ground. Then he will bring out the capstone to shouts of 'God bless it! God bless it!' "

The "mighty mountain" represents the sinful nature of the Devil that many struggle to destroy within themselves. This mountain appears impossible to level to the ground. Likewise, those who struggle with the sinful nature may find it impossible to uproot. However, the Lord intervenes and introduces Zerubbabel who signifies Joshua in the Old Testament and Christ in the New Testament. Zerubbabel leveled the ground, Joshua destroyed his enemies completely and Christ sent us the Holy Spirit to destroy the sinful nature within us, so that Christformation occurs in us. Then, the Capstone, who is Christ, will be formed in us.

1 Peter 2:6–10:
"For in Scripture it says: "See, I lay a stone in Zion, a chosen and precious cornerstone, and the one who trusts in him will never be put to shame." Now to you who believe, this stone is precious. But to those who do not believe, "The stone the builders rejected has become the capstone, and, "A stone that causes men to stumble and a rock that makes them fall." They stumble because they disobey the message—which is also what they were destined for. But you are a chosen people, a royal priesthood, a holy nation, a people belonging to God, that you may declare the praises of him who called you out of darkness into his wonderful light. Once you were not a people, but now you are the people of God; once you had not received mercy, but now you have received mercy."

Christformation journey starts with Christ our Lord and increases into the fullness of Him formed in you. "The stone the builders rejected" refers to those who had considered themselves defenders of their religion and rejected Christ our Lord as their Savior-Messiah. They refused to accept the truth because of their disobedience, not ignorance. Jesus Christ our Lord died brutally by their cruel hands on the cross with the help of the Roman soldiers. He rose from the dead on the third day and became the capstone; the most important stone for building the house that God will live in forever. For Christformation to occur in you, Christ who was rejected by this world must become the capstone of your life.

Every part of the Old Testament journey of God's people out of Egypt corresponds to the New Testament spiritual journey in Christ. How did Christformation occur in the Old Testament believers? Their physical obedience to the leading of God throughout the journey from Egypt to Canaan meant Christformation in them, whereas for us it's a spiritual journey with the leading of God the Holy Spirit into full Christformation in us. The manna, the Rock, the Ten Commandments, the Budding Rod of Aaron, the Ark of the Covenant, the Seven Feasts of the Lord, the Tabernacle of Moses, the Pillar of Cloud by day and the Pillar of Fire by night were the many facets of Christ's divine nature that the chosen people of God encountered on their way from Egypt to Canaan. Christformation occurred in them as they physically obeyed and endured the journey with faithfulness till the end. Those who did not obey God's leading did not have Christformation in them, while we encounter today the divine nature of Christ our Lord in our spiritual journey led by God the Holy Spirit as we choose to obey Him. Winning the war over the sinful nature makes us obedient for full Christformation in us.

E) CHRISTFORMATION IN THE SEVEN APPOINTED FEASTS OF THE LORD

The seven appointed feasts, or festivals, of the Lord in the Old Testament typified Christformation in the people of God whenever they obeyed or ceremonially observed them faithfully. Today, we do not have to observe these feasts ceremonially, but let us read the following passage in the Old Testament to understand how it closely relates to Christformation in us. The Seven Appointed Feasts in the Old Testament signify how Christ our Lord is formed in us progressively.

Leviticus 23:1–44:

"The LORD said to Moses, "Speak to the Israelites and say to them: 'These are my appointed festivals, the appointed festivals of the LORD, which you are to proclaim as sacred assemblies. There are six days when you may work, but the seventh day is a day of sabbath rest, a day of sacred assembly. You are not to do any work; wherever you live, it is a sabbath to the LORD. These are the LORD's appointed festivals, the sacred assemblies you are to proclaim at their appointed times: The LORD's Passover begins at twilight on the fourteenth day of the first month. On the fifteenth day of that month, the LORD's Festival of Unleavened Bread begins; for seven days you must eat bread made without yeast. On the first day, hold a sacred assembly and do no regular work. For seven days, present a food offering to the LORD. And on the seventh day hold a sacred assembly and do no regular work.' " The LORD said to Moses, "Speak to the Israelites and say to them: 'When you enter the land I am going to give you and you reap its harvest, bring to the priest a sheaf of the first grain you harvest. He is to wave the sheaf before the LORD so it will be accepted on your behalf; the priest is to wave it on the day after the Sabbath. On the day you wave the sheaf, you must sacrifice as a burnt offering to the LORD a lamb a year old without defect, together with its grain offering of two-tenths of an ephah of the finest flour mixed with olive oil—a food offering presented to the LORD, a pleasing aroma—and its drink offering of a quarter of a hin of wine. You must not eat any bread, or roasted or new grain, until the very day you bring this offering to your God. This is to be a lasting ordinance for the generations to come, wherever you live. From the day after the Sabbath, the day you brought the sheaf of the wave offering, count off seven full weeks. Count off fifty days up to the day after the seventh Sabbath and then present an offering of new grain to the LORD. From wherever you live, bring two loaves made of two-tenths of an ephah of the finest flour, baked with yeast, as a wave offering of firstfruits to the LORD. Present with this bread seven male lambs, each a year old and without defect, one young bull and two rams. They will be a burnt offering to the LORD, together with their grain offerings and drink offerings—a food offering, an aroma pleasing to the LORD. Then sacrifice one male goat for a sin offering and two lambs, each a year old, for a fellowship offering. The priest is to wave the two lambs before the LORD as a wave offering, together with the bread of the firstfruits. They are a sacred offering to the LORD for the priest. On that same day, you are to proclaim a sacred assembly and do no regular work. This is to be a lasting ordinance for the generations to come, wherever you live. When you reap the harvest of your land, do not reap to the very edges of your field or gather the gleanings of your harvest. Leave them for the poor and for the foreigner residing among you. I am the LORD your God.' " The LORD said to Moses, "Say to the Israelites: 'On the first day of the seventh month, you are to have a day of Sabbath rest, a sacred assembly commemorated with trumpet blasts. Do no regular work, but present a food offering to the LORD.' " The LORD said to Moses, "The tenth day of this seventh month is the Day of Atonement. Hold a sacred assembly and deny yourselves, and present a food offering to the LORD. Do not do any work on that day, because it is the Day of Atonement, when atonement is made for you before the LORD your God. Those who do not deny themselves on that day must be cut off from their people. I will destroy from among their people anyone who does any work on that day. You shall do no work at all. This is to be a lasting ordinance for the generations to come, wherever you live. It is a day of Sabbath rest for you, and you must deny yourselves. From the evening of the ninth day of the month until the following evening you are to observe your Sabbath.' "The LORD said to Moses, "Say to the Israelites: 'On the fifteenth day of the seventh month, the LORD's Festival of Tabernacles begins, and it lasts for seven days. The first day is a sacred assembly; do no regular work. For seven days, present food offerings to the LORD, and on the eighth day hold a sacred assembly and present a food offering to the LORD. It is the closing special assembly; do no regular work. (These are the LORD's appointed festivals, which you are to proclaim as sacred assemblies for bringing food offerings to the LORD—the burnt offerings and grain offerings, sacrifices and drink offerings required for each day. These offerings are in addition to those for the LORD's Sabbaths and in addition to your gifts and whatever you have vowed and all the freewill offerings you give to the LORD.) So beginning with the fifteenth day of the seventh month, after you have gathered the crops of the land, celebrate the festival to the LORD for seven days; the first day is a day of Sabbath rest, and the eighth day also is a day of sabbath rest. On the first day, you are to take branches from luxuriant trees—from palms, willows and other leafy trees—and rejoice before the LORD your God for seven days. Celebrate this as a festival to the LORD for seven days each year. This is to be a lasting ordinance for the generations to come; celebrate it in the seventh month. Live in temporary shelters for seven days: All native-born Israelites are to live in such shelters so your descendants will know that I had the Israelites live in temporary shelters when I brought them out of Egypt. I am the LORD your God.' " So Moses announced to the Israelites the appointed festivals of the LORD."

The seven feasts, or festivals, of the Lord were compulsory for the people of God in the Old Testament to celebrate. The table below is a diagrammatic representation of the seven feasts followed by explanations, given in detail, as to how they correspond with each stage of Christformation in you today.

Seven Appointed Feasts of the Lord (Summary of Types)	
Old Testament	**New Testament**
1. The Sabbath	1. Invitation for Christformation in you.
2. The Passover and the Festival of Unleavened Bread	2. The only qualification needed for Christformation in you. Believing in the completed work of Christ on the cross.
3. Offering the First-fruits	3. Christformation begins through the born again experience in you.
4. The Festival of Weeks	4. Uttermost help comes from God for full Christformation in you, with your complete cooperation to God the Holy Spirit through the Baptism of the Spirit of God.
5. The Festival of Trumpets	5. You will enter into a war with the sinful nature of the Devil in you with full help from the Spirit of God for full Christformation in you.
6. The Day of Atonement	6. You will win the war and overcome the sinful nature of the Devil in you, if you had obeyed God the Holy Spirit who guides you fully to win the war for full Christformation in you.
7. The Festival of Tabernacles	7. Full Christformation has happened in you with the Heavenly Father, His Son and God the Holy Spirit making their home in you permanently.

Diagram 2(b)

The seven appointed feasts of the Lord were mandatory celebrations in Old Testament times. Following are the corresponding verses of fulfillment in the New Testament for Christformation in you.

1) <u>The Sabbath</u>

The following verses are the invitation of the Lord Jesus Christ for full Christformation in you so that you may have true rest from the sinful nature of the Devil. This will be the beginning of the festival when you are invited to feast on the true rest that only comes from Christ our Lord, for He is the Lord of the Sabbath, and true rest can come from no one else. He says, "For my yoke is easy and my burden light" in the verses below. My yoke is the helper; God the Holy Spirit, and my burden; Christformation in you. Isn't that easy and light, if you were to just obey the Holy Spirit's leading to Christ? He will show you the Father when you come to Him through your complete obedience.

Matthew 11:28–30:
"Come to me, all you who are weary and burdened, and I will give you rest. Take my yoke upon you and learn from me, for I am gentle and humble in heart, and you will find rest for your souls. For my yoke is easy and my burden is light."

2) <u>The Passover and the Festival of Unleavened Bread</u>

The blood of the Lamb (Jesus Christ) cleanses you from every sin when you confess and forsake them. This also purifies your conscience and deters you from cherishing sin again. You will realize that He died for your sins on the cross, but He victoriously rose from the dead. Now, He is seated at God's right hand and is interceding so that His divine nature will be fully formed in you. You must obediently "feast" on His pure body and His blood as Christ is the Bread of Life, the heavenly manna of God by which you will live forever.

Matthew 26:26–28:
"While they were eating, Jesus took bread, and when he had given thanks, he broke it and gave it to his disciples, saying, "Take and eat; this is my body." Then he took a cup, and when he had given thanks, he gave it to them, saying, "Drink from it, all of you. This is my blood of the covenant, which is poured out for many for the forgiveness of sins." "

3) <u>Offering the First-fruits</u>

Without true repentance, we can never be born again and can never enter the kingdom of God. The Spirit of God gives birth to our born-again spirit within us the moment we truly repent and turn toward Christ, fully acknowledging Him as Lord and king of our lives. Christformation in us begins in our born-again spirit as we offer our bodies as a living sacrifice to Him for the first time. He never fails those who come with a genuine hunger and thirst for His divine nature.

John 3:5–6:
"Jesus answered, "Very truly I tell you, no one can enter the kingdom of God unless they are born of water and the Spirit. Flesh gives birth to flesh, but the Spirit gives birth to spirit." "

4) The Festival of Weeks

Fifty days after the resurrection of the Lord Jesus Christ, God the Holy Spirit came and filled the 120 disciples who were waiting in Jerusalem. Their waiting symbolized their readiness for God to fill their thirsty souls and spirit with His power from on high to do God's work the same way Christ our Lord had done God the Father's work on earth. Demonstrations of God the Holy Spirit's power were witnessed as soon as He filled them, just as the Lord Jesus Christ had promised to those who genuinely sought to be filled with His power. Feasting from the River of Life began here and continues today for everyone who seeks Christ our Lord. He is God's living water who quenches our thirst forever.

Acts 1:8:
"But you will receive power when the Holy Spirit comes on you; and you will be my witnesses in Jerusalem, and in all Judea and Samaria, and to the ends of the earth."

5) The Festival of Trumpets

Trumpets were used to declare a war. Indeed, your war starts the moment you are led by the power of God the Holy Spirit that has filled you. You become the temple of God, who prepares you for full

Christformation in you. While He is preparing you, there will be war within you between the sinful nature of the Devil and God the Holy Spirit who dwells inside of you. The sinful nature of the Devil will try to hinder Christformation in you. But, "We are more than conquerors through Christ who strengthens us" as stated in Romans 8:37 and "greater is He who is in you than he who is in the world" as mentioned in 1 John 4:4. The victory is confirmed if we obey God the Holy Spirit's leading in this war, step by step through our complete obedience to Him for full Christformation in us. This festival is for feasting on the strength and victory of the Lord Jesus Christ, who is the commander of the Lord's army.

Galatians 5:16–18 (NKJV):
"I say then: Walk in the Spirit, and you shall not fulfill the lust of the flesh. For the flesh lusts against the Spirit, and the Spirit against the flesh; and these are contrary to one another, so that you do not do the things that you wish. But if you are led by the Spirit, you are not under the law."

6) <u>The Day of Atonement</u>

The result of winning the war is the overcoming of all the power of the Enemy—not some, but all. You are promised victory when you trust and totally depend on Christ our Lord to win the war against the sinful nature of the Devil in you. God the Holy Spirit is your true helper when you obey Him and His leading throughout all your battles on earth. As a result, you will deny all ungodliness and worldly lusts and will be purely made Christ's own through His grace and mercy that God has created you for. You will win in Christ our Lord. You will have feasted on Christ's example of total obedience to God the heavenly Father at this stage.

Titus 2:11–14 (NKJV):
"For the grace of God that brings salvation has appeared to all men, teaching us that, denying ungodliness and worldly lusts, we should live soberly, righteously, and godly in the present age, looking for the blessed hope and glorious appearing of our great God and Savior Jesus

Christ, who gave Himself for us, that He might redeem us from every lawless deed and purify His own special people, who will be zealous for good works."

7) The Festival of Tabernacles

You win and overcome all the power of the Enemy through your careful obedience to God the Holy Spirit, who helps you with full Christformation as you successfully put to death the sinful nature of the Devil in you at the same time. As you war, you build. God the heavenly Father dwells within you with His Son through Christformation in you once you fully obey Him. This will happen by the demonstration of God the Holy Spirit's power in you. The Feast of Tabernacles is celebrated when God the heavenly Father, the Son, and God the Holy Spirit dwell in you through full Christformation in you. They make their home in you through a loving, obedient relationship with God's Son by your choosing to obediently feast on Him daily.

John 14:19–23 (NKJV):
"A little while longer and the world will see Me no more, but you will see Me. Because I live, you will live also. At that day, you will know that I am in My Father and you in me, and I in you. He who has My commandments and keeps them, it is he who loves Me. And he who loves Me will be loved by My Father, and I will love him and manifest Myself to him. Judas (not Iscariot) said to Him, "Lord, how is it that You will manifest Yourself to us, and not to the world?" 23 Jesus answered and said to him, "If anyone loves Me, he will keep My word; and My Father will love him, and We will come to him and make Our home with him." "

The concluding passage for the seven feasts of the Lord is in the New Testament, which points to the feeding or feasting on Christ for full Christformation in us.

John 6:52–54:
"Then the Jews began to argue sharply among themselves, 'How can this man give us his flesh to eat?' Jesus said to them, 'Very truly I tell

you, unless you eat the flesh of the Son of Man and drink his blood, you have no life in you. Whoever eats my flesh and drinks my blood has eternal life, and I will raise them up at the last day.' "

The life that will be found in you after you "eat and drink" His flesh and blood is full Christformation in you. Apostle Paul warns us in 1 Corinthians 11 that it is not that easy to partake of the body and blood of Christ. If anyone partakes of it with wrong motives, he will be judged by God. In fact, he warned the Corinthian believers that God's judgment had come on some of them who had partaken with wrong motives.

The main purpose of partaking in the Lord's Supper should be "eat[ing] and drink[ing]" everything of the life of Christ our Lord. The believer is to be filled with Him and be reminded that full Christformation is happening within him or her by the power of God the Holy Spirit. He or she is to obey God the Holy Spirit's leading for this purpose in his or her life. Anyone who takes part in the Lord's Supper for any other reason has taken the Word of God lightly.

You should "feast" on Him so that you can be filled with Him. If you claim you are feasting on Him but your life shows that there is no Christformation in you, you have partaken in vain. This act is a reminder of Christformation in you, and if Christformation is void in you, what's the point of taking part in this?

You should search your heart deeply to determine if Christformation is really happening in you or not. If it is, God the Holy Spirit will give you the true witness in your heart. Do you realize that taking part in all the seven appointed feasts of the Lord symbolizes you feasting on Christ? If you do not "feast" on Him as you should, you will not have full Christformation in you.

F) MILK AND HONEY: "BREAD AND WINE" FOR FULL CHRISTFORMATION IN YOU

Exodus 3:7–9:

"The LORD said, 'I have indeed seen the misery of my people in Egypt. I have heard them crying out because of their slave drivers, and I am concerned about their suffering. So I have come down to rescue them from the hand of the Egyptians and to bring them up out of that land into a good and spacious land, a land flowing with milk and honey—the home of the Canaanites, Hittites, Amorites, Perizzites, Hivites, and Jebusites. And now the cry of the Israelites has reached me, and I have seen the way the Egyptians are oppressing them.' "

In the Old Testament, the "land flowing with milk and honey" was the destination of the people of God who were rescued from Egypt, the land of slavery and suffering. This was God's promise to Moses and the people of Israel.

Milk and honey in the Old Testament corresponds to the bread and wine in the New Testament. We all know that milk and honey are produced by animals, or something of the flesh, whereas bread and wine are produced by a plant through a seed or grain. So we have flesh and seed, but all results in some kind of food that we eat or drink. We have to feed on these to taste their goodness and grow by it. In the Old Testament, the people of God had to physically or ceremonially fulfill all of God's requirements for full Christformation in them while in the New Testament, we have to obey God the Holy Spirit for full Christformation in us.

God the Holy Spirit leads and feeds us with Christ our Lord. The seed of Christformation grows in us in our born-again spirit with the help of God the Holy Spirit, who is the River of Life. He waters it so that full Christformation occurs in us. Let's consider the following verse:

Psalm 81:16:
"But you would be fed with the finest of wheat; with honey from the rock I would satisfy you."

We see here the reference to Christ our Lord and how God the Holy Spirit will feed us with full Christformation. In the Old Testament, Christformation in you was revealed as the "honey from the rock" and in the New Testament as seed to grow into "the finest of wheat" as used for making bread. Today, as we feed on the bread and wine, we are reminded that we are feeding on Christ our Lord for full Christformation in us.

G) CHRISTFORMATION IN THE TABERNACLE OF MOSES

The articles in the tabernacle of God, as illustrated on the following page in Diagram 2(c), best describe Christformation in us, with each of us being the born-again tabernacle of God through Christ who is the Great High Priest. His Spirit is within us as the spirit of glory (*Doxa*) and the baptism of fire that burns away the chaff of the sinful nature of the Devil in us. All these will rise up as incense and glory to the heavenly Father and please Him. God will dwell among His people forever. The tabernacle of God is a picture of full Christformation in us. Let us investigate how this occurs through the passage below.

Hebrews 9:1–10:

"Now the first covenant had regulations for worship and also an earthly sanctuary. A tabernacle was set up. In its first room were the lampstand and the table with its consecrated bread; this was called the Holy Place. Behind the second curtain was a room called the Most Holy Place, which had the golden altar of incense and the gold-covered ark of the covenant. This ark contained the gold jar of manna, Aaron's staff that had budded, and the stone tablets of the covenant. Above the ark were the cherubim of the Glory, overshadowing the atonement cover. But we cannot discuss these things in detail now. When everything had been arranged like this, the priests entered regularly into the outer room to carry on their ministry. But only the high priest entered the inner room, and that only once a year, and never without blood, which he offered for himself and for the sins the people had committed in ignorance. The Holy Spirit was showing by this that the way into the Most Holy Place had not yet been disclosed as long as the first tabernacle was still functioning. This is an illustration for the present time, indicating that the gifts and sacrifices being offered were not able to clear the conscience of the worshiper. They are only a matter of food and drink and various ceremonial washings—external regulations applying until the time of the new order."

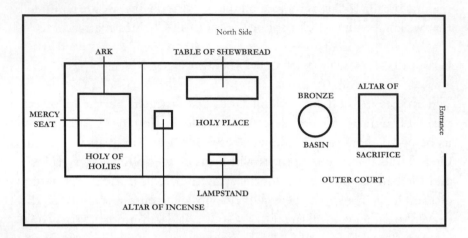

Diagram 2(c)

The articles in the tabernacle were just a picture of what Christformation in you will be. They are the divine nature of the Lord Jesus Christ that begins with the power of the body and blood of the Lamb that brings forgiveness of your sins at the altar of sacrifice when you believe in Him and confess your sins to God through Him. This altar represents His completed work on the cross.

As soon as you have experienced the authority of Christ to forgive you of your sins, the Lord Jesus Christ will be revealed as the Word of God. He took the form of flesh, and you will be made clean by the washing with water through God's Word. He washes till you have no stain, wrinkle, or blemish, and He makes you holy and blameless before God the heavenly Father. The laver, which is a basin with water for cleansing, represents Christ the Word of God who makes you clean through the washing of His word as stated in Ephesians 5:25-26 and John 15:3. However, this would require your obedience to God's Word as mentioned in Matthew 4:4: "Man shall not live by bread alone but by every word that proceeds from the mouth of God." Your obedience begins at the laver by the washing of the Word. At this juncture, God the Holy Spirit is given to you as a deposit as mentioned in 2 Corinthians 5:4-6. You may wonder what this deposit refers to. As stated in Ephesians 1:13-14, the deposit guarantees our inheritance until we are fully redeemed and saved from the clutches of the Devil. What greater inheritance is there as compared to becoming fully like Christ? His leading in your life is the guarantee that Christformation will occur to the fullest through your obedience, following the conviction of your sins. You will grow in your obedience to Him and enter into a deeper relationship with Christ progressively which is symbolized by you entering the Outer Court as you move towards the Holy Place of the tabernacle. It is God the Holy Spirit who leads you at every step, till the end. You will not be able to progress on your own without His help. Before you enter the Holy Place in the tabernacle, there is the altar of incense, which offers fragrance unto the Lord to symbolize a life that pleases Him. God the Holy Spirit brings the fragrance of Christ into your life that makes you acceptable in God's presence. Likewise, in your Christformation, God the Holy Spirit leads you step by step towards full Christformation.

The Lord Jesus Christ will be revealed more and more as you are led into a deeper relationship with Him. Christ's divine nature as the light is formed in you, and you will become a child of Light and no more a child of darkness. The lampstand represents the Lord Jesus Christ as the light to His chosen people.

When His light is formed in your born-again spirit, you will never walk in darkness. Christformation with this divine nature of Christ will make the eternal difference in you. You either belong to the kingdom of Light or the kingdom of darkness. If you belong to Christ, you are in the kingdom of Light. As the Light is formed in you, all darkness will be dispelled in and around you, and the more the Light grows in you from day to day, the more the darkness will be dispelled from you. As you faithfully resist all the temptations of living in darkness, the light of Christ will be fully formed in you. Let's read the following verse that corresponds to the lampstand in the Tabernacle.

John 8:12:
"When Jesus spoke again to the people, he said, 'I am the light of the world. Whoever follows me will never walk in darkness, but will have the light of life.' "

Christ, the Light of life, will be formed and continue to grow in you, which is the sign that you are following Him.

God was and is more concerned about your life in Christ than following rituals. Every article in the tabernacle refers to your life in Christ, particularly Christformation in you. When you continually feed on the Bread of Life, you will be filled with Him. When Christformation takes place, there will be no room for the formation of sin in you. You will no longer aimlessly seek the things of this world to fill the vacuum within you.

The other article on the right was the table of shewbread. Christ our Lord was revealed as the Bread of Life at this table. Let's once again look at another passage that corresponds to the table of shewbread in the New Testament.

John 6:32–35:
"Jesus said to them, "Very truly I tell you, it is not Moses who has given you the bread from heaven, but it is my Father who gives you the true bread from heaven. For the bread of God is the bread that comes down from heaven and gives life to the world." "Sir," they said, "please always give us this bread." Then Jesus declared, "I am the bread of life. Whoever comes to me will never go hungry, and whoever believes in me will never be thirsty." "

There will be no Christformation in you, if you do need feed on the Bread of Life. When Christ is formed in you, there will be no hungering or thirsting for any other thing in this world to fill you, and you will be filled with your eternal inheritance. The bread and water that we consume on this earth fills us with strength for this world, but the Bread of Life that we feed on will form Christ in you forever.

The altar of incense is the other very important article in your life in Christ that brings God the Father's approval in you. The passage in the New Testament below corresponds to this article.

2 Corinthians 2:14–15:
"But thanks be to God, who always leads us in triumphal procession in Christ and through us spreads everywhere the fragrance of the knowledge of him. For we are to God the aroma of Christ among those who are being saved and those who are perishing."

The altar of incense symbolizes the aroma of Christ that is being formed within you. This aroma is the testimony of Jesus in your life. You must fill your life with the aroma (testimony) of Christ, so that you will be pleasing to the heavenly Father.

The difference between those who have Christformation increasing in them and those who are perishing is the testimony of Jesus that is present within them. Those who are perishing will never have the testimony of Jesus because there is no Christformation in them. Judas Iscariot is an example of this truth. He was with Christ but had no testimony of Jesus in him.

Like Judas, we can claim to belong to Christ, but unless the testimony of Jesus pleases God the Father through us, it will all be in vain. The testimony of Jesus comes through Christformation, the forming of the divine nature of Christ permanently in a believer through his or her obedience to Him. Judas did not obey Christ. Let's read the verse below to understand this further.

Revelation 12:11 (NLT)
"And they have defeated him by the blood of the Lamb and by their testimony. And they did not love their lives so much that they were afraid to die."

God's Word is the testimony of Jesus in you when you live obeying it. The Lord Jesus Christ is that Word that is being formed in you. Word became flesh so that He could turn His called, chosen, and faithful flesh into Word through Christformation in them. By your growing obedience to God's Word, this testimony of Christ grows in you. With the power of the blood of the Lamb cleansing you from your sins and your continual obedience to the Word of God in you, the eternal testimony of Christformation is produced in you with the help of God the Holy Spirit.

The altar of incense testifies to the defeat of the Devil through Christformation in you. With this incense of Christ, God the Father's approval will be upon your life. Christformation in you is the incense from the altar. This is how you could offer your bodies as living sacrifices and please the heavenly Father with your obedience to every word that proceeds from His mouth.

Are you able to see the altar of sacrifice and the bronze basin in the verse above in Revelation 12:11? The altar of sacrifice represents the blood of the Lamb, and the bronze basin represents the washing of the Word in your life. With these powers of Christ formed in you fully, the Devil is defeated in your life because you will never cherish the sinful nature of the Devil in you again and will not be afraid to put it to death as a testimony.

The boldness and confidence to come into a deeper relationship with the Lord comes through Christformation in you. You should continually seek full Christformation in you with the help of God the Holy Spirit who dwells within you. You will go through the veil because of the Christformation that is already in you. Without the Christformation that occurs at the altar of sacrifice and the bronze basin, you cannot enter into a deeper relationship with God in the Holy of Holies. The power of the blood of the Lamb and the Word must have been formed in you. In this way, you will have God's full approval.

At the altar of incense, you will enter into a deeper relationship with God in the Holy of Holies. The veil beyond this will appear torn, and you can gain access through a successful Christformation after being washed by the precious blood of the Lamb and the power of the Word of God in your life. We don't see any other way that you could enter into a deeper relationship with God than the way of Christformation in you. God's approval in your life at every stage is important for a deeper relationship with Him. Let's read the verse below to learn what the Bible says about gaining God's approval in your life.

1 Corinthians 11:19:
"No doubt there have to be differences among you to show which of you have God's approval."

Of course, the difference will be Christformation in you through your obedience to God the Holy Spirit and the help He provides for this. The veil will appear torn by your obedience at the previous stage just as the actual veil was torn by Christ's complete obedience to the heavenly Father through His death on the cross. You can enter into a deeper relationship with God through the formation of Christ's obedience in you. This confidence grows in you as Christ's important divine nature is successfully formed in you at the altar of sacrifice, the bronze basin, and the altar of incense. Let's compare the following two passages:

Hebrews 10:19–22:
"Therefore, brothers and sisters, since we have confidence to enter the Most Holy Place by the blood of Jesus, by a new and living way opened for us through the curtain, that is, his body, and since we have a great priest over the house of God, let us draw near to God with a sincere heart and with the full assurance that faith brings, having our hearts sprinkled to cleanse us from a guilty conscience and having our bodies washed with pure water."

2 Corinthians 3:12–18:
"Therefore, since we have such a hope, we are very bold. We are not like Moses, who would put a veil over his face to prevent the Israelites from seeing the end of what was passing away. But their minds were made dull, for to this day the same veil remains when the old covenant is read. It has not been removed, because only in Christ is it taken away. Even to this day when Moses is read, a veil covers their hearts. But whenever anyone turns to the Lord, the veil is taken away. Now the Lord is the Spirit, and where the Spirit of the Lord is, there is freedom. And we all, who with unveiled faces contemplate the Lord's glory, are being transformed into his image with ever-increasing glory, which comes from the Lord, who is the Spirit."

The veil is the body of Christ our Lord that was crucified on the cross. This veil in the tabernacle was torn in two the moment the Lord Jesus Christ breathed His last on the cross. This signified the new, living way through which we can go to the Father without a guilty conscience because of the blood and body of Christ shed and broken for us as a sacrifice for all our sins. We could enter into the Holy of Holies through Christ for full Christformation in us.

In the Holy of Holies are the mercy seat and the ark of the covenant. The ark of the covenant contained the gold jar of manna, Aaron's budding staff, and the stone tablets of the covenant. This ark represents the divine nature of Christ that is to be formed in you with His perfect humanity, divinity, and priesthood qualities like faith, goodness, love and many more as symbolized by the items in the ark stated earlier. The mercy seat of God, with hovering cherubim depicting His glory, signifies the formation of God's glorious presence in you as Emmanuel (God with us), who promises to eternally reside in you through Christformation.

Let us read these verses below:

Hebrews 9:3–5:
"Behind the second curtain was a room called the Most Holy Place which had the golden altar of incense and the gold-covered ark of the covenant. This ark contained the gold jar of manna, Aaron's staff that had budded, and the stone tablets of the covenant. Above the ark were the cherubim of the Glory, overshadowing the atonement cover. But we cannot discuss these things in detail now."

In summary, we could say Christformation starts at the bronze basin as soon as we have been washed with the precious blood of the Lamb that occurs at the altar of sacrifice. God the Holy Spirit leads us to the Word of God, which makes us clean. We are approved of God through our obedience as Christformation begins in us. With this approval of God upon our lives, we go deeper in our relationship with Him, passing the first veil into the Holy Place. The light of the Lord Jesus Christ is formed in us as we continue to obey His Word in our salvation walk in Him. He is also the Bread of Life, who fills us with eternal life as we eat and fill ourselves with Him. God's approval grows in us when Christformation in us starts rising as incense to the Lord through our obedience to the leading of God the Holy Spirit. We will then enter into the Holy of Holies. Full Christformation occurs in us as we faithfully obey God till the end of our days on earth.

SUMMARY: CHAPTER TWO

1) Christformation in You is a Pathway of Obedience to God's Will (Predestination)

Christformation is the revealed pathway of obedience to the Lord, especially to His people whom He has called out from the world. It is God's predestined will from the beginning that we have full Christformation in us at the end of all things. Christformation is the consummation of the Old and the New Testament, the whole will of God fulfilled through the example of the obedience of Christ our Lord. Therefore, Christformation in you is necessary. References: Romans 8:29–30; Colossians 1:15–20.

2) A Promise from God

i) **God made a promise in the garden of Eden** about Christformation in you. God promised that Christ, the Tree of Life, would be revealed to the world at the right time so that we could eat from that tree and live forever. Therefore, Christformation is the fulfillment of God's promise in you, and it is necessary. References: Genesis 3:15; Galatians 4:4.

ii) **God made the same promise to Abraham** that many will be blessed eternally with Christformation in them through his lineage because of his example of faith and obedience to God. God keeps His promise through successful Christformation in you, and therefore, Christformation in you is necessary. References: Genesis 12:1–3; Hebrews 11:8–12.

3) Examples of the Pathway of Obedience to the Lord in the Old Testament

i) **The Journey from Egypt to Canaan** is a picture of full Christformation in you. Every step and stage of that journey represents Christformation in you. Therefore, it is necessary to follow this example of perseverance for the Christformation journey.

71

ii) **Seven Appointed Feasts of the Lord.** Each of the seven appointed feasts of the Lord represents the seven progressive stages of feasting on Christ toward full Christformation in you. Therefore, as it was important for the Old Testament people of God to celebrate the seven feasts, it is important for us to feast in a similar manner on Christ faithfully until He is fully formed within us.

iii) **Milk and Honey, Bread and Wine.** In the Old Testament, feeding on Christ was through physical obedience, as milk and honey were produce of the flesh. In the New Testament, God's people are to feed on Christ's flesh and blood for full Christformation in them. Here, Christ is revealed as seed hidden in the ground, representing Christformation in you.

iv) **Tabernacle of Moses.** Every article, partition, procedure, and practice has semblance to Christformation in you. Therefore, it is necessary to have a vivid picture of the tabernacle in you so that you could obey Christ in all that He commanded in the Gospels toward full Christformation in you.

RUN THE RACE TOWARDS.....
FULL CHRISTFORMATION
IN YOU
HEBREWS 12: 1-2

CHAPTER THREE:
WHERE ELSE IS CHRISTFORMATION
MENTIONED IN THE BIBLE?

A) THE FOUR GOSPELS OF THE LORD JESUS CHRIST

Matthew	
1. The Temptation of Jesus	Chapter 4:1-11
2. The Beatitudes	Chapter 5:1-12
3. Salt and Light	Chapter 5:13-16
4. Fulfilment of the Law	Chapter 5:17-20
5. What is Done in Secret-Giving, Prayer and Fasting	Chapter 6:1-18
6. Treasures in Heaven	Chapter 6:19-24
7. Do not Worry	Chapter 6:25-34
8. Ask, Seek, Knock	Chapter 7:7-12
9. The Narrow and Wide Gate	Chapter 7:13-14
10. A Tree and its Fruit	Chapter 7:15-23
11. The Wise and Foolish Builders	Chapter 7:24-27
12. The Parable of Cloth and Wine	Chapter 9:16-17
13. Finding and Losing	Chapter 10:39
14. Rest for the Weary	Chapter 11:25-30
15. Make a Tree Good	Chapter 12:33-37
16. Evil Spirits Return	Chapter 12:43-45
17. The Parable of the Sower	Chapter 13:3-9
18. The Parable of the Weeds	Chapter 13:24-30
19. The Parables of the Mustard Seed and the Yeast	Chapter 13:31-33
20. Parable of the Hidden Treasure and the Pearl	Chapter 13:44-46
21. Parable of the Net	Chapter 13:47-52
22. Clean and Unclean	Chapter 15:10-20
23. Peter's Confession of Christ	Chapter 16:13-20
24. Take up your Cross	Chapter 16:23-27
25. The Greatest in the Kingdom of Heaven	Chapter 18: 1-9
26. The Parable of the Lost Sheep	Chapter 18:10-14
27. The Rich Young Man	Chapter 19:16-30
28. Parable of the Workers	Chapter 20:1-16
29. A Mother's Request	Chapter 20:20-28
30. The Parable of the Two Sons	Chapter 21:28-32
31. The Parable of the Tenants	Chapter 21:33-44
32. The Parable of the Wedding Banquet	Chapter 22:1-14
33. The Greatest Commandment	Chapter 22:37-39
34. The Seven Woes	Chapter 23:1-39
35. Signs of the End of Age	Chapter 24:4-35
36. The Day and Hour Unknown	Chapter 24:36-51
37. The Parables of the Ten Virgins, Talents, Sheep and Goat	Chapter 25:1-46
38: The Lord's Supper	Chapter 26:26-29
39. In the Garden of Gethsemane	Chapter 26:36-46
40. The Greatest Commission	Chapter 28:18-20

Diagram 3(a)

Mark	
1. The Parable of the New Patch and Wine	Chapter 2:21-22
2. The Parable of the Sower	Chapter 4:3-20
3. The Parable of a Lamp on a Stand	Chapter 4:21-25
4. The Parables of the Growing and Mustard Seed	Chapter 4:26-34
5. Clean and Unclean	Chapter 7:6-23
6. Taking Up Your Cross	Chapter 8:34-37
7. Putting to Death Your Sinful Nature	Chapter 9:42-50
8. The Parable of the Rich Young Man	Chapter 10:17-31
9. The Parable of the Tenants	Chapter 12:1-11
10. The Greatest Commandment	Chapter 12:29-31
11. The Day and Hour Unknown	Chapter 13:32-37
12. The Lord's Supper	Chapter 14:22-25
13. The Signs of the Believer	Chapter 16:15-18

Diagram 3(b)

John	
1. The Word Became Flesh	Chapter 1:1-18
2. Being Born Again	Chapter 3:3-21
3. Living Water	Chapter 4:10-24
4. The Bread of Life	Chapter 6:25-59
5. The Light of the World	Chapter 8:12-30
6. The Children of Abraham and the Devil	Chapter 8:31-47
7. The Shepherd and His Flock	Chapter 10:1-18
8. The Sheep will Listen to My Voice	Chapter 10:25-30
9. Losing and Saving	Chapter 12:23-26
10. Obeying God's Word	Chapter 12:44-50
11. Clean before God	Chapter 13:10-17
12. Love One Another	Chapter 13:34-35
13. In My Father's House	Chapter 14:1-4
14. Lord Jesus The Way	Chapter 14:5-14
15. God The Holy Spirit Promised	Chapter 14:15-31
16. The Vine and the Branches	Chapter 15:1-17
17. The Disciples Hated	Chapter 15:18-27, 16:1-4
18. The Work of God the Holy Spirit	Chapter 16:5-16
19. Grief Turned to Joy	Chapter 16:17-33
20. The Prayers of the Lord Jesus Christ	Chapter 17:1-26
21. Peter Reinstated	Chapter 21:15-19

Diagram 3(c)

Luke	
1. Simeon's Prophecy	Chapter 2:34-35
2. Christ's Growth	Chapter 2:39-40, 52
3. Isaiah's Prophecy	Chapter 3: 4-6
4. Producing Fruit unto Repentance	Chapter 3: 7-12
5. The Temptation of Jesus	Chapter 4:1-13
6. Who is Chosen for Christformation?	Chapter 4:25-27
7. Parable of the New Cloth and Wine	Chapter 5:36-38
8. Blessings and Woes	Chapter 6:20-26
9. Love Your Enemies	Chapter 6:27-36
10. Judging Other	Chapter 6:37-42
11. A Tree and its Fruit	Chapter 6:43-45
12. The Wise and Foolish Builders	Chapter 6:46-49
13. Parable of the Sower	Chapter 8:4-15
14. A Lamp on a Stand	Chapter 8:16-18
15. Lord Jesus' Mother and Brothers	Chapter 8:19-21
16. Take up your Cross	Chapter 9:23-26
17. The Cost of Following Jesus	Chapter 9:57-62
18. The Authority over the Enemy	Chapter 10:18-24
19. The Parable of the Good Samaritan	Chapter 10:30-36
20. The Lord's Prayer	Chapter 11:2-4
21. Asking In Prayer	Chapter 11:5-13
22. Kingdom Divided	Chapter 11:17-28
23. The Lamp of the Body	Chapter 11:33-36
24. The Six Woe	Chapter 11:37-54
25. The Parable of the Rich Fool	Chapter 12:13-21
26. Do Not Worry	Chapter 12:22-34
27. Watchfulness	Chapter 12:35-48
28. The Absence of Christformation in You	Chapter 13:6-9
29. The Parables of the Mustard Seed and the Yeast	Chapter 13:18-21
30. The Narrow Door	Chapter 13:22-30
31. The Parable of the Great Banquet	Chapter 14:15-24
32. The Cost of Being a Disciple	Chapter 14:25-35
33. The Parables of the Lost Sheep, Coin and Son	Chapter 15:1-32
34. The Parables of the Shrewd Manager	Chapter 16:1-18
35. The Parable of the Rich Man and Lazarus	Chapter 16:19-31
36. Sin, Faith and Duty	Chapter 17:1-10
37. The Coming of the Kingdom of God	Chapter 17:20-37
38. The Parable of The Persistent Widow, Pharisee & Tax Collector	Chapter 18:1-14
39. Faith Like a Child	Chapter 18:16-17
40. The Parable of the Ten Minas	Chapter 19:11-27
41. The Parable of the Tenants	Chapter 20:9-18
42. God of the Living	Chapter 20:34-38
43. Signs of the End of Age	Chapter 21:5-36
44. The Last Supper	Chapter 22:14-20
45. The Greatest Among You	Chapter 22:24-35
46. Prayer on the Mount of Olives	Chapter 22:39-46
47. Waiting in Jerusalem	Chapter 24:45-49

Diagram 3(d)

B) IN THE BOOKS OF THE OLD TESTAMENT

References	Relevance to Christformation in You	Specific Messages
The Pentateuch (First five books): • Genesis • Exodus • Numbers • Leviticus • Deuteronomy	Creation, The Fall of Man, Cain and Abel, Noah's Ark, Tower of Babel, Abraham, Melchizedek, Isaac, Jacob, Joseph, Moses, Crossing of the Red Sea, Journey from Egypt to Canaan, the Ten Commandments and the Ceremonial Laws, the Tabernacle of Moses, The Seven Appointed Feasts of the Lord, Crossing of Jordan River, Entering and Conquering Canaan Land.	• The sinful nature of the Devil in man. • Obedience to the Lord God and types of Christformation in you.
Leaders of God's People: Joshua, Judges, Kings, Priests	The lives of Joshua, Queen Esther, David, Solomon and some of the judges and kings who obeyed God in adverse situations. The sinful nature of the Devil in man.	Eternal leadership of Christ our Lord.
Major and Minor Prophets of God	The prophecies and lives of Ezra, Nehemiah, Samuel, Isaiah, Jeremiah, Elijah, Elisha, Ezekiel, Daniel, Hosea, Jonah, Zechariah, Habakkuk, Malachi and all the other prophets of God. The sinful nature of the Devil in man.	God's message through His prophets and prophecies about Christformation in you.
Poetic Books	Psalms, Proverbs, Songs of Solomon, Lamentations, Job.	
Individual characters	Hannah, Rahab, Naaman, Enoch, Johnathan and many others like them.	

Diagram 3(e)

C) THE OLD TESTAMENT PROPHETS OF GOD

Prophets	Scripture Passage(s)	Relevance to Christformation in You
Isaiah	1. Chapter 4:2-6 2. Chapter 6:1-13 3. Chapter 7:1-25 4. Chapter 8:12-18 5. Chapter 9:6-7 6. Chapter 10:20-23 7. Chapter 11:1-16 8. Chapter 12-Chapter 31 9. Chapter 32-Chapter 51 10. Chapter 52-Chapter 66	1. The Branch of the Lord. 2. The Holy Seed. 3. The Fertile Land 4. A Stumbling Stone 5. A Child is born 6. The Remnant 7. The Branch from Jesse 8. The Strength for Battle 9. Kingdom of Righteousness 10. Eternal Victory
Jeremiah	1. Chapter 1-Chapter 11 2. Chapter 12-Chapter 22 3. Chapter 23-Chapter 29 4. Chapter 30-Chapter 39 5. Chapter 40-Chapter 52	1. Salvation Prophecy 2. Deliverance Promise 3. The Righteous Branch 4. Restoration Promise 5. Full Restoration

Ezekiel	1. Chapter 1-Chapter 10
	2. Chapter 11-Chapter 24
	3. Chapter 25-Chapter 32
	4. Chapter 33-Chapter 36
	5. Chapter 37:1-28
	6. Chapter 38-Chapter 39
	7. Chapter 40-Chapter 48
		1. The Living Creatures
		2. Judgement-Parables
		3. Prophecy over Land
		   a. Watchman
		   b. Valley of Dry Bones
		   c. Prophecy
		   d. New Temple

Daniel	1. Chapter 1-Chapter 6 2. Chapter 7-Chapter 12	1. God's Power Shown 2. Prophecy and Signs

Diagram 3(f)

D) THE NEW TESTAMENT APOSTLES OF CHRIST

Apostles of Christ	Scripture Passage(s)	Relevance to Christformation in You
James	Chapter 1-Chapter 5	Obedience to Christ our Lord in all areas of life is required for Christformation in you.
Peter	1 Peter: Chapter 1- Chapter 5	Learning obedience to Christ through sufferings for full Christformation in you.
	2 Peter: Chapter 1-Chapter 3	Making every effort for full Christformation in you
Jude	Verses 1-25	Perseverance for full Christformation in you.
John	1 John 2 John 3 John	Walking as Jesus Did: Through obedience

Diagram 3(g)

E) THE BOOK OF ACTS

Scripture Passage(s)	Relevance to Christformation in You
Chapter 1 & 2	Baptism of God the Holy Spirit on believers
Chapter 3-Chapter 8	Demonstration of God's Power in His disciples
Chapter 9-Chapter 28	Demonstration of God's power in Apostle Paul's Conversion and consequent ministry

Diagram 3(h)

F) PAULINE EPISTLES

Epistles	Relevance to Christformation in You
Romans 1 & 2 Corinthians Galatians Ephesians Philippians Colossians 1 & 2 Thessalonians Hebrews	The divine nature of Christ our Lord revealed for Christformation in you. This would require our total obedience to Christ through God the Holy Spirit for full Christformation in you
1 & 2 Timothy Titus Philemon	Following the Great Shepherd for full Christformation in you

Diagram 3(i)

G) THE BOOK OF REVELATION

Scripture Passage(s)	Relevance to Christformation in You
1. Chapter 1-Chapter 3	Overcoming the sinful nature of the Devil in you for full formation of Christ's divine nature in you
2. Chapter 4-Chapter 18	The authority of Christ our Lord in executing judgment and for full Christformation in you
3. Chapter 18-Chapter 22	Restoration of the Garden of Eden fellowship with God through Christformation in you

Diagram 3(j)

SUMMARY: CHAPTER THREE

Section A	Christormation was extensively mentioned about in the four gospels; Matthew, Mark, Luke and John, through the teachings and parables of the Lord.
Section B	The Old Testament has many structural examples of Christformation; written for your knowledge and as practical examples of faith with obedience.
Section C	The patriarchs and the prophets of God in the Old Testament had prophesied about Christformation.
Section D	The apostles of Christ explained about Christformation to believers.
Section E	The book of Acts, in particular has many accounts of Christformation in believers.
Section F	The general and Pauline epistles contain teachings about Christformation.
Section G	The book of Revelation has many parables about Christformation.

Diagram 3(k)

The big picture of Christformation from the book of Genesis to Revelation is made available to you for easy referencing through the related passages and verses given. We urge you to search the scriptures to learn more truths about Christformation. You will realize God's perfect plan for those who obey Christ through these scriptures. Both the Old and the New Testaments have a similar message of obedience to Christ. In the Old Testament, obedience to Christ is measured by the keeping of God's laws or regulations, observing ceremonies and celebrations of festivals which all pointed to Christformation. The New Testament became a necessity when the laws of God were not obeyed during Old Testament times. Anyone who had disobeyed any of the laws of God would have disobeyed all. In this way, the Lord Jesus Christ came to fulfill the laws of

God. He obeyed all of God's commandments. Now, you who believe and obey Christ will have His divine nature formed in you fully. Therefore, the Old Testament is a physical or structural example of Christformation. We should never commit the folly of discarding or omitting the Old Testament. Many parts of the Old Testament were written as practical examples of Christformation for you.

CHRISTFORMATION
IS THE TESTIMONY OF CHRIST
IN YOU

REVELATION 12: 11

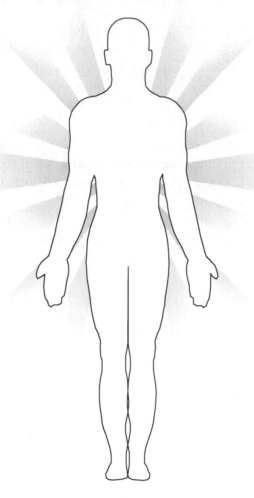

Chapter Four:
How Does Christformation
Occur in You?

First, you must be born again in your spirit for Christformation to begin in you. If you are born again but do not obey Christ, you will have no Christformation in you. Instead, you might be filled with evil spirits! You must choose to obey Christ until the end for full Christformation to occur in you.

You have to actively cooperate with God the Holy Spirit by making every effort toward Christformation in you at all times. Your willful disobedience to Christ will disrupt and even abort Christformation in you. God the Holy Spirit is your promised helper for Christformation in you and will guide you into everything necessary for full Christformation in you. God the Holy Spirit, who dwells within you, makes you a temple of the Holy Spirit. God demonstrates His power through Christformation in that temple.

A) Christformation is the Demonstration of the Power of God—the Holy Spirit—in You

1 Thessalonians 1:4–5:
"For we know, brothers and sisters loved by God, that he has chosen you, because our gospel came to you not simply with words but also with power, with the Holy Spirit and deep conviction. You know how we lived among you for your sake."

The power of the Word of God, especially the gospel of the Lord Jesus Christ, is demonstrated in your life by God the Holy Spirit through Christformation in you. You will need to allow the full demonstration of His power in your life if you are to experience full Christformation in you, which cannot be forced upon you—you must allow it to happen in your life. You must obey the leading of God the Holy Spirit in your entire walk with Christ for full Christformation in you. You should be actively sowing into your born-again spirit the growth of Christformation in you through your obedience to Christ and His Word, which has the power of God the Holy Spirit to turn them into Christformation in you when you obey.

1 Corinthians 2:3–5:

"I came to you in weakness with great fear and trembling. My message and my preaching were not with wise and persuasive words, but with a demonstration of the Spirit's power, so that your faith might not rest on human wisdom, but on God's power."

Christformation in you is the demonstration of God's power through the gospel of the Lord Jesus Christ as you are counseled and assisted closely by God the Holy Spirit who lives within you. The demonstration of God the Holy Spirit is further witnessed through the successful transformation of the sinful mind into the mind of Christ. God the Holy Spirit helps in the transformation of the mind of the believer through the Christformation that has already occurred in the born-again spirit. If Christformation has not occurred in the believer's born-again spirit because of his or her disobedience to God the Holy Spirit, there will be no transformation of the mind. The believer's faith rests on God's power and not on his or her own strength.

John 16:12–16:

" "I have much more to say to you, more than you can now bear. But when he, the Spirit of truth, comes, he will guide you into all the truth. He will not speak on his own; he will speak only what he hears, and he will tell you what is yet to come. He will glorify me because it is from me that he will receive what he will make known to you. All that belongs to the Father is mine. That is why I said the Spirit will receive from me what he will make known to you." Jesus went on to say, "In a little while you will see me no more, and then after a little while you will see me." "

God the Holy Spirit guides you into all truth when you obey His leading, not for your own head knowledge, as mistakenly perceived by many, but for full Christformation to occur in you. God the Holy Spirit only speaks what He hears. From the verses above, you know that God the Holy Spirit is a person, for He hears and speaks. He will also tell you what is yet to come.

What is "yet to come"? The Lord Jesus is yet to come, and He is coming back for sure. God the Holy Spirit will constantly remind you of this. What else is "yet to come?" The end of the age is yet to come, and it is surely coming soon. He will remind you of this too. What else? Full Christformation in you is yet to come, but it is only going to happen when you fully obey His leading until the end. He will keep assuring you of this! What will God the Holy Spirit receive from the Lord Jesus Christ that He will make known to you? Let us look into the verses below for the answers.

1 Corinthians 2:9–15:
"However, as it is written: "What no eye has seen, what no ear has heard, and what no human mind has conceived"— the things God has prepared for those who love him—these are the things God has revealed to us by his Spirit. The Spirit searches all things, even the deep things of God. For who knows a person's thoughts except their own spirit within them? In the same way, no one knows the thoughts of God except the Spirit of God. What we have received is not the spirit of the world, but the Spirit who is from God, so that we may understand what God has freely given us. This is what we speak, not in words taught us by human wisdom but in words taught by the Spirit, explaining spiritual realities with Spirit-taught words. The person without the Spirit does not accept the things that come from the Spirit of God but considers them foolishness, and cannot understand them because they are discerned only through the Spirit. The person with the Spirit makes judgments about all things, but such a person is not subject to merely human judgments."

What are these that no eye has seen, no ear heard, and no mind conceived? What are these things that God had prepared for those who love Him? God the Holy Spirit dwells within you through Christ our Lord so that you may understand the deep things that God has freely given you. What has He freely given you? He has freely given you the exceptional ability to understand and accept everything that comes from our Living God through Christ our Lord. Only God the Holy Spirit could reveal them to you when He dwells in you!

You can discern and make right judgments only through God the Holy Spirit who dwells within you. How can accurate discernment and good judgment be in you if you consider the leading and guidance of God the Holy Spirit as foolishness? There is a vast difference between mere human judgments and God the Holy Spirit-led judgments. A person who is subject to merely human judgments cannot understand judgments that come from God the Holy Spirit. In the first place, if you don't have Him in you, how can you understand anything that comes from God? How can Christ be formed in you if you cannot discern the leading of God the Holy Spirit for Christformation in you? The divine nature of Christ— spiritual judgment, discernment, fear of the Lord, and understanding—is only revealed and formed in those who obey the leading of God the Holy Spirit. Let us also read what the passage below says about this.

Matthew 13:10–16:
"The disciples came to him and asked, "Why do you speak to the people in parables?" He replied, "Because the knowledge of the secrets of the kingdom of heaven has been given to you, but not to them. Whoever has will be given more, and they will have abundance. Whoever does not have, even what they have will be taken from them. This is why I speak to them in parables: 'Though seeing, they do not see; though hearing, they do not hear or understand.' In them is fulfilled the prophecy of Isaiah: 'You will be ever hearing but never understanding; you will be ever seeing but never perceiving. For this people's heart have become calloused; they hardly hear with their ears, and they have closed their eyes. Otherwise they might see with their eyes, hear with their ears, understand with their hearts and turn, and I would heal them.' But blessed are your eyes because they see and your ears because they hear."

How can you obey if you cannot understand what God is saying to you? How can Christformation in you occur if you do not obey the leading and guidance of God the Holy Spirit? He does not say anything on His own. He only says what He hears from God and Christ. In fact, He says everything about Christ our Lord to you. As for the heavenly Father, all that He had said and still says is about Christ, just as when the Lord Jesus Christ was on earth, He said everything about the heavenly Father and forewarned us about welcoming and obeying God the Holy Spirit. Christ reminded us that God the Holy Spirit would come to fill His place on earth during His physical absence.

John 16:7–11:
"But very truly I tell you, it is for your good that I am going away. Unless I go away, the Advocate will not come to you; but if I go, I will send him to you. When he comes, he will prove the world to be in the wrong about sin and righteousness and judgment: about sin, because people do not believe in me; about righteousness, because I am going to the Father, where you can see me no longer; and about judgment because the prince of this world now stands condemned."

God the Holy Spirit is the most important person for Christformation in you. He is sent by Christ our Lord to help you with full Christformation in you. Your obedience to His leading and guidance will benefit you with full Christformation in you. This is vital. When you do not obey Him, you will be void of Christformation in you. The evil prince of this world will do all he can to disrupt and even abort Christformation in you by tempting you to disobey God. Only when you obey Him, the power of God the Holy Spirit will be demonstrated in you. The misdeeds of the sinful nature of the Devil in you will be put to death with God the Holy Spirit's power within you.

The full armor of God is Christformation in you. Only with Christformation could you ward off the attacks of the Evil One. Righteousness, truth, the gospel, faith, the Word, and salvation can only come through Christformation in you, and Christformation comes through your obedience to God's Word. Let us read the passage from the book of Ephesians to learn more about this.

Ephesians 6:10–18:
"Finally, be strong in the Lord and in his mighty power. Put on the full armor of God, so that you can take your stand against the devil's schemes. For our struggle is not against flesh and blood, but against

the rulers, against the authorities, against the powers of this dark world and against the spiritual forces of evil in the heavenly realms. Therefore put on the full armor of God, so that when the day of evil comes, you may be able to stand your ground, and after you have done everything, to stand. Stand firm then, with the belt of truth buckled around your waist, with the breastplate of righteousness in place, and with your feet fitted with the readiness that comes from the gospel of peace. In addition to all this, take up the shield of faith, with which you can extinguish all the flaming arrows of the evil one. Take the helmet of salvation and the sword of the Spirit, which is the word of God. And pray in the Spirit on all occasions with all kinds of prayers and requests. With this in mind, be alert and always keep on praying for all the Lord's people."

Standing against the Devil's schemes is no ordinary task. Each of you may have varied experiences handling the Devil, especially with the sinful nature of the Devil. Bear in mind that the Devil has about six thousand years of experience handling man, starting with Adam and Eve. So if you are going to stand against the Devil's schemes, you need to have strength that has more than six thousand years in practical experience. You can't imagine anyone with that strength besides the Lord Jesus Christ, who said, "Before Abraham, I Am."

Unless Christ our Lord's divine nature is formed in you, you cannot stand against the Devil's schemes. The breastplate of righteousness, the belt of truth, the ever-readiness of the gospel shoes for peace, the shield of faith, the sword of the Spirit, the helmet of salvation, and an attitude of continual praying in the Spirit for all the people of God, who are purchased by the blood of Jesus Christ our Lord, are to be formed in you. The exhortation to put on this full armor of God is the encouragement to allow full Christformation in you.

You must choose to allow the divine nature of Christ our Lord to be formed in you. It will never be forced on you. God the Holy Spirit dwells within you to help you with full Christformation in you, but only when you fully yield yourself to His leading and guidance.

B) An Explanation from the Parable of the Sower

The Parable of the Sower best explains how Christformation occurs in you. This parable is one of the first parables that were expounded by the Lord Jesus Christ to His twelve disciples. Christformation in you is a long and gradual sowing and reaping process. Let's study this passage together to understand the related truths.

Matthew 13:18–23:
" "Listen then to what the parable of the sower means: When anyone hears the message about the kingdom and does not understand it, the evil one comes and snatches away what was sown in their heart. This is the seed sown along the path. The seed falling on rocky ground refers to someone who hears the word and at once receives it with joy. But since they have no root, they last only a short time. When trouble or persecution comes because of the word, they quickly fall away. The seed falling among the thorns refers to someone who hears the word, but the worries of this life and the deceitfulness of wealth choke the word, making it unfruitful. But the seed falling on good soil refers to someone who hears the word and understands it. This is the one who produces a crop, yielding a hundred, sixty, or thirty times what was sown." "

Christformation in you is about your response to God's Word when you first hear it. It is very important that you understand it as God intends and not interpret it to your own liking. Most of the time, God's Word is not understood the way He intends. If it was, it would produce the intended Christformation in you in the end. In fact, the apostle Paul likened full Christformation in you to the complications of childbirth in Galatians 4:19, "My dear children, for whom I am again in the pains of childbirth until Christ is formed in you." He was saying to the believers that any hindrance or lack of interest in God's Word on your part and the world's influence can abort Christformation in you, which is what the Devil would like to see happen in you. But as it is said in 1 John 4:4; "greater is He that is in you than he that is in the world." For those who are overcomers of the sinful nature of the Devil through their obedience to God's Word, God the Holy Spirit will help develop full Christformation in them.

The gradual process of sowing and reaping in obedience to God's Word for full Christformation in you is the main message of the Parable of the Sower. Any cause for stunted growth or aborting of Christformation in you will show your personal disobedience to God's Word. So you have to be careful when you hear God's Word each time. What God requires of you in obedience to His word will result in Christformation in you. How much you yield yourself to the leading and guidance of God the Holy Spirit will determine how much Christformation occurs in you. In this way, you will learn that God cannot be deceived. What you sow is what you will reap through your obedience to God's Word. If you keep sowing with misdeeds from the sinful nature of the Devil in you, you will only reap destruction through eternal death. But if you keep sowing with good deeds from the divine nature of Christ, Christformation will occur in you.

The testimony of Jesus is formed in you through your obedience to God's Word with the help of God the Holy Spirit. When you understand God's word clearly, you want to obey Him. When you obey Him, Christformation occurs in you. Let's read the passage below.

Galatians 6:7–10:
"Do not be deceived: God cannot be mocked. A man reaps what he sows. The one who sows to please his sinful nature, from that nature will reap destruction; the one who sows to please the Spirit, from the Spirit will reap eternal life. Let us not become weary in doing good, for at the proper time we will reap a harvest if we do not give up. Therefore, as we have opportunity, let us do good to all people, especially to those who belong to the family of believers."

If God's Word is sown in you and you want to obey Him rather than the sinful nature of the Devil in you, there should be no reason why there won't be Christformation in you.

If you keep hearing the Word of God but obey only the sinful nature of the Devil in you, how can the divine nature of Christ be formed in you? "Sowing to please the flesh" means pleasing the sinful nature of the Devil in you, which is indirectly pleasing the Devil. This is how the Devil will claim ownership of you. How can you say you belong to God when you keep obeying the sinful nature of the Devil in you? Obedience to God's Word is sowing Christformation in you. At harvest time, you will reap full Christformation in you if you have fully obeyed Christ and His words.

The Parable of the Sower is about obedience to the Lord for full Christformation in you. The full formation of Christ's divine nature is what you will reap eternally. If you offer your life fully to the Lord Jesus Christ with obedience to His Word, you are led and guided by God the Holy Spirit within you. Didn't Christ our Lord warn us that we can claim to belong to Him in this world and yet continue sinning and do evil like anyone else that does not belong to Him? Let's read this passage below to grasp this important truth.

Matthew 7:22–24:
"Many will say to me on that day, 'Lord, Lord, did we not prophesy in your name and in your name drive out demons and in your name perform many miracles?' Then I will tell them plainly, 'I never knew you. Away from me, you evildoers!' Therefore everyone who hears these words of mine and puts them into practice is like a wise man who built his house on the rock."

Take note of the word *many*. *Many* will claim to have belonged to Him and have worked or ministered to others in His name but continued doing evil at the same time. You may ask, "What is the evil that they might have done?" All disobedience to God's Word is evil. Those who have an ongoing relationship with Christ our Lord are those who obey Him. Those who do not obey Him do not have a relationship with Him. That's why He said to them, "I never knew you."

Is it possible to do His work when you do not have a relationship with Him? Yes! But you must be ready to face the consequences of your own actions for such pretense. You can pretend to be doing His work, but Christformation in you requires your obedience to God's Word. Let's look at another passage that speaks about this.

James 1:21–25:
"Therefore, get rid of all moral filth and the evil that is so prevalent and humbly accept the word planted in you, which can save you. Do not merely listen to the word, and so deceive yourselves. Do what it says. Anyone who listens to the word but does not do what it says is like someone who looks at his face in a mirror and, after looking at himself, goes away and immediately forgets what he looks like. But whoever looks intently into the perfect law that gives freedom, and continues in it—not forgetting what they have heard, but doing it—they will be blessed in what they do."

You must humbly accept the Word planted in you, but before that, you have to rid yourself of pleasing the sinful nature of the Devil in you. You must consider the sinful nature of the Devil in you as moral filth. Otherwise, it will be difficult for you to humbly accept the Word planted in you, as humbly accepting the Word planted in you will lead to your doing as it says. God's Word is not meant for entertaining our ears, but for us to learn obedience to God. God's Word sown in us must produce His desired fruit, which is full Christformation in us.

The Lord Jesus Christ Himself is that Word of God that is sown in us. When we obey God's Word, we are obeying Christ. By obeying Him, His divine nature is formed within us.

C) An Explanation from the Parable of the Hidden Treasure or Pearl

Matthew 13:43–46:
"Then the righteous will shine like the sun in the kingdom of their Father. Whoever has ears, let them hear. The kingdom of heaven is like treasure hidden in a field. When a man found it, he hid it again, and then in his joy went and sold all he had and bought that field. Again, the kingdom of heaven is like a merchant looking for fine pearls. When he found one of great value, he went away and sold everything he had and bought it."

If you do not see or understand God's kingdom to be "like treasure hidden in a field," you will be void of Christformation in you because you will not see or understand the importance of seeking it with all your heart, mind, and strength. Fine pearls are rare, expensive, and difficult to find. There is a high price to pay for a quality pearl. Once you have found one, you would willingly pay the full price to buy it. So, is Christformation as valuable to you as treasure hidden in a field? If so, you would want to give up all of the sinful nature of the Devil in you in order to have full Christformation.

Also, Christformation in you is hidden and is secretly formed in your born-again spirit with the help of God the Holy Spirit, just like the precious pearl in an oyster that is hidden deep down on the seabed. When you understand that Christformation is the kingdom of God in you, you will start getting rid of the sinful nature of the Devil in you as you will view it as moral filth, even though you had at one time treasured it. Apostle Paul sternly warned the Roman believers about living to please the sinful nature of the Devil in them, even after believing in the Lord Jesus Christ. Let's be warned as we read this key verse for Christformation in you.

Romans 8:13:
"For if you live according to the sinful nature, you will die; but if by the Spirit you put to death the misdeeds of the body, you will live."

Living according to the flesh is willfully pleasing the sinful nature of the Devil in you. If you live like this, you will surely have eternal and spiritual death after your physical death. If you actively put to death the misdeeds of the body, which are the results of obeying the sinful nature of the Devil in you, you will surely live, as Christ will be formed in you eternally when you obey His Word. You "put to death the misdeeds of the body" not in your own strength but by obeying God the Holy Spirit.

You have to buy the highly valued pearl or "treasure hidden in a field" through the full submission of your life to God. You must seek Christ with all your heart, mind, and strength for full Christformation in you. You will have to humbly accept that full Christformation in you is the greatest treasure in your life, and you are committed to obeying the leading of God the Holy Spirit in you. You will have to accept that Christformation in you does not come easily as it requires you to "sow with tears" through your obedience to Christ.

Christformation in you is as gold refined in fire. You have to work out Christformation in you through your obedience to God's Word with fear and trembling through the guidance and leading of God the Holy Spirit. You will have to carry your cross by putting to death the sinful nature of the Devil in you. By denying the pleasing of your flesh, full Christformation in you will be produced with the help of God the Holy Spirit.

You must make every effort to ensure that full Christformation occurs in you so that your faith in the Lord Jesus Christ, the heavenly Father, and God the Holy Spirit will show through your full obedience to them. Apostle Paul desired to see this happen in the believers when he instructed Titus as to what he should teach them as stated in the passage below.

Titus 2:11–15 (NLT):
"For the grace of God has been revealed, bringing salvation to all people. And we are instructed to turn from godless living and sinful pleasures. We should live in this evil world with wisdom, righteousness, and devotion to God, while we look forward with hope to that wonderful day when the glory of our great God and Savior, Jesus Christ, will be revealed. He gave his life to free us from every kind of sin, to cleanse us, and to make us his very own people, totally committed to doing good deeds. You must teach these things and encourage the believers to do them. You have the authority to correct them when necessary, so don't let anyone disregard what you say."

By receiving the grace of God, the end result should be your turning from godless living and sinful pleasures. This would mean that if you do not turn away from godless living and sinful pleasures, you are very far away from God's grace, and continuing to live like that would mean that you didn't really experience God's grace in the first place. If you had, you would have turned away from your godless living and sinful pleasures.

Wisdom, righteousness, and devotion to God can only fill you if Christ is formed in you. All these are of His divine nature that is to be formed in you. The glory of our great God and Savior will be revealed as full Christformation in you, and we should look forward to this with great hope. "He gave his life to free us from every kind of sin, to cleanse us, and to make us his very own people, totally committed to doing good deeds." Isn't this what the apostle James means in the passage below?

James 3:13–18:
"Who is wise and understanding among you? Let him show it by his good life, by deeds done in the humility that comes from wisdom. But if you harbor bitter envy and selfish ambition in your hearts, do not boast about it or deny the truth. Such "wisdom" does not come down from heaven but is earthly, unspiritual, of the devil. For where you have envy and selfish ambition, there you find disorder and every evil practice. But the wisdom that comes from heaven is first of all pure; then peace-loving, considerate, submissive, full of mercy and good fruit, impartial and sincere. Peacemakers who sow in peace raise a harvest of righteousness."

If you have believed in the Lord Jesus Christ, your faith should result in successful Christformation in you. If Christformation in you isn't the harvest of your salvation, your faith was useless. There will be nothing to show your true faith in Him. You were disobedient to the leading and guidance of God the Holy Spirit for Christformation in you.

In the book of Revelation, we witness Christ our Lord rebuking those who were not willing to commit themselves to Christformation. They were deluded into thinking that they would be saved as long as they believed in Christ without making any other effort in their walk with God. Here, Christ our Lord is saying that if you believe, your actions should follow. Otherwise, what you believe is pointless.

Revelation 3:14–18:
" "To the angel of the church in Laodicea write: These are the words of the Amen, the faithful and true witness, the ruler of God's creation. I know your deeds, that you are neither cold nor hot. I wish you were

either one or the other! So, because you are lukewarm—neither hot nor cold—I am about to spit you out of my mouth. You say, 'I am rich; I have acquired wealth and do not need a thing.' But you do not realize that you are wretched, pitiful, poor, blind, and naked. I counsel you to buy from me gold refined in the fire, so you can become rich; and white clothes to wear, so you can cover your shameful nakedness; and salve to put on your eyes, so you can see."

The Lord Jesus Christ counsels you to buy something from Him. "Buy what?" you may ask. Buy "gold refined in the fire," which is full Christformation in you, "so you can become rich; and have white clothes to wear, so you can cover your shameful nakedness; and salve to put on your eyes, so you can see." Christformation in you will be "tested in fire." How else would you know it is pure gold?

You must be willing to give up godless living and sinful pleasures in exchange for Christformation in you, no matter how difficult it gets. As mentioned in Revelation 3:18, you are counseled to buy gold refined in fire (pay the price) for Christformation in you. Only then will you be rich in God's eyes. You will have white clothes to "cover your shameful nakedness," and salve to put on your eyes, so that you could see God clearly. This is a reminder of the beatitude in Matthew 5:8 where only the pure can see God. This parable speaks about full Christformation in you.

The pathway to full Christformation requires your full obedience to Christ through the leading of God the Holy Spirit. Without Christformation in you, you will be wretched, pitiful, poor, blind, and naked. If you are willing to lose everything of this world—especially its pleasures—by denying yourself the sinful nature of the Devil, you will in the end save your life eternally through full Christformation in you. Let's read the passage below to understand its meaning carefully and to make the necessary effort to live by it.

Luke 9:22–24:
"And he said, 'The Son of Man must suffer many things and be rejected by the elders, chief priests, and teachers of the law, and he must be killed and on the third day be raised to life.' Then he said to them all,

'If anyone would come after me, he must deny himself and take up his cross daily and follow me. For whoever wants to save his life will lose it, but whoever loses his life for me will save it.' "

"Come after me" is your decision to obey Christ our Lord and all His commandments until the end. "He must deny himself" is your decision to put to death all the misdeeds of the flesh willingly and, in this way, crucifying the sinful nature of the Devil in you with its passions and evil desires. "Take up your cross" is your decision to willingly suffer ridicule, shame, oppression, persecution, and all kinds of opposition from the Enemy and his allies so that full Christformation occurs in you. "Follow me" is your decision to obey the leading and guidance of God the Holy Spirit, whom Christ our Lord had appointed as your helper and counselor for full Christformation in you.

D) An Explanation from the Parable of the Growing Seed, Mustard Seed, and Yeast

Mark 4:26–32:
"He also said, "This is what the kingdom of God is like. A man scatters seed on the ground. Night and day, whether he sleeps or gets up, the seed sprouts and grows, though he does not know how. All by itself the soil produces grain—first the stalk, then the head, then the full kernel in the head. As soon as the grain is ripe, he puts the sickle to it, because the harvest has come." Again he said, "What shall we say the kingdom of God is like, or what parable shall we use to describe it? It is like a mustard seed, which is the smallest of all seeds on earth. Yet when planted, it grows and becomes the largest of all garden plants, with such big branches that the birds can perch in its shade." "

The kingdom of God is Christformation in you. Christ is the King of kings and Lord of lords appointed by the heavenly Father. Jesus Christ our Lord and King fills everything of His kingdom. So it is right that as His eternal subjects, bought by His precious blood shed at the cross of Calvary, that we be filled with Him through full Christformation in us.

The parable of the growing seed best explains this Christformation in you. Christformation starts from within a believer in his or her born-again spirit, but this cannot be seen with our physical eyes. God the heavenly Father, the Lord Jesus Christ, God the Holy Spirit, and your born-again spirit will be the only ones who will know everything about the Christformation that's occurring in you; the world and the people around you might not know it. "Night and day, whether he sleeps or gets up, the seed sprouts and grows, though he does not know how." Even we might not know how or when exactly the divine nature of Christ our Lord is formed within us, but at harvest time, we will realize it.

The stalk, the head, and the full kernel are where the grain or the fruit is housed. The grain does not just appear but grows gradually into one with the help of the stalk, head, and kernel. When the "grain is ripe" means that the harvest (putting in the sickle) time has come. Take note that there is a time for the grain to become ripe. Christformation seed sown into your born-again spirit will grow into a stalk, head, and kernel, meaning the full transformation of your mind into the mind of Christ and the clothing of your body with the imperishable, Christ-conformed body.

It is not harvest time until the plant has fully grown with the grain or fruit of full Christformation in you. It is God, the owner of the ground, who decides when the grain is ripe, not you and me who merely house the grain or fruit. This is what the Lord Jesus Christ meant when He said that He is going to prepare a place for us. Let us read these verses where He had said these things to understand how it relates to Christformation in you.

John 14:1–14:
" "Do not let your hearts be troubled. You believe in God; believe also in me. My Father's house has many rooms; if that were not so, would I have told you that I am going there to prepare a place for you? And if I go and prepare a place for you, I will come back and take you to be with me that you also may be where I am. You know the way to the place where I am going. Thomas said to him, "Lord, we don't know where you are going, so how can we know the way?" Jesus answered, "I am the way and the

truth and the life. No one comes to the Father except through me. If you really know me, you will know my Father as well. From now on, you do know him and have seen him." Philip said, "Lord, show us the Father and that will be enough for us." Jesus answered: "Don't you know me, Philip, even after I have been among you such a long time? Anyone who has seen me has seen the Father. How can you say, 'Show us the Father'? Don't you believe that I am in the Father, and that the Father is in me? The words I say to you I do not speak on my own authority. Rather, it is the Father, living in me, who is doing his work. Believe me when I say that I am in the Father and the Father is in me; or at least believe on the evidence of the works themselves. Very truly I tell you, whoever believes in me will do the works I have been doing, and they will do even greater things than these, because I am going to the Father. And I will do whatever you ask in my name, so that the Father may be glorified in the Son. You may ask me for anything in my name, and I will do it."

This was another parable the Lord Jesus Christ spoke regarding Christformation in you to His disciples. "The way, the truth, and the life" is Christ's divine nature that must be formed in you first if you are going to be joined with the heavenly Father, God the Son, and God the Holy Spirit for eternity. The Lord Jesus was saying that He was going to the heavenly Father to prepare us to be joined to Him. How can this happen except that we be like Christ in every way, in truth and in life? He was exalted to that position at the right hand of the heavenly Father because of His perfect obedience to Him, even to the point of death on the cross. Consider this verse below.

Hebrews 1:3:
"The Son is the radiance of God's glory and the exact representation of his being, sustaining all things by his powerful word. After he had provided purification for sins, he sat down at the right hand of the Majesty in heaven."

These words that came from the mouth of the Lord Jesus Christ were from the heavenly Father. Whatever Christ said on earth still rings in the minds of those who read the Word of God and understand it with the help of God the Holy Spirit who indwells them. Christ is the exact representation of the heavenly Father's being and is seated at His right hand because He did what no one else could do for us. He learned perfect obedience to God the heavenly Father while on earth as a human being, taking upon Himself the flesh of a man through the virgin birth by the power of God the Holy Spirit. He was faithful to God as His only begotten Son and provided purification for sins before He was seated at the right hand of God. Now, He intercedes for us so that full Christformation occurs within us as we obey God the Holy Spirit, who guides us to Him. He is interceding so that His divine nature be made known to man while on earth and be fully formed in those who believe in Him.

In Mark 4:30–32, Jesus says, "What shall we say the kingdom of God is like, or what parable shall we use to describe it? It is like a mustard seed, which is the smallest of all seeds on earth. Yet when planted, it grows and becomes the largest of all garden plants, with such big branches that the birds can perch in its shade." This parable of the mustard seed explains Christformation in you. The mustard seed represents the insignificant Christ as described in Isaiah 53: 2-3. However, the planting of this insignificant seed signifies Christ's atoning sacrifice on the cross. This corresponds to John 12: 24-25, whereby the seed must die. Through His sacrificial death and victorious resurrection, He revealed Himself as the Tree of life, which is represented as the largest of all garden plants. And we who have His divine nature formed in us are the big branches that even non-believers take refuge in. In times of peril, they will turn to us for answers to their problems or to seek shelter from their woes. This is because they would have seen the demonstration of God's power in our lives. But unknown to them, the source of this power is the Christformation that has occurred in us. Upon experiencing this same power in their lives, these same people may then be drawn to believe in Christ eventually.

With full Christformation in us, we will be a blessing to many. Just imagine how immense that tree would be if all those who have full Christformation were to gather together. It all started with one act of Christ on the cross. It's no wonder then that the apostle Paul said in Galatians 6:14, "May I never boast except in the cross of our Lord Jesus Christ, through which the world has been crucified to me, and I to the world."

The parable of the yeast also explains Christformation in you:

Matthew 13:33–34:
"He told them still another parable: 'The kingdom of heaven is like yeast that a woman took and mixed into about sixty pounds of flour until it worked all through the dough.' Jesus spoke all these things to the crowd in parables; he did not say anything to them without using a parable."

Yeast was often used by the Lord Jesus Christ to describe the different natures found in man. The Lord often referred to the sinful nature of the Devil in man, especially hypocrisy, as yeast. Hypocrisy is the sin of pretension, which is acted out of the sinful nature of the Devil but executed in the name of God. The Devil's intention through this is to create confusion. However, in this parable, the Lord Jesus Christ did not refer to yeast as hypocrisy. Instead, He emphasized that, like yeast, His divine nature needs to fully work through the born-again spirit and fill it.

You must allow the yeast, which is the initial portion of His divine nature sown into you to work through until the whole divine nature of Christ is fully formed in you. The verse below will help you understand this parable in its totality. Take note of the word *until* in this verse. The child that is growing in the womb is not delivered until the growth is complete. This parable above is about full growth. A loaf of bread is not fully sized to a standard loaf unless the yeast has worked fully in it. Likewise, Christformation will be incomplete if the divine nature of Christ is not fully formed in you.

Galatians 4:19:
"My dear children, for whom I am again in the pains of childbirth until Christ is formed in you."

E) THE COST OF BEING A DISCIPLE

Matthew 28:18–20:
"Then Jesus came to them and said, 'All authority in heaven and on earth has been given to me. Therefore go and make disciples of all nations, baptizing them in the name of the Father and of the Son

and of the Holy Spirit, and teaching them to obey everything I have commanded you. And surely I am with you always, to the very end of the age.' "

"Go and make disciples of all nations," the Lord commissioned His disciples. But what is the best way to make disciples? The best way is Christformation in them. After accepting them as one of the brethren through water baptism, you are to teach them to obey everything the Lord Jesus Christ had commanded. Obedience to the Lord is very important for Christformation in you. Without obedience to the Lord, there will be no Christformation in you. Let's look at another passage below that confirms what is being said here.

Luke 14:25–35:
"Large crowds were traveling with Jesus, and turning to them he said: "If anyone comes to me and does not hate father and mother, wife and children, brothers and sisters—yes, even their own life—such a person cannot be my disciple. And whoever does not carry their cross and follow me cannot be my disciple. Suppose one of you wants to build a tower. Won't you first sit down and estimate the cost to see if you have enough money to complete it? For if you lay the foundation and are not able to finish it, everyone who sees it will ridicule you, saying, 'This person began to build and wasn't able to finish.' Or suppose a king is about to go to war against another king. Won't he first sit down and consider whether he is able with ten thousand men to oppose the one coming against him with twenty thousand? If he is not able, he will send a delegation while the other is still a long way off and will ask for terms of peace. In the same way, those of you who do not give up everything you have cannot be my disciples. Salt is good, but if it loses its saltiness, how can it be made salty again? It is fit neither for the soil nor for the manure pile; it is thrown out. Whoever has ears to hear, let them hear." "

The word *hate* means obedience to the Lord in all circumstances, as the greatest test for obedience to the Lord will come through your loved ones if they do not seek the will of God as you do. You will be tested through and through by them because they live under the same roof as you, and you cannot escape bumping into or facing them on a daily basis. How you conduct your life with them may affect your fervency in the Lord. You might be tempted to compromise your steadfastness so that conflicts between you and your family members or close ones are avoided. You may even resort to giving in to their demands or wishes even though you know that what they are asking for may not be in line with God's word. As a result, you might be forced to practice double standards between outsiders and loved ones. Guilt may set in unconsciously and wreck your walk with the Lord.

The Lord Jesus warns about being firm in taking a stand against anything that might hinder full Christformation in you, whether it be your close family members or anyone else. Taking a firm stand against pleasing the sinful nature of the Devil is part and parcel of carrying your cross while following Christ our Lord through the careful leading and guidance of God the Holy Spirit toward full Christformation in you.

"This person began to build and wasn't able to finish." The decision is yours to obey God the Holy Spirit till the end for full Christformation in you. You should be able to make the decision to follow Christ till the end through Christformation in you with the indispensable help of God the Holy Spirit. You should decide to learn obedience to God through God the Holy Spirit from the start of your spiritual birth in Christ. You should grow in obedience to the Lord through the formation of Christ's divine nature in you. Do you obey Him only when it is convenient for you? Do you give up obeying Him or should you give up obeying the sinful nature of the Devil in you? You should make the decision and be resolute about it till the end.

Without obeying Christ, there will be no Christformation in you. Count the eternal cost now. Inside a believer, there will be war between the sinful nature of the Devil and God the Holy Spirit, who helps through His counsel so that we will choose Christformation in us. Many believers give up the fight and are overwhelmed by the sinful nature of the Devil in them. They have surrendered themselves to defeat and do not know that the full armor of God in Ephesians 6:10–18 is full Christformation in them.

When you have diligently sowed Christformation in yourself with the help of God the Holy Spirit, you will have the divine nature of Christ, such as His righteousness, truth, peace, faith, the hope of your salvation, and the Word of God sown into you to ward off every attack of the Devil. You should count this cost and choose to fill yourself with Christ well ahead of the battles. You can do this with prayer and intercession with the help of God the Holy Spirit within you.

"In the same way, those of you who do not give up everything you have cannot be my disciples." This is the actual cost of following Christ through God the Holy Spirit for full Christformation in you. You have to give up everything that seeks to please the sinful nature of the Devil in you rather than God the Holy Spirit who indwells you. You have to forgo the evil passions and desires completely in order to be Christ's disciple. If you keep obeying the sinful nature of the Devil in you, you will have the second death, which is your spiritual death eternally. This will occur simply because you chose to disobey God the Holy Spirit for Christformation in you. You sowed eternal destruction to yourself when you were given the choice to do otherwise.

"Salt is good, but if it loses its saltiness, how can it be made salty again? It is fit neither for the soil nor for the manure pile; it is thrown out. Whoever has ears to hear, let them hear." Though you claim you are saved, your salvation will make no sense to God if you do not love Him. As stated in John 14:23-24, if you love the Lord Jesus, you would listen to Him and be on the path of obedience to God, which leads to full Christformation in you. Furthermore, consider this, how can you be saved if you do not even love Christ? And if you heartlessly shun His pure love and continue on the path of disobedience after supposedly believing in the Lord Jesus, are you worthy of eternal life in Christ? You may find out at the end that you have not been His salt on earth and it will be too late for you then. The time would have arrived for God to dispose for good, anything that has lost its saltiness on this earth. The salt that God had expected in you is obedience to Him. If you do not obey Him, of what use will you be to Him on the present earth or the new heaven and earth that are coming soon?

F) CHRISTFORMATION AS THE ARMOR OF GOD

2 Corinthians 4:6–12:
"For God, who said, "Let light shine out of darkness," made his light shine in our hearts to give us the light of the knowledge of God's glory displayed in the face of Christ. But we have this treasure in jars of clay to show that this all-surpassing power is from God and not from us. We are hard pressed on every side, but not crushed; perplexed, but not in despair; persecuted, but not abandoned; struck down, but not destroyed. We always carry around in our body the death of Jesus, so that the life of Jesus may also be revealed in our body. For we who are alive are always being given over to death for Jesus' sake, so that his life may also be revealed in our mortal body. So then, death is at work in us, but life is at work in you."

There is an ongoing battle between light and darkness on this earth, until the Devil, the False Prophet, the Antichrist, the demons that follow the Devil, and all the rebellious children of the Devil are thrown into the lake of fire at the great white throne judgment. But the eternal light of Christ that is already formed within you will continue to shine through Christformation; not only during your time on this earth but also in the new heaven and new earth. Remember, when you walk in obedience to Christ, you will never walk in darkness as stated in John 8:12. Instead, your light will shine wherever there is darkness and this will lead many who seek deliverance out of it.

Christformation in you is the eternal treasure in jars of clay. This all-surpassing power of God the Holy Spirit is demonstrated in your life through successful Christformation in you, in spite of the many trials and tribulations of your faith, as the apostle Paul says in the passage above.

Apostle Paul says that when the death of the sinful nature of the Devil was initiated in him with the help of God the Holy Spirit, it brought forth a hunger and thirst for the life of Christformation not only in himself but in others too. "I'll die, so that you'll live", as it is said in 2 Corinthians 5:15, was the kind of life the Lord Jesus led. The apostles of Christ were led the same way.

When Christformation is growing in you, you will be led by God the Holy Spirit to put to death the misdeeds of the sinful nature of the Devil more and more each day. Through the counseled obedience and help of God the Holy Spirit in you, you will overcome all the power of the Enemy in you. Your sacrifice is necessary for Christformation in you. Let's see what the following passage of Scripture says about this sacrifice.

Romans 12:1–2:
"Therefore, I urge you, brothers and sisters, in view of God's mercy, to offer your bodies as a living sacrifice, holy and pleasing to God—this is your true and proper worship. Do not conform to the pattern of this world, but be transformed by the renewing of your mind. Then you will be able to test and approve what God's will is—his good, pleasing and perfect will."

The heavenly Father's good, pleasing, and perfect will for you is full Christformation in you. It starts with you, as you are an object of His mercy now through Christ's completed work on the cross at Calvary. Since you have believed in Him, you will have to offer up your body as a living sacrifice; a true act of worship to Him. The greatest way to worship God is to forsake the sinful nature of the Devil in you and actively allow Christformation in your born-again spirit that will transform your mind into the renewed mind of Christ.

There will be no time or thought left for pleasing the sinful desires that come from the sinful nature of the Devil in you. If you can't stop pleasing the sinful nature, you would need to ask yourself this question: Have I conformed to the pattern of this world by doing everything else except being led and assisted by God the Holy Spirit into full Christformation? Look into the passage in the gospel of John that speaks about true and proper worship.

John 4:23–24:
"Yet a time is coming and has now come when the true worshipers will worship the Father in the Spirit and in truth, for they are the kind of worshipers the Father seeks. God is spirit, and his worshipers must worship in the Spirit and in truth."

Worshipping the heavenly Father "in the Spirit and in truth"; we can't see anything beyond full Christformation in this statement. Worshipping in the Spirit is being obedient to God the Holy Spirit, who leads and guides us towards full Christformation. Worshipping in truth is obeying all the commandments of Christ, who is "the way, the truth, and the life," and no man can ever face or please the heavenly Father without his or her obedience to all that Christ our Lord commanded. Worship is about obedience, and obedience is about Christformation in you. How much you obey God the Holy Spirit's leading is how much you will have Christformation in you. Apostle Paul admits that it is difficult to sow Christformation in oneself but that is the one and only thing that will remain in us forever.

You will not be able to go to the heavenly Father without Christformation in you. If you say you have believed in Him, He will ask, "Where is the fruit of your repentance?" The fruit of your repentance is obedience to God, for obedience produces the kind of worshipers the Father seeks. God the heavenly Father is seeking those who will be obedient to Him like Christ His beloved Son. Let's look at the verses below and apply them to our lives.

Hebrews 5:7–10:
"During the days of Jesus' life on earth, he offered up prayers and petitions with fervent cries and tears to the one who could save him from death, and he was heard because of his reverent submission. Son though he was, he learned obedience from what he suffered and, once made perfect, he became the source of eternal salvation for all who obey him and was designated by God to be high priest in the order of Melchizedek."

"He became the source of eternal salvation for all who obey Him." If there is no obedience to Christ, there will be no salvation. In the Great Commission, He said "Make disciples by teaching them to obey my commandments." If they truly obey His commandments, whatever confession they make outwardly of their salvation, like water baptism, will be acceptable of God.

But if you profess that you belong to Christ, but do not obey His commandments, how can He become the source of eternal salvation in you? If you argue that you cannot be freed from the sinful nature of the Devil within you, how can He be the high priest in the order of Melchizedek for you? He can't be your High Priest if he hasn't set you free from your sins! Melchizedek lives forever, but sin doesn't. The very reason God sent Adam and Eve out of the garden was because He did not want sin to live forever. He promised after the fall of man that He would put an end to sin through His beloved Son, the Lord Jesus Christ, and He did! He was designated by God the heavenly Father to free you from the sinful nature of the Devil sown in you through the disobedience of Adam and Eve in the garden of Eden. Christformation in you is the permanent armor of God against the attacks of the Devil, who attempts to make you succumb again and again to his sinful nature in you. Let's look at the full armor of God and what it consists of.

Ephesians 6:10–18:
"Finally, be strong in the Lord and in his mighty power. Put on the full armor of God, so that you can take your stand against the devil's schemes. For our struggle is not against flesh and blood, but against the rulers, against the authorities, against the powers of this dark world and against the spiritual forces of evil in the heavenly realms. Therefore put on the full armor of God, so that when the day of evil comes, you may be able to stand your ground, and after you have done everything, to stand. Stand firm then, with the belt of truth buckled around your waist, with the breastplate of righteousness in place, and with your feet fitted with the readiness that comes from the gospel of peace. In addition to all this, take up the shield of faith, with which you can extinguish all the flaming arrows of the evil one. Take the helmet of salvation and the sword of the Spirit, which is the word of God. And pray in the Spirit on all occasions with all kinds of prayers and requests. With this in mind, be alert and always keep on praying for the entire Lord's people."

All these pieces of armor that produce righteousness, peace, faith, word, and salvation in you do not just come on you like that. They are formed in your born-again spirit and mind through your continual obedience to the leading and guidance of God the Holy Spirit. All the above is the divine nature of Christ that will be formed in you as you obey Christ our Lord. Christformation occurs in you as you obey Christ through the Spirit of God. Protection comes when God the Holy Spirit comes into you, but full protection comes when God the Son and the heavenly Father dwell in you through full Christformation. That is what God the Holy Spirit is leading you toward. Meditate on the verse below carefully, and you will be able to have full Christformation in you when you live as it says.

John 14:23:
"Jesus replied, 'Anyone who loves me will obey my teaching. My Father will love them, and we will come to them and make our home with them.' "

G) RUNNING THE RACE OF CHRISTFORMATION IN YOU WITH PERSEVERANCE TO THE END

Hebrews 12:1–2:
"Therefore, since we are surrounded by such a great cloud of witnesses, let us throw off everything that hinders and the sin that so easily entangles. And let us run with perseverance the race marked out for us, fixing our eyes on Jesus, the pioneer and perfection of faith. For the joy set before him he endured the cross, scorning its shame, and sat down at the right hand of the throne of God."

Someone asked us once, "Why don't we just walk? Do we have to run in this race?" Why is our walk with the Lord likened to a race by the writer of the book of Hebrews? Walking is alright, and you may walk if you want to. But if someone ever challenges you to a race, wouldn't you want to take that challenge? Do you know who challenges your faith daily? It is the Devil, who prowls around like a hungry lion seeking to devour you. Do you think that the challenger would just settle for walking when he can run ahead of you to the finish line and at the same time defeat you, to your shame?

You know that the challenger is in the business of prowling, seeking whomever he may devour. Are you ever ready for any challenge? This is what the writer of Hebrews is encouraging you to do. There are many entangling hindrances on the way. Are you ready to face them? Are you ready to throw off everything that hinders you on your way to victory? Are you prepared to overcome everything that may slow you down or even stop you? Do you know that you are surrounded by "spectators," encouraging us on? "Who are these 'great cloud of witnesses'?" you may want to know. "What are they hoping to see or witness?" The answer to this is in the following passage:

Hebrews 11:39–40:
"These were all commended for their faith, yet none of them received what had been promised, since God had planned something better for us so that only together with us would they be made perfect."

We are all made perfect through the completed work of Christ on the cross of Calvary. Why are they still witnessing if Christ had already completed the work? The "great cloud of witnesses" is made up of those who lived during the Old Testament times and had obeyed God with their commendable faith in Him. But they could only wait for what had been promised to them, as God had planned something better for us who live during the New Testament times. This "something better" is Christ our Lord, who took the form of flesh, died, and was raised to life again. Now "only together with us would they be made perfect." What does that mean? They are waiting and watching to see how we would finish the race, now that we can "fix our eyes on Jesus, the Author and Finisher," whom they couldn't see because He wasn't revealed to them in human form and the work wasn't completed on the cross yet during their time. Now that the Savior has been revealed and has won and made a public spectacle of the Devil through His glorious work of redemption on the cross, purchasing us with the precious blood of the Lamb, that "something better" is about to be completed. That "something better" is also mentioned elsewhere in the book of Hebrews:

Hebrews 7:11–28:
"If perfection could have been attained through the Levitical priesthood—and indeed the law given to the people established that priesthood—why was there still need for another priest to come, one in the order of Melchizedek, not in the order of Aaron? For when the priesthood is changed, the law must be changed also. He of whom

these things are said belonged to a different tribe, and no one from that tribe has ever served at the altar. For it is clear that our Lord descended from Judah, and in regard to that tribe Moses said nothing about priests. And what we have said is even more clear if another priest like Melchizedek appears, one who has become a priest not on the basis of a regulation as to his ancestry but on the basis of the power of an indestructible life. For it is declared: "You are a priest forever, in the order of Melchizedek." The former regulation is set aside because it was weak and useless (for the law made nothing perfect), and a better hope is introduced, by which we draw near to God. And it was not without an oath! Others became priests without any oath, but he became a priest with an oath when God said to him: "The Lord has sworn and will not change his mind: 'You are a priest forever.' " Because of this oath, Jesus has become the guarantor of a better covenant. Now there have been many of those priests, since death prevented them from continuing in office; but because Jesus lives forever, he has a permanent priesthood. Therefore he is able to save completely those who come to God through him, because he always lives to intercede for them. Such a high priest truly meets our need—one who is holy, blameless, pure, set apart from sinners, exalted above the heavens. Unlike the other high priests, he does not need to offer sacrifices day after day, first for his own sins, and then for the sins of the people. He sacrificed for their sins once for all when he offered himself. For the law appoints as high priests men in all their weakness; but the oath, which came after the law, appointed the Son, who has been made perfect forever."

"Jesus has become the guarantor of a better covenant" and the formation of this "guarantor" in you ensures a better and everlasting covenant between you and God. Furthermore, "because Jesus lives forever, he has a permanent priesthood," which leads you to become a part of His royal and eternal priesthood upon His formation in you. Also, according to this promise, His perfection is being formed in you, reiterated in the verse, "For the law appoints as high priests men in all their weakness; but the oath, which came after the law, appointed the Son, who has been made perfect forever."

The Old Testament "cloud of witnesses" did not live to see the coming of Christ, but we have seen and continue to see. Because He has been made perfect forever, you who believe and obey Him will also be made perfect forever through full Christformation in you.

Why must you run this race with perseverance to the finish line? Christformation in you does not happen without your effort. Time and again, the apostle Paul advised to "make every effort" possible for full Christformation in you. No race can be won without effort. You may need a good coach, but in the end it is your own effort, commitment, and performance that will win you a prize. The Lord Jesus warned against becoming complacent where you may carelessly abort God's work in you completely.

Luke 13:23–25:
"Someone asked him, 'Lord, are only a few people going to be saved?' He said to them, 'Make every effort to enter through the narrow door, because many, I tell you, will try to enter and will not be able to. Once the owner of the house gets up and closes the door, you will stand outside knocking and pleading, "Sir, open the door for us." But he will answer, "I don't know you or where you come from." ' "

The "narrow door" is the main entrance that leads to full Christformation in you, your obedience to all that the Lord Jesus has commanded. Many do not want to obey, but still want Christ to be formed in them. Many look for shortcuts, but there are no shortcuts in Christ's kingdom. Some think that if they give lots of money for a religious cause they will be accepted by God. After a while, you will be disillusioned. Sadly, you will realize later that you had entered through the wrong door.

You should give to the work of the Lord generously but that may not necessarily mean that you are obedient to the Lord in all that He had commanded you do. This is how "many will try to enter and will not be able to." They will think that they had made it, but the Lord will say, "I don't know you or where you come from." You will still be outside the kingdom of God, knocking and pleading, "Sir, open the door for us."

But, there is good news for you today! The door is still open through obedience in running the race of successful Christformation in you. The "cloud of witnesses" are still watching and waiting to see when the owner of the house gets up and closes the door with the race ending there. It will be too late for you then. So, turn now to Him fully and run the race of full Christformation in you assisted very closely by God the Holy Spirit within you. Listen to Him, and you will win. But first, throw off everything of the sinful nature of the Devil in you that will hinder you from winning this race that promises the best eternal prize: full Christformation in you. What can be compared to it? This is what apostle Paul said about this prize:

Philippians 3:13–15:
"Brothers and sisters, I do not consider myself yet to have taken hold of it. But one thing I do: Forgetting what is behind and straining toward what is ahead, I press on toward the goal to win the prize for which God has called me heavenward in Christ Jesus. All of us, then, who are mature should take such a view of things. And if on some point you think differently, that too God will make clear to you."

SUMMARY: CHAPTER FOUR

1) Christformation is the Demonstration of the Power of God—the Holy Spirit—in You

Christformation is the work of God the Holy Spirit in you, who was sent to help you with Christformation in you. He helps you right from the conviction of sin to the born-again experience of the spirit until there is full Christformation in you. Of course, your cooperation is also necessary in order for Christformation to occur in you. Without your obedience to all that Christ has commanded, there will be no Christformation in you. This is how Christformation will occur in you: The more you obey Christ, the more Christformation will occur within you. God the Holy Spirit will help your soul (mind) to be transformed into the mind of Christ. This is the demonstration of His power in you.

2) The Parables of Christ Explain How Christformation Occurs in You

i) **Parable of the Sower.** Explains Christformation in you to the fullest. The seed is the Word of God and can be sown in four different types of ground. The word of God is formed in you as you obey it. When the word of God is obeyed, the Word of God, who is Christ, is formed in you. Christ is the Word of God that must be formed in you. Word became flesh so that all flesh that obeys the Word will become like the Word. You must hear, understand, accept, and obey the Word so that the Word will be formed in you. How much you obey the Word determines how much Christformation will occur in you.

ii) **Parable of the Hidden Treasure or Pearl.** Hidden treasure or pearls are valuables that may meet all your earthly needs and wants. Likewise, all the needs and wants of the born-again spirit will be met once Christ, who is likened to a hidden treasure or pearl, is fully formed in you. You will give up pleasing the sinful nature of the Devil in you and seek the eternal divine nature of Christ to be formed in you.

iii) **Parable of the Growing Seed, Mustard Seed, and Yeast**. Christformation will fill your born-again spirit, which in turn will transform the soul (mind) in a growing manner as in a seed. This growth will fill the whole born-again spirit and soul as you fully obey the Word of God brought into remembrance in you by God the Holy Spirit. These parables of the mustard seed and the yeast confirm that full Christformation in you is possible.

3) **Christformation in You Occurs as You Pay the Price**

i) **The cost of being a disciple** is making the right decision to give up pleasing the sinful nature of the Devil in you completely and putting its misdeeds to death in you. You must be willing to obey Christ until the end and live by the leading of God the Holy Spirit, who helps you with full Christformation in you.

ii) **Christformation as the Armor of God**. You must be willing to pay the price to be engaged in a war against the Devil and the demons, not in your own strength but with the help of God the Holy Spirit, until the divine nature of Christ is formed in you. Righteousness is one aspect of the divine nature of Christ that must be formed in you, which, once formed in you, becomes the breastplate of righteousness in you. Likewise, all the other aspects of the divine nature of Christ must be formed in you through your willingness to fight the Enemy so that you attain full Christformation in the end.

iii) **Getting Involved in the Race of Christformation**. You must be willing to be in strict training to enter the race and win the prize, which is full Christformation in you. The strict training will come from God the Holy Spirit, requiring your total obedience to everything Christ had commanded. You will need to pay the price to win the eternal prize by counting everything as loss to gain Christformation in you fully.

CHRISTFORMATION
IS THE RICHEST OF FARE
IN YOU

ISAIAH 55: 1-3

CHAPTER FIVE:
WHO WILL HAVE CHRISTFORMATION?

A) THERE ARE ONLY TWO KINDS OF OBJECTS

Romans 9:22–25:
"What if God, although choosing to show his wrath and make his power known, bore with great patience the objects of his wrath—prepared for destruction? What if he did this to make the riches of his glory known to the objects of his mercy, whom he prepared in advance for glory—even us, whom he also called, not only from the Jews but also from the Gentiles? As he says in Hosea: 'I will call them "my people" who are not my people; and I will call her "my loved one" who is not my loved one.' "

There are only two kinds of objects that God created. If you understand this truth clearly, you will know why certain people behave in such a deplorable manner even when they are surrounded with examples of good behavior in this world. They continue being evil, not because it's in their power to do so, but because God had decided to bear with great patience these objects of His wrath—those already prepared for destruction. But why does God have to bear with great patience those whom He is about to destroy?

Not only must we bear evil on earth, God also bears with great patience these deplorable objects of His wrath. In this world, you are either an object of His mercy or an object of His wrath. If you are an object of His mercy, you will be filled with His loving-kindness. But if you are an object of His wrath, you will not be able to escape destruction in the end. However, He will bear with you for a little while more. "But why would He do so?" you may ask. "Why delay destruction on the objects of His wrath? Don't they deserve a speedy punishment?" No. Their destruction is delayed for the sake of the objects of His mercy.

Reflect on what had happened in Egypt. Pharaoh refused to set the people of God free when Moses went to their rescue. God wanted "to make the riches of His glory known to the objects of his mercy, those he had prepared in advance for glory." "So, how did He do that in the past?" you may ask. He bore with great patience by demonstrating His power through the ten plagues that hit Egypt one after another. God was very patient even with those who deserved instant punishment. Pharaoh was given ten different forms of punishment to let the people of God break free from their slavery in Egypt.

Consider how great God's patience was even to the objects of His wrath. He brought about the ten plagues that Pharaoh had earned for himself and the Egyptians through his persistent stubbornness, but God showed forth the riches of His glory through His long-suffering patience to those who test Him. He showed the hidden riches of His patience to the objects of His mercy. Why then did He display His long-suffering nature and patience to His objects of mercy? It is because He wanted that same patience and long-suffering nature to be formed in the objects of His mercy. Christformation can only occur in the objects of His mercy; it can never occur in the objects of His wrath, for they are already prepared in advance for destruction. On the contrary, the objects of His mercy are prepared for eternal *doxa* glory of the heavenly Father through full Christformation in them. This *doxa* glory of God will be explained thoroughly in the conclusion of chapter seven.

The four Gospels provide an example of an object of His wrath, who pretended to be an object of His mercy. But he was later exposed for his sins and had to face the consequences of living a life of deceit and malice. We all know that the disciples of Christ our Lord were supposedly objects of His mercy, but one of them was not. Does that surprise you? Judas Iscariot was not an object of His mercy. Only objects of His mercy will eventually have Christformation in them. How much Christ was formed in each of the disciples depended on their personal obedience to all that Christ had commanded. In the same way today, God the Holy Spirit guides each believer to obey God's Word. Each believer sows to Christformation in himself with the help of God the Holy Spirit within him. Those who believe but refuse to obey Christ will have no Christformation in them. Those who only claim that they are born again but do not have Christformation in them are like Judas Iscariot, the objects of His wrath. Let's read the following passage to understand how serious this sin of pretension can be.

1 John 3:4–6:
"Everyone who sins breaks the law; in fact, sin is lawlessness. But you know that he appeared so that he might take away our sins. And in him is no sin. No one who lives in him keeps on sinning. No one who continues to sin has either seen him or known him."

The Lord Jesus took the form of flesh to take away our sins, and we are still playing around with this eternally lethal thing called sin. In Christ, there was no sin at all. This truth is something that many cannot comprehend or understand. It is difficult to understand this truth because all men and women in this world have sin within them, but Christ our Lord alone had none in Him. Although He was born in the human flesh, He had no sin in Him. What had happened to the sinful nature of the Devil that was sown in Adam and Eve in His case? Why did it not have any power over Christ? Why was the Devil made to look so powerless in Christ? The sinful nature of the Devil had no power over the Lord Jesus Christ even though He had taken the form of flesh because He had no sin in Him. Well, he tried to tempt Him in the wilderness at His weakest point physically after He had fasted for forty days and forty nights, but this evil plan failed. The Devil even tried to persecute Christ, using his children who were in positions of authority. But that too failed.

Finally at the cross, he killed Him, but the Lord Jesus Christ overcame death and resurrected to life again. The Devil's powerlessness over God, His angels, and mankind became a public spectacle. Never before had a man overcome the Devil in every way. He became the firstborn of God to destroy all the power and the works of the Devil on earth. The Devil stands condemned before God forever with the victory of Christ over sin. From then on, anyone who continues to obey the sinful nature of the Devil will die not only a physical death but also with a second, or spiritual death and be thrown into the lake of fire for eternity. Let's read about this in the passage below.

Revelation 21:6–8:

"He said to me: 'It is done. I am the Alpha and the Omega, the Beginning and the End. To the thirsty I will give water without cost from the spring of the water of life. Those who are victorious will inherit all this, and I will be their God and they will be my children. But the cowardly, the unbelieving, the vile, the murderers, the sexually immoral, those who practice magic arts, the idolaters, and all liars—they will be consigned to the fiery lake of burning sulphur. This is the second death.' "

Christ our Lord is the Alpha and Omega, the beginning and the end of everything that God created. You cannot live on this earth and just ignore Him. Everyone will be judged by what the Lord Jesus Christ had done on earth. If you were truly thirsty for victory over sin and desired to be an overcomer, you would have eventually come to Him. If you don't come to Him because of unbelief or fear that you would be persecuted like Him, and continue obeying the vile, sinful nature of the Devil in you, you deserve to be consigned to the fiery lake of burning sulphur forever as your second death.

The same passage says, "Those who are victorious will inherit all this, and I will be their God and they will be my children." Victorious in what? Victorious over sin. "Inherit all this"; what is this? Christformation in you, which is the inheriting of the fullness of Christ in you. How else could God the heavenly Father be your God and you be His child if you are not filled with Christ His only begotten Son? Only Christ could please the heavenly Father, and no one can go to Him unless he or she is filled with Christ His Son. Therefore, Christformation can only happen in those who are objects of His mercy. If you were to study the passage below you would realize that inheriting Christ in His fullness is only for those born out of a promise from God and not for ordinary children. Pharaoh was born an ordinary child because he was not born out of a promise from God but from an ordinary relationship between a man and his wife. On the other hand, Moses was born out of a promise from God; and so is every one of you who has Christformation within you. You have a promise of God over your life. Let's read the passage below and differentiate between the two.

Galatians 4:28–31:

"Now you, brothers and sisters, like Isaac, are children of promise. At that time, the son born according to the flesh persecuted the son born by the power of the Spirit. It is the same now. But what does Scripture say? 'Get rid of the slave woman and her son, for the slave woman's son will never share in the inheritance with the free woman's son.' Therefore, brothers and sisters, we are not children of the slave woman, but of the free woman."

Hagar is the slave woman likened to the present Jerusalem, which is still in bondage, and Ismael was her son, who will never share in the inheritance of Christformation. If you have Christformation increasing in you, it's God's promise fulfilled in your life. All those who belong to the Jerusalem above that is at God's right hand now, as described in Hebrews 12: 22-24, will have Christformation in them. All those who belong to the slave woman will never have Christformation in them because they are objects of God's wrath. However, all those who have the promise of God fulfilled in them through Christformation are objects of His mercy.

B) An Explanation from the Parables of the Lost Sheep, Coin, and Son

We have three parables in one chapter describing who will have Christformation in them. Let's read the three different parables below to understand the truths about Christformation in them.

Luke 15:6–7:

"Then he calls his friends and neighbors together and says, 'Rejoice with me; I have found my lost sheep.' I tell you that in the same way there will be more rejoicing in heaven over one sinner who repents than over ninety-nine righteous persons who do not need to repent."

Luke 15:9–10:

"And when she finds it, she calls her friends and neighbors together and says, 'Rejoice with me; I have found my lost coin.' In the same way, I tell you, there is rejoicing in the presence of the angels of God over one sinner who repents."

Luke 15:31–32:
" 'My son,' the father said, 'you are always with me, and everything I have is yours. But we had to celebrate and be glad, because this brother of yours was dead and is alive again; he was lost and is found.' "

The first parable is about one straying sheep out of a flock of one hundred. The point stressed here by the Lord was repentance, which is turning away from sins committed with remorse in heart, as the psalmist prayed in Psalm 38:18, "I confess my iniquity; I am troubled by my sin." In this parable, the sheep had strayed from the shepherd. The sheep needed to fully trust the shepherd and follow him wherever he went. Christformation can never occur in you if you haven't truly repented. But if you do, that would require making the personal decision to forsake pleasing the sinful nature of the Devil in you from where all sins start. The Lord Jesus Christ said that sin comes from within you from the sinful nature of the Devil sown in you through the disobedience of Adam and Eve in the garden of Eden. From one man came sin, and now we have been introduced to the last Adam, "the one man from whom righteousness comes." Let's compare these passages to understand the message clearly.

Mark 7:20–23:
"He went on: 'What comes out of a person is what defiles them. For it is from within, out of a person's heart, that evil thoughts come—sexual immorality, theft, murder, adultery, greed, malice, deceit, lewdness, envy, slander, arrogance and folly. All these evils come from inside and defile a person.' "

And in the book of Romans it says:

Romans 5:19:
"For just as through the disobedience of the one man the many were made sinners, so also through the obedience of the one man the many will be made righteous."

Finally, this passage in 1 Corinthians says:

1 Corinthians 15:45–49:

"So it is written: 'The first man Adam became a living being"; the last Adam, a life-giving spirit. The spiritual did not come first, but the natural, and after that the spiritual. The first man was of the dust of the earth; the second man is of heaven. As was the earthly man, so are those who are of the earth; and as is the heavenly man, so also are those who are of heaven. And just as we have borne the image of the earthly man, so shall we bear the image of the heavenly man."

From these verses, we learn that not only will the Lord forgive when you truly repent of all your sins as the psalmist did in Psalms 66:18. He asked God that he be cleansed from *all* his sins, never to cherish obeying the sinful nature of the Devil again. You will start "bearing the image of the heavenly man" who is the Lord Jesus Christ once you do this. The Old Testament believers did not have this opportunity but you do because of the Lord Jesus Christ's completed work on the cross. Christformation will begin to occur in you; you will start becoming like Him with His divine nature as you obey all that He has commanded.

Take special note of the ninety-nine righteous persons who did not need to repent. Can this be true? Yes, they did not need to repent because God had truly forgiven them. This is so because; they had never returned to please the sinful nature after that. They themselves knew within their hearts through the witness of God the Holy Spirit as it is in the book of Romans:

Romans 4:7–8:

"Blessed are those whose transgressions are forgiven, whose sins are covered. Blessed is the one whose sin the Lord will never count against them."

But there will be more rejoicing in heaven over one sinner who repents than the ninety-nine who do not need to repent. Christformation occurs only in those who have truly repented of all their sins, meaning they do not return to pleasing the sinful nature of the Devil in them but have decided to turn away from pleasing that evil nature for good.

The second parable is about a woman who had ten silver coins but lost one. As soon as she found it, she celebrated with her neighbors. To a woman, these coins mean much. In the same way, even the angels in heaven know when one who was lost (one who did not know that he had sinned) is convicted of his sin by God the Holy Spirit and truly repents. He would then feel sorry for sinning and never return to pleasing the sinful nature of the Devil in him. The angels too are interested in the things that happen in and around a believer in Christ, especially Christformation in you that follows one's true repentance. The angels are ministering spirits of God who help with Christformation in us.

Hebrews 1:14:
"Are not all angels ministering spirits sent to serve those who will inherit salvation?"

The third parable is the most appropriate parable for explaining Christformation in you. The parable of the lost son is commonly used to explain the gospel of the Lord Jesus Christ to someone who hasn't heard about Him before. It is an appealing story about a son who demands his way out of the family because he feels he should lead an enjoyable life of his own by pleasing the sinful nature of the Devil in him. His argument to his father was, "If I have such a nature in me, why can't I satisfy it?" The father knew that the son was ignorant of the fact that this evil nature would destroy him if he tried to satisfy it. Yet the son insisted upon his birthright. It grieved the father to see his son succumb to the sinful nature of the Devil in him.

The presence of sin hurts all parties. Just one selfish person can wreck the whole family, and here is an example of such a person. Because the prodigal son was celebrated upon his return from sinful living, the faithful son developed a self-righteous anger which caused his reluctance to meet his brother, even though he returned safe and sound from the destructive path that he chose. The Bible says that the father pleaded with the faithful son. However, he arbitrarily refused the father. His answer displayed antipathy and indicated a certain sense of regret for not pursuing a hedonistic lifestyle like his brother. In fact, he even began to question if his prior obedience to his father was worthwhile. Do you see how the selfishness of the prodigal son had affected the life of the faithful son?

This is the decadence of sinful living; it's contagious, worse than tuberculosis. Just the presence of sin destroys and even more so when it is practiced. Wasn't sin contagious from Eve to Adam? Sin can be passed on by anyone to anyone as long as the sinful nature of the Devil is not put to death in them. That's why the apostle Paul refers to the sinful nature of the Devil as the "earthly nature" in the book of Colossians. Let's read what it says here.

Colossians 3:5–10:
"Put to death, therefore, whatever belongs to your earthly nature: sexual immorality, impurity, lust, evil desires and greed, which is idolatry. Because of these, the wrath of God is coming. You used to walk in these ways, in the life you once lived. But now you must also rid yourselves of all such things as these: anger, rage, malice, slander, and filthy language from your lips. Do not lie to each other, since you have taken off your old self with its practices and have put on the new self, which is being renewed in knowledge in the image of its Creator."

If you have decided to put on the new self, which is the same as allowing Christformation in you, why must you go back to pleasing the sinful nature of the Devil in you again? At one time, you lived pleasing the sinful nature in you and, like the lost son in the parable, you nearly destroyed your life. So why should you live like that again?

Apostle Paul warns you to put to death whatever belongs to the sinful nature of the Devil in you. It may seem like this nature would do you some earthly good, for that's what Adam and Eve concluded with the evil persuasion of the Devil in the garden of Eden. But instead it turned out to be an irrevocable curse for all who were involved, including the Devil. It separated the best of relationships, for that's what sin does best! It tragically separated Adam and Eve from God. All such things as these: anger, rage, malice, slander, and filthy language and lying to each other are all harmful for healthy relationships. In fact, any sin you practice from the sinful nature of the Devil in you is harmful to your relationship with others. In one way or the other, it will separate you from the best of relationships.

Ponder deeply upon what God is saying here in this passage. So, before it's too late and it destroys your relationship with God eternally, you should get rid of the sins mentioned above. You should make every effort toward full Christformation in your born-again spirit, which will transform your mind into the mind of Christ. In this way, you will have sown greatly into your eternal "house" that is being built at God's right hand now as you obediently sow. Apostle Paul encouraged the believers in the Colossian province with these words:

Colossians 3:1–3:
"Since, then, you have been raised with Christ, set your hearts on things above, where Christ is, seated at the right hand of God. Set your minds on things above, not on earthly things. For you died, and your life is now hidden with Christ in God."

"Set you hearts and minds on things above, not on earthly things" is a very clear reference to Christformation in you. What are these things above? These things above have much do with your Christ-conformed body. He is the perfect One whom we should be conformed to. God will not be pleased if we do not become like Him with His divine nature formed within us; that is, if we keep claiming we belong to Him. Perfection is in Him, and when His divine nature is fully formed within us, we will be made perfect too.

It takes faith to be able to see things above, where Christ is seated at the right hand of God. It takes faith to set your heart and mind on obedience for full Christformation in you. It takes faith to be able to see that your life is hidden with Christ in God through Christformation in you. The celebration that happened when the lost son returned to his father in the parable was for Christformation in him. The celebration is a picture of the forming of Christ's divine nature within you after you have truly repented of your sins. Let's look at these verses to observe what happens in the gospel according to Luke:

Luke 15:21–24:

"The son said to him, 'Father, I have sinned against heaven and against you. I am no longer worthy to be called your son.' But the father said to his servants, 'Quick! Bring the best robe and put it on him. Put a ring on his finger and sandals on his feet. Bring the fattened calf and kill it. Let's have a feast and celebrate. For this son of mine was dead and is alive again; he was lost and is found.' "

The lost son had finally come to the realization that his father always has the best reserved for him. This was just cause for the celebrations. We say this because the best that can happen to a truly repentant child of God is Christformation in him or her. The robe, the ring, the sandals and the feast symbolically refer to full Christformation in the one who was lost, but is now found. This took place as soon as the lost son (who felt unworthy to belong to his father) genuinely repented. Likewise, for any born again child of God, the robe signifies the new born again spirit in Christ, while the ring signifies the new relationship as the bride to the bridegroom. The sandals represent the new walk and ministry that would arise from this new relationship. Finally, the feast signifies the feasting on Christ for full Christformation to occur in us. All these are offered to us by the heavenly Father through His only begotten Son.

The misdeeds that originate from the sinful nature of the Devil will be put to death through a life of obedience to God the Holy Spirit within. True repentance, or turning away from the sinful nature of the Devil, is precious to God. This can only come by believing in Christ and all that He had accomplished on the cross at Calvary.

After all that God has said through these three parables about Christformation, if you continue gratifying the sinful nature of the Devil, whose fault will that be? Only yours! Yes, it is truly yours and not God's fault because you have not obeyed Him. Until the day you decide to turn away from the sinful nature of the Devil in true repentance, you are still a lost son, and there will be no Christformation in you.

C) An Explanation from the Parable of the Wise and Foolish Builders and Virgins

Luke 6:46–49:

"Why do you call me, "Lord, Lord," and do not do what I say? As for everyone who comes to me and hears my words and puts them into practice, I will show you what they are like. They are like a man building a house, who dug down deep and laid the foundation on rock. When a flood came, the torrent struck that house but could not shake it, because it was well built. But the one who hears my words and does not put them into practice is like a man who built a house on the ground without a foundation. The moment the torrent struck that house, it collapsed and its destruction was complete."

If you call upon Jesus Christ as Lord, you should obey everything He commands you to do. If you do not put everything He commands into practice, how then is He your Lord? "As for everyone who comes to me and hears my words and puts them into practice, I will show you what they are like," the Lord Jesus Christ said to His disciples. "They are like a man building a house." You may ask, "What house?"

Building a house is an individual's responsibility. The house is the building that gives you shelter from the rain, scorching sun, floods, and all other kinds of possible danger. How and where you build that house is very important if it is really going to give you shelter. If you build a house and if it doesn't give you shelter, it won't be a house. The Lord Jesus Christ made a promise to the disciples upon the completion of His work on the cross at Calvary; before His exaltation to the right hand side of the Father. He said in John 14:1-6, that He would help them build that eternal shelter in God. Let's look at what He says in the passage below.

John 14:1–4:

" "Do not let your hearts be troubled. You believe in God; believe also in me. My Father's house has many rooms; if that were not so, would I have told you that I am going there to prepare a place for you? And if I go and prepare a place for you, I will come back and take you to be with me that you also may be where I am. You know the way to the place where I am going." "

When the Lord Jesus Christ said, "I will go and prepare a place for you in my Father's house, which has many rooms," we may be drawn to think that He is preparing a physical structure in heaven for us. However, in this passage, Christ was not referring to a physical structure but a spiritual house. In the physical context, a house is a shelter, but in matters of the spirit, God is our shelter. The house mentioned in this passage refers to Christ because His divine nature is to be built in us. The forming of Christ in us is also the same as building Christ in us. When His divine nature is fully built in us, only then the triune God will come and dwell in us. When God says He will dwell in us, He is saying He will dwell in those who have Christ's divine nature fully built in them. He dwells in us because we dwell in Christ. Christ is our eternal dwelling place. In making Christ our dwelling place, the Most High God becomes our dwelling place. Without Christ being revealed to us, we cannot see the Most High God. Psalm 91:9–10 says, "If you make the Most High your dwelling—even the LORD, who is my refuge—then no harm will befall you, no disaster will come near your tent."

If Christ is to be built in us, what are these many rooms then? Perhaps we mistook these rooms for our physical residence in heaven. However, the "many rooms" are actually the many parts of the divine nature of Christ that are to be formed in us. If Christ is the house and the many rooms are the many parts of His divine nature, what more is there for Him to prepare in heaven?

First, He is "preparing" by interceding for us to respond to all that He commands with total obedience. Second, Christ sends our helper, the Holy Spirit, to lead and guide us to every truth so that His divine nature is formed in us. Finally, He prepares all His called, chosen, and faithful believers to be shown to the Father as His perfect bride through full Christformation in them. "The place that He will take us to" is our eternal abode with God the Father as Christ's perfect bride. In fact, the Lord Jesus said the prayer below for us while He was on this earth so that this may come to pass at God's appointed time.

John 17:20-23:

" "My prayer is not for them alone but I pray also for those who will believe in me through their message, that all of them may be one, Father, just as you are in me and I am in you. May they also be in us so that the world may believe that you have sent me. I have given them the glory that you gave me, that they may be one as we are one—I in them and you in me—so that they may be brought to complete unity. Then the world will know that you sent me and have loved them even as you have loved me."

The above explains what Christ is doing for you. And this is what is required of you. You should dig down deep and lay the foundation of your life on the Rock, Jesus Christ our Lord. If you have done this, only then are you a wise builder in God's eyes. You should begin building your house through obedience with Christformation in you. Then, you should continue building upon what you have started until there is full Christformation in you. Apostle Paul warns through the passage below that the foundation will determine the quality of the house that is being built.

1 Corinthians 3:10–15:

"By the grace God has given me, I laid a foundation as a wise builder, and someone else is building on it. But each one should build with care. For no one can lay any foundation other than the one already laid, which is Jesus Christ. If anyone builds on this foundation using gold, silver, costly stones, wood, hay or straw, their work will be shown for what it is, because the Day will bring it to light. It will be revealed with fire, and the fire will test the quality of each person's work. If what has been built survives, the builder will receive a reward. If it is burned up, the builder will suffer loss but yet will be saved—even though only as one escaping through the flames."

Christformation does not occur in you without your obedience to all that Christ commands. So the foundation is built through your obedience to Christ. But thereafter you should not cease obeying Him, as your measure of obedience decides the material that the rest the house is built with. If from the start you have obeyed Christ, you will have matured in Him so that you can build full Christformation in you through your growing obedience. Endurance, patience, and perseverance will be some of the gold needed to build full Christformation in you. But how would you develop perseverance if you have not been willing to suffer for your faith? How would you develop character if you had not persevered in your faith? These are some vital parts of the divine nature of Christ that are to be formed in increasing measure within your born-again spirit so that full Christformation occurs in you. Consider the following verses:

Romans 5:3–5:
"Not only so, but we also rejoice in our sufferings, because we know that suffering produces perseverance; perseverance, character; and character, hope. And hope does not disappoint us, because God has poured out his love into our hearts by the Holy Spirit, whom he has given us."

As stated in James 1:2-4, if you persevere with obedience till the end, and are willing to be tested with fire (trials and testing through suffering) towards attaining full Christformation, then your genuine faith in God will be proven. As a result, you will be spared from shame in God's presence as indicated in Revelations 16:15. But a life lacking Christformation in you is a life lacking obedience to Christ. You will then be at a loss when the storms of this life hit. You must persevere till full Christformation has been successful in you, just as God had predestined for you from the beginning. You will be tested to corroborate if all the qualities of Christ's divine nature had been successfully formed in you.

The more you obey the Word of God, the more Christ's divine nature will be formed in you, as explained in the parable of the sower. The parable of the wise and foolish builders reaffirms this, "As for everyone who comes to me and hears my words and puts them into practice, his house will be well built, ready to face any storms of life and survive till the end."

The parable of the ten virgins describes what your attitude should be toward full Christformation in you. Let's also look into these verses below and be warned.

Matthew 25:1–13:
"At that time, the kingdom of heaven will be like ten virgins who took their lamps and went out to meet the bridegroom. Five of them were foolish and five were wise. The foolish ones took their lamps but did not take any oil with them. The wise ones, however, took oil in jars along with their lamps. The bridegroom was a long time in coming, and they all became drowsy and fell asleep. At midnight the cry rang out: "Here's the bridegroom! Come out to meet him!" Then, all the virgins woke up and trimmed their lamps. The foolish ones said to the wise, "Give us some of your oil; our lamps are going out." "No," they replied, "there may not be enough for both us and you. Instead, go to those who sell oil and buy some for yourselves." But while they were on their way to buy the oil, the bridegroom arrived. The virgins who were ready went in with him to the wedding banquet. And the door was shut. Later, the others also came. "Lord, Lord," they said, "open the door for us!" But he replied, "Truly I tell you, I don't know you." Therefore keep watch, because you do not know the day or the hour."

This parable teaches us about Christformation in you as likened to oil in a lamp. Christformation in you is the oil while the born-again spirit in you is likened to the lamp. How can there be light if there isn't oil in the lamp? Similarly, how can the testimony of Christ shine through you if Christ's divine nature is not formed in you?

If there is no Christformation in you, how can Christ be glorified through you? How can you be a blessing to others if the blessings that come from Christ are not formed in you first? How can Christ our Lord, who is the bridegroom, claim ownership of you if His divine nature isn't formed within you? The very reason He went away was to give His bride ample time to have His nature formed in her when He returns. When the wisdom of God is formed in you, you will be found with Christformation. Only those who have Christ, the wisdom of God, will be ready with full Christformation for the Bridegroom.

The foolish virgins said to the wise, "Give us some of your oil; our lamps are going out." Here is the warning that, if there is no Christformation in you, you are likened to "lamps giving out no light." When you start depending on the testimonies of fellow believers in Christ in order to survive your Christian life and do not have the hunger, thirst or urgency of your own to build your own testimony through obedience to Christ, soon you will burn out yourself. The testimony of Jesus will not be found in you at all because you are always depending on others and not on Christ to build your life in Him. "The wise ones, however, took oil in jars along with their lamps." "Oil in jars" refer to you who have filled yourselves with Christformation. You are the ones who had realized the need to attain full Christformation. You took the trouble to know what will prepare you for the bridegroom's (Christ's) second coming. You made every effort towards full Christformation in you. This verse also refers to those who have been obedient to God the Holy Spirit, who guides them to full Christformation, especially those who hunger and thirst for it.

The five wise virgins were ready with full Christformation in them. How were the foolish virgins not ready for the bridegroom? "The bridegroom was a long time in coming, and they all became drowsy and fell asleep." Apostle Paul warned the Thessalonian believers about "falling asleep." Let's read the verses that explain more about being caught unprepared through our own carelessness.

1 Thessalonians 5:6–8:
"So then, let us not be like others, who are asleep, but let us be awake and sober. For those who want to sleep will sleep at night, and those who want to get drunk will get drunk at night. But since we belong to the day, let us be sober, putting on faith and love as a breastplate, and the hope of salvation as a helmet."

Faith, hope, and salvation that come from Christ can only be formed in those who are awake and sober like the five wise virgins. It's this hope in Christ that makes you want to fill yourself with Christformation in you for His appearance as the Bridegroom. Those who live like the five foolish virgins, who did not see the need for Christformation in themselves, will be locked out of God's kingdom when Christ our Lord returns. They will have nothing in them that will identify them with Christ as His Bride.

The foolish virgins did not sow Christformation in themselves with the help of God the Holy Spirit in their born-again spirits and therefore weren't ready. They went to sleep regarding God the Holy Spirit's leading and guidance toward Christformation in them. They did not recognize the importance of developing Christformation in them until the bridegroom came. Only then did they realize that something was missing in them. But it was too late to "buy" oil, or Christformation.

The foolish virgins knew that there would be a price to pay for full Christformation in them, and yet they did not care to make every effort to buy in advance. They thought they could pursue the matter when it was more convenient for them. But it was too late for the foolish virgins to make the decision at the hour the bridegroom appeared.

The Lord Jesus rebuked His church in Sardis and Laodicea when they took pride in the things of this world and their earthly possessions but were asleep when it came to Christformation in them. He counseled them to pay the price for full Christformation in them. Let's compare these two following passages while we take heed of their warnings.

Revelation 3:1–6:

"These are the words of him who holds the seven spirits of God and the seven stars. I know your deeds; you have a reputation of being alive, but you are dead. Wake up! Strengthen what remains and is about to die, for I have found your deeds unfinished in the sight of my God. Remember therefore, what you have received and heard; hold it fast, and repent. But if you do not wake up, I will come like a thief, and you will not know at what time I will come to you. Yet you have a few people in Sardis who have not soiled their clothes. They will walk with me, dressed in white, for they are worthy. The one who is victorious will, like them, be dressed in white. I will never blot out the name of that person from the book of life, but will acknowledge that name before my Father and his angels. Whoever has ears, let them hear what the Spirit says to the churches."

Revelation 3:13–18:

"To the angel of the church in Laodicea write: These are the words of the Amen, the faithful and true witness, the ruler of God's creation. I know your deeds, that you are neither cold nor hot. I wish you were either one or the other! So, because you are lukewarm—neither hot nor cold—I am about to spit you out of my mouth. You say, "I am rich; I have acquired wealth and do not need a thing." But you do not realize that you are wretched, pitiful, poor, blind, and naked. I counsel you to buy from me gold refined in the fire, so you can become rich; and white clothes to wear, so you can cover your shameful nakedness; and salve to put on your eyes, so you can see."

Your worldly reputation can be deceiving, as it may not reflect the truth about you. Apostle Paul was very careful about receiving praise from sinful men. To them, "bitter will be sweet and sweet will be bitter" as stated in Isaiah 5:20-21. In this statement, "You have a reputation of being alive, but you are dead," the Lord Jesus is rebuking the believers in Laodicea with the truth about them. Certainly it is not a sugar-coated rebuke that the world would like to hear. You live a life that is contrary to the praises that you receive from others. How would you like that comment made about you? Your reputation does not say the right thing about the real you. You can deceive man, but you cannot deceive God.

Your boasting of being something you are not will come to a tragic end in God's presence one day. Many will find out the truth about themselves at the judgment of the great white throne. Here the Lord Jesus Christ is rebuking you to change your ways while you are still on earth, as He rebuked the believers whom He still loved in Sardis.

Don't go to sleep without being victorious with Christformation in you. If you fall asleep, how can you be victorious? Again, to the believers at Laodicea, Jesus says to stop their evil boastings of who they are and what they have gained on this earth materially. The things of this world do not last; instead seek full Christformation in you that will last, which will please the heavenly Father eternally. "You say, 'I am rich; I have acquired wealth and do not need a thing.' " But the Lord Jesus says,

"Do not boast to the world because you do not realize that you are wretched, pitiful, poor, blind, and naked." Worldly wealth may make you self-sufficient in this world, but not eternally. Eternally, you need Christformation in you, for eternal life is found only in Christ, who was the Tree of Life in the garden of Eden that God sealed off as soon as Adam and Eve ate from the tree of death in disobedience to God.

The parable of the wise and foolish virgins is a reminder of what happens when a believer of Christ falls asleep and does not actively sow or add Christformation in him- or herself through the guidance of God the Holy Spirit. You as the temple of God the Holy Spirit are supposed to be a new creation in Christ with His divine nature formed within you.

D) The Seven Churches in Revelation

Take note that there is a common requirement from the Lord Jesus Christ to all the seven churches: "To him who overcomes ... I will give ..." Let's compare these seven passages.

1) Revelation 2:7 (Ephesus Church):

"He who has an ear let him hear what the Spirit says to the churches. *To him who overcomes*, I will give the right to eat from the tree of life, which is in the paradise of God" (emphasis added).

2) Revelation 2:11 (Smyrna Church):

"He who has an ear let him hear what the Spirit says to the churches. *He who overcomes* will not be hurt at all by the second death" (emphasis added).

3) Revelation 2:17 (Pergamum Church):

"He who has an ear let him hear what the Spirit says to the churches. *To him who overcomes*, I will give some of the hidden manna. I will also give him a white stone with a new name written on it, known only to him who receives it" (emphasis added).

4) Revelation 2:26–29 (Thyatira Church):

"*To him who overcomes* and does my will to the end, I will give authority over the nations—He will rule them with an iron scepter; he will dash them to pieces like pottery—just as I have received authority from my Father. I will also give him the morning star. He who has an ear, let him hear what the Spirit says to the churches" (emphasis added).

5) Revelation 3:5–6 (Sardis Church):

"*He who overcomes* will, like them, be dressed in white. I will never blot out his name from the book of life, but will acknowledge his name before my Father and his angels. He who has an ear let him hear what the Spirit says to the churches" (emphasis added).

6) Revelation 3:12–13 (Philadelphia Church):

"*Him who overcomes* I will make a pillar in the temple of my God. Never again will he leave it. I will write on him the name of my God and the name of the city of my God, the new Jerusalem, which is coming down out of heaven from my God; and I will also write on him my new name. He who has an ear let him hear what the Spirit says to the churches" (emphasis added).

7) Revelation 3:21–22 (Laodicean Church):

"*To him who overcomes*, I will give the right to sit with me on my throne, just as I overcame and sat down with my Father on his throne. He who has an ear let him hear what the Spirit says to the churches" (emphasis added).

"To him who overcomes" is a message to an individual person and is repeated to believers in all seven churches. Though the message was given to the entire church, the Lord Jesus Christ wanted every believer to be "one who overcomes." "Overcome what?" you may ask. Overcome the sinful nature of the Devil in you.

In His entire message to the seven churches, Jesus wanted the believers to overcome some form of weakness that was evidently a hindrance toward Christformation in them. The seven churches had believers with some form of sin in them that He wasn't pleased with. He was reminding them that if they continue pleasing the sinful nature of the Devil in them and not listen to and obey God the Holy Spirit, they would not have Christformation in them. He warned the believers that only if they overcame the sinful nature of the Devil in them would Christ's divine nature be formed within them. This is impossible without His help.

First, the believers must overcome all their weaknesses. Many sins are committed through our weaknesses. However, some are through outright rebellion toward the Lord. These sins have no chance of escape from the coming judgment, He warned sternly. Here, to all the believers in the seven churches, He was encouraging them to give up pleasing the sinful nature of the Devil in them completely so that full Christformation would occur in them by the power of God the Holy Spirit.

Every good gift comes from Christ the Lord Himself. What does that mean to you? These gifts are various qualities of His divine nature that are to be formed in you. How can they be formed in you, if you do not give up everything of the Devil's nature within you? How can you be of two natures at the same time? You have to give up one of them. Christ had warned His disciples in Matthew 7:17-19, "You will never find bad fruit on a good tree." In addition to this, the apostle Paul warns us with these words:

2 Corinthians 6:14–18:

"Do not be yoked together with unbelievers. For what do righteousness and wickedness have in common? Or what fellowship can light have with darkness? What harmony is there between Christ and Belial? What does a believer have in common with an unbeliever? What agreement is there between the temple of God and idols? For you are the temple of the Living God. God has said: "I will live with them and walk among them, and I will be their God, and they will be my people." "Therefore come out from them and be separate," says the Lord. "Touch no unclean thing, and I will receive you. I will be a Father to you, and you will be my sons and daughters," says the Lord Almighty."

Who you obey in your life must be distinctly clear. You cannot claim to belong to Christ but still obey the sinful nature of the Devil in you. So, who do you belong to? Stop obeying the sinful nature of the Devil in you. Be freed from slavery to it. When the Lord Jesus said in John 8:35-37, "So if the Son sets you free, you will be free indeed," He was referring to setting you free from the sinful nature of the Devil in you. For only He who was without any sin can free you.

But this does not come without your obedience to everything He has commanded. You must obey the Son before He sets you free. Touch no unclean thing, and God will receive you. If you touch anything unclean, He will not receive you as His child. What is this "unclean" thing? We have dealt with this in the earlier chapters, but it is worth repeating as a reminder:

Mark 7:20–23:
"He went on: "What comes out of a man is what makes him 'unclean.' For from within, out of men's hearts, come evil thoughts, sexual immorality, theft, murder, adultery, greed, malice, deceit, lewdness, envy, slander, arrogance, and folly. All these evils come from inside and make a man 'unclean.' " "

Be separated from this unclean sinful nature of the Devil in you that produces the above-mentioned sins. They will defile you in God's sight if you touch any one of them. If you want to be His son or daughter, you must not touch them. These evils that "come from inside" are from the sinful nature of the Devil sown in you through the disobedience of one man—Adam. Now through the obedience of one man—Christ—will come the righteousness of God. The same obedience of Christ to the Father will be formed in you eternally when you obey Christ by putting to death the sinful nature of the Devil in you with the help of God the Holy Spirit.

"To him who overcomes, I will give the right to sit with me on my throne, just as I overcame and sat down with my Father on his throne." So it is the one who overcomes the sinful nature of the Devil fully in him who will be seated with Christ on His throne. He humbled himself and took the lowly form of a man in this world, yet He overcame the Devil by resisting him even to the point of death on the cross.

The believers of Christ in the seven churches were warned that if they did not make every effort necessary to overcome the sinful nature of the Devil, they would not have Christformation in them. The right to eat from the Tree of Life can only be given to you after you have overcome the sinful nature of the Devil in you. Joshua and the people of God, who survived the Sinai wilderness, entered Canaan and defeated their enemies one by one. Likewise, we who believe in Christ our Lord must also defeat all aspects of the sinful nature, overcoming one part after another through our obedience so that Christ will be formed in us fully. Canaan represents full Christformation in us.

If you were to take note of the believers' evil practices in the aforementioned seven churches, you would be shocked to realize that some of them still practiced idolatry, witchcraft, sorcery, debauchery, deception, sexual immorality, greed, covetousness, malice, dishonesty, adultery, fornication, robbery, theft, cheating, lying and many other forms of outright disobedience to the Lord. And they did so even though they claimed to be His. The stern rebuke from the Lord Jesus Christ was for them.

You cannot enter God's kingdom by obeying the sinful nature of the Devil in you. Let's read the following verses to understand this truth further:

Galatians 5:19–21 (NLT):
"When you follow the desires of your sinful nature, the results are very clear: sexual immorality, impurity, lustful pleasures, idolatry, sorcery, hostility, quarrelling, jealousy, outbursts of anger, selfish ambition, dissension, division, envy, drunkenness, wild parties, and other sins like these. Let me tell you again, as I have before, that anyone living that sort of life will not inherit the kingdom of God."

E) THE NEW JERUSALEM

You should read the following passage carefully to understand in whom Christformation will occur. One thing we are certain of: Christformation will never occur in those without a divine promise over their lives, as Christformation in you is the result of a promise from God. Hagar had a child, Ishmael, an ordinary child, who was born without any promise from God. Isaac was born out of God's promise to Abraham and Sarah. Let's read on:

Galatians 4:21–28:

"For it is written that Abraham had two sons, one by the slave woman and the other by the free woman. His son by the slave woman was born according to the flesh, but his son by the free woman was born as the result of a divine promise. These things are being taken figuratively: The women represent two covenants. One covenant is from Mount Sinai and bears children who are to be slaves: This is Hagar. Now Hagar stands for Mount Sinai in Arabia and corresponds to the present city of Jerusalem, because she is in slavery with her children. But the Jerusalem that is above is free, and she is our mother. For it is written: "Be glad, barren woman, you who never bore a child; shout for joy and cry aloud, you who were never in labor; because more are the children of the desolate woman than of her who has a husband." Now you, brothers and sisters, like Isaac, are children of promise."

Christformation will never occur in someone who does not have the promise of God. Who are those with the promise of God for Christformation in them? They who belong to the New Jerusalem (the heavenly Jerusalem, not the earthly Jerusalem) will have Christformation in them. "But the Jerusalem that is above is free, and she is our mother." New Jerusalem will bear, wean, and nurture the children of God to mature to full Christformation in them. From the beginning of time, God had promised that these children of His would have Christformation in them. Ordinary children of the slave woman represented by Hagar will have no Christformation in them.

Now, there are two women who represent two covenants. One is a covenant of slavery to the sinful nature of the Devil while the other is the covenant of freedom from the sinful nature of the Devil. One will be bound, and the other free; that's the difference. The child that belongs to Hagar will grow to become more and more like the Devil, and the child who belongs to Sarah will grow more and more to become like Christ. The sinful nature of the Devil will grow in the ordinary children of Hagar, but the divine nature of Christ will be fully formed in the children of promise through Sarah. "Now you, brothers and sisters, like Isaac, are children of promise." What is the promise? Full Christformation in you. Let us read another passage that explains this clearly.

Hebrews 12:18–24:

"You have not come to a mountain that can be touched and that is burning with fire; to darkness, gloom and storm; to a trumpet blast or to such a voice speaking words that those who heard it begged that no further word be spoken to them, because they could not bear what was commanded: "If even an animal touches the mountain, it must be stoned to death." The sight was so terrifying that Moses said, "I am trembling with fear." But you have come to Mount Zion, to the city of the living God, the heavenly Jerusalem. You have come to thousands upon thousands of angels in joyful assembly, to the church of the firstborn, whose names are written in heaven. You have come to God, the Judge of all, to the spirits of the righteous made perfect, to Jesus the mediator of a new covenant, and to the sprinkled blood that speaks a better word than the blood of Abel."

The Lord Jesus Christ is the mediator of the new covenant, which is the covenant of freedom from the sinful nature of the Devil. The blood of Christ that was shed for us on Calvary has power to cleanse us permanently from all sins, which the first covenant of the blood of bulls and goats did not have. The blood of Abel was the sacrificial blood of the first Adam, but it has no power to permanently cleanse us from our sins. With the new covenant through Christ, all our sins are washed away permanently by the blood of the Lamb of God shed for us on the cross.

In the passage above, these covenants are represented figuratively by two mountains—Sinai and Zion. One is of the "earthly Jerusalem" while the other is of the "heavenly Jerusalem." Those who belong to Mount Zion will have Christformation in them, and those who belong to Mount Sinai will never have Christformation in them. Those who have Christformation in them have their names written in heaven because they belong to the last Adam, who is from heaven. The first Adam is from this earth, and those who belong to him live only to obey the earthly nature of the Devil in them.

Remember, the Devil and one-third of the host of demons, who were the fallen angels, were "thrown to the earth like lightning" and that's how the earthly nature came about. The "church of the firstborn" in Mount Zion will have full Christformation in them for they are the "spirits of the righteous made perfect" through full Christformation in them. Christ's divine nature will be fully formed in their born-again spirits. Let us look at another corresponding passage in the Bible.

Revelation 21:1–4:
"Then I saw "a new heaven and a new earth," for the first heaven and the first earth had passed away, and there was no longer any sea. I saw the Holy City, the New Jerusalem, coming down out of heaven from God, prepared as a bride beautifully dressed for her husband. And I heard a loud voice from the throne saying, "Look! God's dwelling place is now among the people, and he will dwell with them. They will be his people, and God himself will be with them and be their God. He will wipe every tear away from their eyes. There will be no more death or mourning or crying or pain, for the old order of things has passed away."

"Prepared as a bride beautifully dressed for her husband" is full Christformation in the children of God. This is New Jerusalem. God the heavenly Father, the Son of God, and God the Holy Spirit will "make their home" in all those who have full Christformation in them. This is the ultimate will of God. This does not happen until you obey all that Christ had commanded you so that His divine nature is fully formed within you. Christformation in you is for eternity; there will be no more death or mourning, crying, or pain. The sinful nature of the Devil brings sorrow, guilt, pain, first death to the flesh, and second death to the spirit when you fully obey it. However, full Christformation in you will bring God's eternal dwelling place among you. Obeying the sinful nature of the Devil will be the thing of the past once Christ is fully formed in you.

Full Christformation in the believers will occur just the way God has planned it from the beginning. This will be completed on Mount Zion. The promise of Christformation will be fulfilled in all those who have obeyed Him fully without the presence of the sinful nature of the Devil in them anymore. These will be the called, chosen, and faithful believers in Christ who "had not touched that unclean thing," which means those who had never found it pleasurable to obey the sinful nature of the Devil in them but had "put it to death" in obedience to the leading of God the Holy Spirit while they were on earth. Let's witness what happens on Mount Zion through these verses in the book of Revelation:

Revelation 14:1–5:
"Then I looked, and there before me was the Lamb, standing on Mount Zion, and with him 144,000 who had his name and his Father's name written on their foreheads. And I heard a sound from heaven like the roar of rushing waters and like a loud peal of thunder. The sound I heard was like that of harpists playing their harps. And they sang a new song before the throne and before the four living creatures and the elders. No one could learn the song except the 144,000 who had been redeemed from the earth. These are those who did not defile themselves with women, for they remained virgins. They follow the Lamb wherever he goes. They were purchased from among mankind and offered as firstfruits to God and the Lamb. No lie was found in their mouths; they are blameless."

Christ's and the heavenly Father's name were "written on the foreheads," which is an indication of full Christformation in them. "No one could learn the song except the 144,000 who had been redeemed from the earth" meant no one could learn obedience to all that Christ had commanded like they did on earth. They were careful not to defile themselves by obeying the sinful nature of the Devil in them and remained vigilant as the five wise virgins in Matthew 25, who kept themselves pure and ready for the bridegroom at his sudden return. "They were purchased from among mankind and offered as firstfruits to God and the Lamb. No lie was found in their mouths; they are blameless." Only the blameless will have full Christformation in them.

They had no trace of belonging to the "father of all lies" who is the Devil. The divine nature of Christ was fully formed in them just as the precious stones that were found on the walls of the Holy City beautified the City of God. Let's read about this.

Revelation 21:18–21:
"The wall was made of jasper, and the city of pure gold, as pure as glass. The foundations of the city walls were decorated with every kind of precious stone. The first foundation was jasper, the second sapphire, the third chalcedony, the fourth emerald, the fifth sardonyx, the sixth carnelian, the seventh chrysolite, the eighth beryl, the ninth topaz, the tenth chrysoprase, the eleventh jacinth, and the twelfth amethyst. The twelve gates were twelve pearls, each gate made of a single pearl. The great street of the city was of pure gold, like transparent glass."

All the precious stones mentioned in this passage represent the divine nature of Christ that is formed in each believer to beautify the city of God eternally and bring glory to the heavenly Father. Now they will all have the same divine nature and sin will not be found in God's presence anymore. This will be the new heaven and new earth.

F) Those Fully Obedient to God the Holy Spirit (Led by the Spirit)

Romans 8:14–17:
"For those who are led by the Spirit of God are the children of God. The Spirit you received does not make you slaves, so that you live in fear again; rather, the Spirit you received brought about your adoption to sonship. And by him we cry, *"Abba,* Father." The Spirit himself testifies with our spirit that we are God's children. Now if we are children, then we are heirs—heirs of God and co-heirs with Christ, if indeed we share in his sufferings in order that we may also share in his glory."

Christformation does not occur in you if you obey the sinful nature of the Devil in you. Christformation occurs in you only when you are led by the Spirit of God. "Being led by the Spirit of God" means that you are obedient to His leading and guidance toward full Christformation in you. Without your total obedience to Him, full Christformation will not occur in you. You will only become heirs of God and co-heirs of Christ with full Christformation in you. This can only happen if you have been fully obedient to the leading and guidance of God the Holy Spirit even though you have had to endure sufferings in order to resist pleasing the sinful nature. When you do this, you will surely share in His glory through full formation of Christ's divine nature in you.

Sonship through Christformation comes when you obey God the Holy Spirit at all costs. The children of God will have Christformation in them because only Christ can please the heavenly Father. He will be pleased with you if you have all the divine nature of Christ formed in you. Let us refer to another passage in 1 John.

1 John 3:2–3:
"Dear friends, now that we are children of God, what we will be has not yet been made known. But we know that when Christ appears, we shall be like him, for we shall see him as he is. All who have this hope in him will purify themselves, just as he is pure."

No one is without sin as Christ our Lord is. He is pure, and you will be pure like Him through Christformation in you. If your hope comes from God the Holy Spirit, you will yearn to be like Him and for His pure, divine nature to be formed in you with the help of God the Holy Spirit. Your total dependence will be on Him for full Christformation in you, because you do not know what you will be until you see Him when He appears. But for now, God the Holy Spirit will lead you to a life of faith and full Christformation in you. Without this faith in Him, you can never please God the heavenly Father.

You must be led by God the Holy Spirit with every step made towards full Christformation in you. You cannot do this in your own strength, and no man can help you. The Holy Spirit is your helper and counselor that Christ our Lord said He would send once He returned to the heavenly Father's right side. He said in John 16:13-15 that God the Holy Spirit will "guide you into everything of me. Nothing He says or does is His, He will take what is mine and give it to you" for a full

Christformation in you. The fruit and gifts of the Holy Spirit are the divine nature of Christ that must be formed in you. The fruit is the nature of Christ that you must eat from, and the gifts are given to you by Christ through God the Holy Spirit. Let us read to understand these very important truths about the fruit and gifts of the Spirit and how they apply to Christformation in you in the two following passages.

Galatians 5:22–25 (NLT):
"But the Holy Spirit produces this kind of fruit in our lives: love, joy, peace, patience, kindness, goodness, faithfulness, gentleness, and self-control. There is no law against these things! Those who belong to Christ Jesus have nailed the passions and desires of their sinful nature to his cross and crucified them there. Since we are living by the Spirit, let us follow the Spirit's leading in every part of our lives."

1 Corinthians 12:1–11:
"Now about the gifts of the Spirit, brothers and sisters, I do not want you to be uninformed. You know that when you were pagans, somehow or other you were influenced and led astray to mute idols. Therefore I want you to know that no one who is speaking by the Spirit of God says, "Jesus be cursed," and no one can say, "Jesus is Lord," except by the Holy Spirit. There are different kinds of gifts, but the same Spirit distributes them. There are different kinds of service, but the same Lord. There are different kinds of working, but in all of them and in everyone it is the same God at work. Now to each one the manifestation of the Spirit is given for the common good. To one there is given through the Spirit a message of wisdom, to another a message of knowledge by means of the same Spirit, to another faith by the same Spirit, to another gifts of healing by that one Spirit, to another miraculous powers, to another prophecy, to another distinguishing between spirits, to another speaking in different kinds of tongues, and to still another the interpretation of tongues. All these are the work of one and the same Spirit, and he distributes them to each one, just as he determines."

Love, joy, peace, patience, kindness, goodness, faithfulness, gentleness, and self-control are all aspects of the divine nature of Christ our Lord. They can only be formed in you as a result of your obedience to God the

Holy Spirit in you. There is no other way that the divine nature of Christ can be formed in you, except through God the Holy Spirit. He is the Spirit of Christ; therefore the divine nature of Christ appears as the fruit of the Spirit that must be formed in you through your life of obedience to Him. He guides you step by step as detailed in Galatians 5:16-25. This fruit can only be formed in your born-again spirit through your obedience to the leading and guidance of God the Holy Spirit in you. He will lead you to put to death all the misdeeds of the sinful nature in you, but your total obedience to Him is required. In this way, you will be guided to eat from the Tree of Life and fill yourself with His divine nature until it is formed in you for eternity. You will be reminded of the way of the cross all along, which is death to the sinful nature of the Devil in you. "Since we are living by the Spirit, let us follow the Spirit's leading in every part of our lives" in order that full Christformation occurs in you.

The following verses describe the gifts of God.

James 1:16–17:
"Don't be deceived, my dear brothers and sisters. Every good and perfect gift is from above, coming down from the Father of the heavenly lights, who does not change like shifting shadows."

The gifts of the Spirit originate from Christ our Lord and are aspects of His divine nature meant to be formed in you. They can only be formed in you through your obedience to the leading and guidance of God the Holy Spirit. There is no other way except through obedience to Him. What you think, do, and say are guided by Him once you believe in Christ and are born again in your spirit. The Holy Spirit is your helper and counselor that Christ our Lord and the heavenly Father has sent to you for full Christformation in you. You were never meant to be an orphan on this earth. The gifts are for spiritual purposes in your life and for others.

The manner in which you come to Christ will be the same way others will come to Him: through your obedience to all that He has commanded you. There is no other way you can come to Him and be filled with Him.

If you are filled with Him, you will be filled with His gifts in you and will be of great blessing to others. Many will learn about Christ from the works and service that God the Holy Spirit produces through you, but you must be obedient to Him in order for this to occur through you. Whatever happens through you is because Christ is formed in you.

God the Holy Spirit will manifest through you for the glory of God. God is glorified whenever there is obedience to Christ, but the Devil is glorified whenever there is disobedience to Christ.

The gifts of the Spirit are aspects of Christ's divine nature that were manifested through His ministry on earth. Christ our Lord obeyed the heavenly Father with His works and prayer. He ministered to needs according to the will of the Father and not as He wished. He knew the will of the Father and obeyed it.

The gifts of the Spirit are about serving God as He has willed for us and not about doing His work as we wish it to be. When we do His work according to His will, we glorify Him. In what other way can we glorify Him except when we obey God the Holy Spirit to do His work? He will remind us about the Lord Jesus Christ obediently doing God's work in all that the heavenly Father had willed through Him. We need to obey God the Holy Spirit to do His work on earth.

How can we obey God to do His work according to His will if Christ's obedience isn't formed in us first? The gifts of the Spirit come as we are ready for Christformation in us and will flow out of the fruit of the Spirit in us, which is the formation of Christ's divine nature. As we grow and mature with Christformation, our ministry through the gifts of the Spirit will bring greater glory to God. "For this reason I remind you to fan into flame the gift of God" says Apostle Paul to young Timothy in the verses below. We will be filled with power, love, and self-discipline, which are also other aspects of the divine nature of Christ to be formed in us as mentioned in that same passage.

2 Timothy 1:6–7:
"For this reason I remind you to fan into flame the gift of God, which is in you through the laying on of my hands. For God did not give us a spirit of timidity, but a spirit of power, of love, and of self-discipline."

G) The Called, Chosen, and Faithful of Christ

Revelation 17:14:
"They will make war against the Lamb, but the Lamb will overcome them because he is Lord of lords and King of kings—and with him will be his called, chosen, and faithful followers."

The kingdom of darkness is at war against the Lord Jesus Christ who is the King of kings and the Lord of lords. But it has only known Him as the Lamb of God thus far since His first coming. However, He is about to be revealed as the 'Rider on the White Horse' to judge and make war at His glorious second coming. The kingdom of darkness is about to confront the greatest One of God as revealed in Revelation 19: 11-21.

All kings will bow before Him and confess that He is the Lord of lords. With Him will be those who are like Him with the divine nature of Christ formed in them. They will be those who obeyed the call of God to be separated unto Him while they were on earth. They will also be those who were chosen by the heavenly Father from the beginning of time to be the exact representation of Christ on earth through full Christformation in them by the power of God the Holy Spirit leading and guiding them. They will also be those who learned the obedience of Christ and have proven faithful till the end and will have overcome the sinful nature of the Devil in them. They will have inherited eternal life in Christ. With full Christformation in them, they will be ready to fight the Enemy once and for all because, while on earth, they had been fighting the Enemy daily.

Full Christformation occurs in those who are called, chosen, and faithful followers of Christ. Let us read another passage related to this.

Romans 8:29–30:

"For those God foreknew he also predestined to be conformed to the image of his Son, that he might be the firstborn among many brothers and sisters. And those he predestined, he also called; those he called, he also justified; those he justified, he also glorified."

God has chosen you to be conformed to the image of His Son so that He might be the firstborn among many brothers and sisters. Those whom he has chosen by predestination and who have responded to His call, He makes right before God, washing them with the precious blood of the Lamb and glorifying them with full Christformation in them. What could glorify the heavenly Father more than to witness those whom He has chosen from the beginning to be conformed into the image of His Son?

Who exactly are these called, chosen, and faithful followers of Christ? How did they conduct their lives in order for Christ to be fully formed in them? What was required of them? What does the Word of God say about them? Let's find out from the following Bible passages.

Revelation 12:17:

"Then the dragon was enraged at the woman and went off to wage war against the rest of her offspring—those who keep God's commands and hold fast their testimony about Jesus."

They were those who kept God's commandments and held fast to Christformation in them, which is the testimony that they truly belonged to Jesus their Savior and Lord through their personal obedience to Him.

Matthew 24:12–13:

"Because of the increase of wickedness, the love of most will grow cold, but the one who stands firm to the end will be saved."

They will be those who will stand firm till the end in spite of the temptation to continue obeying the sinful nature of the Devil in them. They will be the overcomers of this world, its pleasures and passions.

Daniel 11:33–35:

"Those who are wise will instruct many but for a time they will fall by the sword or be burned or captured or plundered. When they fall, they will receive a little help, and many who are not sincere will join them. Some of the wise will stumble so that they may be refined, purified, and made spotless until the time of the end, for it will still come at the appointed time."

They will be those who will be refined, purified, and made spotless from the blemishes of the sinful nature of the Devil in them through many tests and trials of their faith.

Revelation 20:4–5:

"I saw thrones on which were seated those who had been given authority to judge. And I saw the souls of those who had been beheaded because of their testimony about Jesus and because of the word of God. They had not worshiped the beast or its image and had not received its mark on their foreheads or their hands. They came to life and reigned with Christ a thousand years. (The rest of the dead did not come to life until the thousand years were ended.) This is the first resurrection."

They will be those who had resisted receiving the beast's mark of ownership (serving or returning allegiance to him in exchange for the pleasures of this world). They will have to go through all kinds of trials and tribulations for their faith in order to remain in Christ till the end. They will prove their faithfulness to Christ, laying down their lives for the purposes of His kingdom.

In all of the called, chosen, and faithful ones, Christ's divine nature will be formed in them eternally. We see a similar passage in the Old Testament that speaks of faithfulness, whereby the living creatures that represent Christ-likeness never did anything on their own. Wherever the Spirit led them, they went faithfully; that was the secret of their obedience. We too must be led by the Spirit towards full Christformation; faithfully following Him till the end and not turning to the right or left in self-will. Let's read the passage below to understand this better.

Ezekiel 1:4–17:

"I looked, and I saw a windstorm coming out of the north—an immense cloud with flashing lightning and surrounded by brilliant light. The center of the fire looked like glowing metal, and in the fire was what looked like four living creatures. In appearance, their form was that of a man, but each of them had four faces and four wings. Their legs were straight; their feet were like those of a calf and gleamed like burnished bronze. Under their wings on their four sides, they had the hands of a man. All four of them had faces and wings, and their wings touched one another. Each one went straight ahead; they did not turn as they moved. Their faces looked like this: Each of the four had the face of a man, and on the right side each had the face of a lion, and on the left the face of an ox; each also had the face of an eagle. Such were their faces. Their wings were spread out upwards; each had two wings, one touching the wing of another creature on either side, and two wings covering its body. Each one went straight ahead. Wherever the spirit would go, they would go, without turning as they went. The appearance of the living creatures was like burning coals of fire or like torches. Fire moved back and forth among the creatures; it was bright, and lightning flashed out of it. The creatures sped back and forth like flashes of lightning. As I looked at the living creatures, I saw a wheel on the ground beside each creature with its four faces. This was the appearance and structure of the wheels: They sparkled like chrysolite, and all four looked alike. Each appeared to be made like a wheel intersecting a wheel. As they moved, they would go in any one of the four directions the creatures faced; the wheels did not turn about as the creatures went."

The four living creatures were very much like the Son of Man and they moved in perfect unity towards a set purpose. Ezekiel prophesied about the mark of obedience of those who believe in the Son of Man, as revealed in the gospels of the Lord Jesus Christ. There will be some who will obey all that Christ had commanded. In them, Christ will be fully formed. God the Holy Spirit is seen to have an indispensable role in making this come true in believers. In this way, the four Gospels of The Way, The Truth and The Life will be fulfilled in them. This passage in Ezekiel is actually a prophecy of what is to come through Christ. God the Holy Spirit would bring about this unity and conformity to

Christ in all that they do and say as a living testimony among men. The humanity, divinity, servanthood, and authority of Christ would be formed in all those who would obey the leading of God the Holy Spirit toward their full obedience to the gospel of Christ. Where there is full obedience to Christ, there will be full Christformation in them.

SUMMARY: CHAPTER FIVE

There are only two kinds of objects in this world: objects of God's mercy and objects of God's wrath. Christformation can only occur in the objects of God's mercy, never in the objects of His wrath.

Objects of God's mercy are marked by their obedience to the Lord while the objects of His wrath are marked by their disobedience to Him. Objects of God's mercy live pleasing God the Holy Spirit in them whereas objects of God's wrath live pleasing the sinful nature of the Devil in them. Objects of God's mercy are born out of a promise from God whereas objects of God's wrath are born into this world as ordinary children. Objects of God's mercy are lost and then found again, but objects of God's wrath will never be found again. Objects of God's mercy are wise, but objects of God's wrath will act foolishly.

As in the seven churches of the book of Revelation, the objects of God's mercy will be overcomers of the Devil. They will be citizens of the New Jerusalem above. They were always led and assisted by God's Spirit while on earth, and their names are written in the Book of Life. These are the called, chosen, and faithful ones of God. The following table clearly indicates the distinction between the two objects.

Objects of God's Mercy	Objects of God's Wrath
Christformation Occurs in them	Christformation does not occur in them
Marked by obedience to the Lord	Marked by disobedience to the Lord
Live pleasing God the Holy Spirit	Live pleasing the sinful nature of the Devil
Born of God's promise	Born as ordinary children of God
Lost and found	Lost and never found
Wise	Foolish
Overcomers of the Devil	Defeated by the Devil
Citizens of New Jerusalem	Citizens of Old Jerusalem
Were always led by God's Spirit	Were never led by God's Spirit
Called, chosen and faithful of Christ	Failed children of God.
Their names were found written in the Book of life.	Their names were not found written in the Book of life.

Diagram 5(a)

CHRISTFORMATION
IS THE FORMATION OF THE DIVINE NATURE OF CHRIST IN YOU

2 PETER 1: 3-11

Chapter Six:
Who Is Involved with
Your Christformation?

A) God the Father

Ephesians 1:3–10:
"Praise be to the God and Father of our Lord Jesus Christ, who has blessed us in the heavenly realms with every spiritual blessing in Christ. For he chose us in him before the creation of the world to be holy and blameless in his sight. In love he predestined us for adoption to sonship through Jesus Christ, in accordance with his pleasure and will—to the praise of his glorious grace, which he has freely given us in the One he loves. In him we have redemption through his blood, the forgiveness of sins, in accordance with the riches of God's grace that he lavished on us. With all wisdom and understanding, he made known to us the mystery of his will according to his good pleasure, which he purposed in Christ, to be put into effect when the times reach their fulfillment—to bring unity to all things in heaven and on earth under Christ."

"To bring unity to all things in heaven and on earth under Christ" is the heavenly Father's will. From everything He did from the beginning of time, we can see that all His purposes were centered on Christ, His only begotten Son. Every one of the Father's blessings is found in His Son so that He who has the Son has all the blessings of the Father. Even before He created the world and everything in it, the Father willed that, if we are to be holy and blameless in His sight, it can be only through Christ His Son—through Christformation in us.

God the Father's grace is only found in Christ. The highest form of His grace towards us is the forgiveness of sins, without which we can never see or hear Him, as He is without any sin. We can only be redeemed from our sins through the provision of Christ's blood shed for us on the cross of Calvary. We would all be doomed if we did not have the Father's grace given to us through His Son.

God the Father knew that the sinful nature of the Devil, which was sown into Adam and Eve at the garden of Eden by the Devil's wiles and deception, must be put to death. How could that be put to death forever in us except through His Son? The sinful nature of the Devil in us brings death, but the Lord Jesus Christ brings eternal life. So when we put to death the misdeeds of the sinful nature of the Devil by the power of God the Holy Spirit within us, He leads us toward full Christformation as we obey everything Christ commands us to do.

The many prayers of the Lord Jesus suggest the involvement of the heavenly Father in Christformation within us. Let's read some of them.

John 17:20–23:
" "My prayer is not for them alone. I pray also for those who will believe in me through their message, that all of them may be one, Father, just as you are in me and I am in you. May they also be in us so that the world may believe that you have sent me. I have given them the glory that you gave me, that they may be one as we are one—I in them and you in me—so that they may be brought to complete unity. Then the world will know that you sent me and have loved them even as you have loved me."

Here the Lord Jesus prayed that everything good starts with the heavenly Father. "I in them and you in me—so that they may be brought to complete unity." It's Christformation in you that will eventually bring complete unity in God's love because His love is formed in each of us permanently. All who have believed will be made complete in Christ through full Christformation. The Lord Jesus Christ prayed to the Father that "I, you, and they who believe may become one." How will this unity occur? Through full Christformation in us because the Father is in Christ, and Christ is in the Father, and the Lord Jesus Christ prayed that "may they also be in us."

The greatest glory to God is when "we are all made one in Christ." The famous gospel verse quoted in almost all evangelistic meetings, John 3:16, speaks of God's eternal purpose for all who believe in Him.

John 3:16:
"For God so loved the world that he gave his one and only Son, that whoever believes in him shall not perish but have eternal life."

We cannot be one with God the Father and His Son if we do not have eternal life in us. Eternal life is found in Christ, for He is the Tree of Life, revealed to us so that we can eat from Him and have eternal life in us. We have another passage to confirm what Christ had said about this.

John 10:28–30:
"I give them eternal life, and they shall never perish; no one will snatch them out of my hand. My Father, who has given them to me, is greater than all; no one can snatch them out of my Father's hand. I and the Father are one." "

With Christformation in you, no one can snatch you out of God's hand. What about the rest? Can they be snatched? Yes! Just read the parable of the sower carefully. You will learn that only those who obeyed all that Christ commanded had Christformation in them, and they could not be snatched out of God's hand. As for the rest of them, the Devil could easily snatch them away, one way or another. This was the same in the garden where the "true vine" was planted. Let's read the opening verses of the following parable.

John 15:1–4:
" "I am the true vine, and my Father is the gardener. He cuts off every branch in me that bears no fruit, while every branch that does bear fruit he prunes so that it will be even more fruitful. You are already clean because of the word I have spoken to you. Remain in me, as I also

remain in you. No branch can bear fruit by itself; it must remain in the vine. Neither can you bear fruit unless you remain in me."

God the heavenly Father is likened to the owner of the vineyard in this parable. It is He who decides which branch will remain on the vine. Branches that do not have Christformation in them will be cut off and thrown into the fire. The branches that have Christformation in them will be pruned through many trials and sufferings to produce full Christformation in them. Those who remain in Christ by obeying Him fully, no matter how difficult it gets, will have full Christformation in them in the end. This is one way that God disciplines us.

Let's read and understand another corresponding passage.

Hebrews 12:4–11:
"In your struggle against sin, you have not yet resisted to the point of shedding your blood. And have you completely forgotten this word of encouragement that addresses you as a father addresses his son? It says, "My son, do not make light of the Lord's discipline, and do not lose heart when he rebukes you because the Lord disciplines the one he loves, and he chastens everyone he accepts as his son." Endure hardship as discipline; God is treating you as his children. For what children are not disciplined by their father? If you are not disciplined—and everyone undergoes discipline—then you are not legitimate, not true sons and daughters at all. Moreover, we have all had human fathers who disciplined us, and we respected them for it. How much more should we submit to the Father of spirits and live! They disciplined us for a little while as they thought best; but God disciplines us for our good, in order that we may share in his holiness. No discipline seems pleasant at the time, but painful. Later on, however, it produces a harvest of righteousness and peace for those who have been trained by it."

How can you share in His holiness unless there is Christformation in you? Christformation occurs in you when you obey the Lord in all your circumstances. Discipline, rebukes, chastisement, and hardships will result in Christformation in you. What more if you struggle against sin with all your heart, mind (soul), and strength? Won't there then be full Christformation in you? Isn't Christformation in you the sharing in His holiness? If you have to go through such painful discipline, will you not gain full Christformation in you?

As you suffer for your faith, you will have the harvest of Christ's righteousness in you eternally. The heavenly Father disciplines you in this way so that you will put to death the sinful nature of the Devil in you and obey Christ for full Christformation. The heavenly Father disciplines you so that you will have full Christformation in you.

B) GOD THE SON

Colossians 1:15–20:

"The Son is the image of the invisible God, the firstborn over all creation. For in him all things were created: things in heaven and on earth, visible and invisible, whether thrones or powers or rulers or authorities; all things have been created through him and for him. He is before all things, and in him all things hold together. And he is the head of the body, the church; he is the beginning and the firstborn from among the dead, so that in everything he might have the supremacy. For God was pleased to have all his fullness dwell in him, and through him to reconcile to himself all things, whether things on earth or things in heaven, by making peace through his blood, shed on the cross."

From this passage we know that all those who believe in Christ will eventually be filled with Him because He is the firstborn over all creation. Wait a minute; we were taught that Adam was the first man created on this earth. Adam was of this earth, and we all physically resemble Adam, but that's about it. The body like Adam's dies and is returned to the earth as dust.

The Lord Jesus Christ is from heaven, and all who believe in Him will become like Him through Christformation in them. All supremacy belongs to the Lord Jesus Christ on earth, in heaven, and even underneath the earth because all power and authority has been given to Him by the Father. All the fullness of God the Father is in Christ our Lord. When we are filled with Christ, we are also filled with the Father, as the divine nature of Christ that is formed within us is also the divine nature of the heavenly Father. Even though Christ lowered Himself to be a human being, He was faithful and obeyed the heavenly Father's will for Him to make peace through His death on the cross, which made it possible to reconcile all things on earth and in heaven to God. Christ is the Alpha and Omega, the beginning and the end, the author and finisher of Christformation in everyone who believes and obeys Him till the end. Let's read the following passage, which tells us more about this.

Hebrews 12:1–2:

"Therefore we also, since we are surrounded by so great a cloud of witnesses, let us lay aside every weight, and the sin which so easily ensnares us, and let us run with endurance the race that is set before us, looking unto Jesus, the author and finisher of our faith, who for the joy that was set before Him endured the cross, despising the shame, and has sat down at the right hand of the throne of God."

The Lord Jesus Christ is the author and finisher of your journey of faith that ends with full Christformation in you. He is always interceding for you so that you will finish the race of Christformation in you successfully. He is an example of endurance for you to follow so that you will also be lifted up with Him to where He is now through your faith in Him. He experienced the joy of doing the heavenly Father's will no matter what shame it brought Him in the eyes of the world. He was faithful and will faithfully lead you to full Christformation if you throw away everything that hinders you from obeying all of His commands. He is the One who apportioned this grace to you. Let us read what is said about Christformation in you in the passage below.

Ephesians 4:7–13 (TNIV):

"But to each one of us grace has been given as Christ apportioned it. This is why it says: "When he ascended on high, he took many captives and gave gifts to his people." (What does "he ascended" mean except that he also descended to the lower, earthly regions? He who descended is the very one who ascended higher than all the heavens, in order to fill the whole universe.) So Christ himself gave the apostles, the prophets, the evangelists, the pastors, and teachers to equip his people for works of service so that the body of Christ may be built up until we all reach unity in the faith and in the knowledge of the Son of God and become mature, attaining to the whole measure of the fullness of Christ."

Until you attain the whole measure of the fullness of Christ through full Christformation in you, God's work is not complete in you. You too could disrupt, delay, or abort it by turning to the sinful nature of the Devil in you again, continuing a life of sin that will bring eternal destruction. You can easily get entangled in sin that will hinder Christformation in you. But you must realize that Christ Himself has apportioned God's grace to each one of us who believe in Him. This grace is for full Christformation in us because only that will remain in us forever. As each believer is filled with Christ, he or she will be equipped for God's work on earth.

Through the individual equipping of the believer, the body of Christ will be built up, and we will reach a unity of the Spirit in the faith and in the knowledge of Christ our Lord. When we have reached this unity in these two important areas of our lives in Christ, it will then be a sure sign that we have become mature with Christformation in us. It is Christ our Lord who gives us the five-fold ministry such as the ministry of the apostles, prophets, evangelists, pastors and teachers which is mentioned in Ephesians 4:11-13 so that this happens. The following passage from the Bible confirms this truth.

1 John 2: 1–6 (TNIV):

"My dear children, I write this to you so that you will not sin. But if anybody does sin, we have an advocate with the Father—Jesus Christ, the Righteous One. He is the atoning sacrifice for our sins, and not only for ours but also for the sins of the whole world. We know that we have come to know him if we keep his commands. Those who say, "I know him," but do not do what he commands are liars, and the truth is not in them. But if anyone obeys his word, love for God is truly made complete in them. This is how we know we are in him: whoever claims to live in him must live as Jesus did."

Christ is the atoning sacrifice and the advocate with the Father for our sins. Those who belong to Him do not continue sinning but entrust themselves to the power of God the Holy Spirit to put to death all the misdeeds of the sinful nature of the Devil in them. If we claim that we belong to Christ, we will obey Christ at all costs. If we do not obey all that He has commanded us, can we boldly claim that we belong to Him? The answer is a big NO. How can Christformation occur in us if we keep obeying the sinful nature of the Devil and not obey the leading of God the Holy Spirit? If we live in Him, He will live in us, and we will live as Jesus did on earth. He had no sin in Him, and so we will be. With the help of God the Holy Spirit, we will be able to put to death all the acts of the sinful nature of the Devil and build full Christformation in us.

We must live as Jesus did. He is the Shepherd and the Apostle of our new life in Him as mentioned in Hebrews 3:1. When we hear His voice, we must follow Him towards full Christformation. Let us read the supporting passage below.

John 10:14–18 (TNIV):
" "I am the good shepherd; I know my sheep and my sheep know me—just as the Father knows me and I know the Father—and I lay down my life for the sheep. I have other sheep that are not of this sheep pen. I must bring them also. They too will listen to my voice, and there shall be one flock and one shepherd. The reason my Father loves me is that I lay down my life—only to take it up again. No one takes it from me, but I lay it down of my own accord. I have authority to lay it down and authority to take it up again. This command I received from my Father." "

Salvation in Christ is not just about having the elated feeling of being saved. It is an obedient walk of faith upon hearing the Shepherd's voice and following Him for full Christformation in you till the end. He leads you to greener pasture and sometimes even through the valley of the shadow of death, but you need not fear because He is leading you. The end result will be full Christformation in you if you completely trust in Him. In the end, there will be only "one flock and shepherd," as John 10:15-16 says. And finally, the divine nature of that one shepherd will be formed in you fully.

You who have followed Him till the end will be one flock through Christformation. You will all be one because you have become like Him with His divine nature formed in you permanently. You will all appear like Him forever to the pleasure and fulfilled will of the heavenly Father. He knows those who are His. You will become useful to the Master with full Christformation in you, for now and eternity. The passage below will help you understand this truth better.

2 Timothy 2:19–21:
"Nevertheless, God's solid foundation stands firm, sealed with this inscription: 'The Lord knows those who are his,' and, 'Everyone who confesses the name of the Lord must turn away from wickedness.' In a large house there are articles not only of gold and silver, but also of wood and clay; some are for special purposes and some for common use. Those who cleanse themselves from the latter will be instruments for special purposes, made holy, useful to the Master and prepared to do any good work."

As indicated in 2 Timothy 2:19, God's solid foundation is His holiness and this holiness of God is revealed through the Lord Jesus Christ by the power of God's Spirit in us. That is how the Lord knows those who are His. Anyone who does not obey Him isn't standing on God's solid foundation. The Lord knows that those who are His will obey Him. His sheep will listen to His voice and follow Him. When you listen to Him, you will turn away from all wickedness.

Full Christformation is hindered when we do not turn away from wickedness fully. This is one of God's fair "sowing and reaping" principle for us. We sow for eternal purposes what might also be useful for His earthly purposes through us. "Those who cleanse themselves from the latter will be instruments for special purposes, made holy." How else could we be instruments for special purposes unless Christformation has begun in us?

There will be no room for wickedness in us when we are made holy in New Jerusalem through full Christformation. There is no power on earth like the power of the blood of Christ. God the Holy Spirit fills us with this power as mentioned in John 16:13-15. Satan cannot withstand this power in us, as the power of the blood of Christ paves the way for Christformation in us.

Let us read the passage in the book of Hebrews to understand the power of the blood of Christ in and around us. We have victory over the Devil through Christ's blood, and God the Holy Spirit helps us experience this victory.

Hebrews 9:13–15:

"The blood of goats and bulls and the ashes of a heifer sprinkled on those who are ceremonially unclean sanctify them so that they are outwardly clean. How much more, then, will the blood of Christ, who through the eternal Spirit offered himself unblemished to God, cleanse our consciences from acts that lead to death, so that we may serve the living God! For this reason Christ is the mediator of a new covenant, that those who are called may receive the promised eternal inheritance—now that he has died as a ransom to set them free from the sins committed under the first covenant."

C) GOD THE HOLY SPIRIT

Romans 8:8–10 (NLT):

"That's why those who are still under the control of their sinful nature can never please God. But you are not controlled by your sinful nature. You are controlled by the Spirit if you have the Spirit of God living in you. (And remember that those who do not have the Spirit of Christ living in them do not belong to him at all.) And Christ lives within you, so even though your body will die because of sin, the Spirit gives life because you have been made right with God."

If the Spirit of God isn't within you, it will be impossible for Christformation to occur in you. The Spirit of God helps you to work out Christformation in you because you have been made right with God. He leads you toward full Christformation in you when you obey His leading and guidance to be made perfect. He speaks and warns you when you step out of the pathway of full Christformation in you, knowingly or unknowingly. You are required to listen to Him and obey all that Christ has commanded whenever He brings them into remembrance in you.

Full Christformation is the whole life of Christ formed in you. The divine nature of Christ needs to be formed in you, and God the Holy Spirit will help you with this. If you are a believer who continues obeying the sinful nature of the Devil in you, the Spirit of God cannot help you with Christformation. You will have to decide to give up obeying the sinful nature of the Devil in you first before the Holy Spirit can help you with Christformation in you. If you are a slave to wickedness, you cannot serve God in righteousness at the same time.

Romans 8:26–27 (NLT):
"And the Holy Spirit helps us in our weakness. For example, we don't know what God wants us to pray for. But the Holy Spirit prays for us with groaning that cannot be expressed in words. And the Father who knows all hearts knows what the Spirit is saying, for the Spirit pleads for us believers in harmony with God's own will."

God the Holy Spirit helps us in our state of weakness. He helps us to know what God's will is for us whenever we do not know what to do next. He helps us with our secret pain and agony, which we aren't able to articulate to God in prayer, for many reasons. He brings our prayers in His own words to God the Father and helps us with our secret needs that are within God's will for us. He also helps to bring God's comforting answers to us.

God the Holy Spirit is the greatest comforter we have on earth. Many of us have difficulty comforting someone who is grieving over the death of a loved one, but God the Holy Spirit comforts them best. We conclude this through testimonies of believers who have gone through unbearable grief. He comforts us when we have failed in the things of God. He also comforts and assures us when we miss the mark and fall into sinning unknowingly, gently convicting us of our sin.

All things work for our own good, and God the Holy Spirit helps us to understand that these trials and the testing of our faith work out Christformation in us eternally when we obey God's Word at all costs.

Let's read the passage below to better understand God the Holy Spirit.

2 Corinthians 3:16–18 (NLT):
"But whenever someone turns to the Lord, the veil is taken away. For the Lord is the Spirit, and wherever the Spirit of the Lord is, there is freedom. So all of us who have had that veil removed can see and reflect the glory of the Lord. And the Lord—who is the Spirit—makes us more and more like him as we are changed into his glorious image."

The Spirit of the Lord brings you nearer to God the Father and the Lord Jesus Christ. The veil that did not allow those who were in the tabernacle to enter and see the glory of the Lord in the Old Testament is removed the moment the Spirit of the Lord comes into you through the sacrificial death of Christ on the cross. He gives you freedom to come to God while leading and guiding you to all truth about Christ our Lord. It is God the Holy Spirit who makes you more and more like Christ with His divine nature formed in you.

When full Christformation occurs in you, you will be changed into His glorious image in your born-again spirit. This will transform your mind into the mind of Christ. God the Holy Spirit helps you closely with this when you obey Him. When you have surrendered your life to His leading and guidance, you will not be blind to the things of God anymore. You will be enabled to see Christ clearly so that you can obey all that He has commanded.

Isaiah 11:1–3:
"A shoot will come up from the stump of Jesse; from his roots a Branch will bear fruit. The Spirit of the LORD will rest on him— the Spirit of wisdom and of understanding, the Spirit of counsel and of might, the Spirit of the knowledge and fear of the LORD—and he will delight in the fear of the LORD. He will not judge by what he sees with his eyes, or decide by what he hears with his ears."

The divine nature of Christ our Lord is found in the Spirit of the Lord. Isaiah prophesied that the Spirit of the Lord would first rest in fullness on the Lord Jesus Christ, who would be the firstborn of God the heavenly Father. The Lord Jesus Christ is the branch and will bear the fruit of Christformation in all those who believe in Him and are found faithful.

Those without the fear of the Lord will never have Christformation in them, as the fear of the Lord is the beginning of wisdom and understanding. The one who has Christ formed within him will delight in the fear of the Lord. For some, the fear of the Lord is burdensome, but it should never be because the Lord Jesus Christ delighted Himself in the fear of the Lord while He was on earth. If you are ever going to please the heavenly Father, you must revere the Lord. Likewise, you also cannot please Him unless you have the divine nature of Christ formed within you.

The end result of having these aspects of the divine nature of Christ formed in you; through the power of the Spirit of the Lord, will be your right actions in all your dealings with others. Just, righteous behavior will spring forth from these successfully formed aspects of Christ in you. The Lord Jesus Christ will teach and instruct you through His Spirit in you. He will make you a useful instrument of righteousness with full Christformation in you and will empower you through God the Holy Spirit who indwells you. Let us read the prophecy below that highlights this indispensable and much-needed empowering.

Joel 2:28–32:
" "And afterward, I will pour out my Spirit on all people. Your sons and daughters will prophesy, your old men will dream dreams, your young men will see visions. Even on my servants, both men and women, I will pour out my Spirit in those days. I will show wonders in the heavens and on the earth, blood and fire and billows of smoke. The sun will be turned to darkness and the moon to blood before the coming of the great and dreadful day of the LORD. And everyone who calls on the name of the LORD will be saved; for on Mount Zion and in Jerusalem there will be deliverance, as the LORD has said, even among the survivors whom the LORD calls."

This prophecy was fulfilled on that spectacular day of Pentecost, fifty days after the Passover feast. When He appeared to the disciples, the Lord commanded them to wait in Jerusalem for forty days after He had resurrected from the dead and before He ascended to heaven to the Father's right hand. The first prayer meeting of the 120 disciples in Jerusalem was the glorious start to the acts of God the Holy Spirit on earth to lead the lost sheep back to Christ the Great Shepherd. Signs and wonders followed the empowerment of the believers of Christ in Jerusalem. Ever since the first outpouring of the power of God on His people in Acts 2:16-21, signs and wonders that accompany a believer of Christ, had and will continue on until the second coming of the Lord.

Most importantly, God the Holy Spirit fills believers as a guarantee of full Christformation in them if they obey His leading till the end. God will show signs and wonders in and around the believer so that many will fully turn to God in true repentance. God the Holy Spirit helps each believer to put to death all the misdeeds of the sinful nature of the Devil, provided they obey His leading toward Christformation in them.

When a believer obeys all that Christ has commanded, there will be full Christformation in him or her. Let us read two passages that confirm this truth.

Ephesians 1:11–14:
"In him we were also chosen, having been predestined according to the plan of him who works out everything in conformity with the purpose of his will, in order that we, who were the first to put our hope in Christ, might be for the praise of his glory. And you also were included in Christ when you heard the message of truth, the gospel of your salvation. When you believed, you were marked in him with a seal, the promised Holy Spirit, who is a deposit that guarantees our inheritance until the redemption of those who are God's possession—to the praise of his glory."

2 Corinthians 1:21–22:

"Now it is God who makes both us and you stand firm in Christ. He anointed us, set his seal of ownership on us, and put his Spirit in our hearts as a deposit, guaranteeing what is to come."

Do not grieve God the Holy Spirit by obeying the sinful nature of the Devil in you, for that will temporarily halt or hinder Christformation in you. You must cooperate with Him as He leads and guides you to put to death all the misdeeds of the sinful nature of the Devil in you. When you do not cooperate with Him, you grieve Him, as you have intentionally delayed full Christformation in you.

Do not blaspheme Him, for you will permanently abort Christformation in you. You blaspheme Him by rebelling against His will that is aligned to God the heavenly Father's will and purpose for you in Christ our Lord. Do not put out the Spirit's fire in you and others by becoming a lukewarm believer that Christ will spew out of His mouth.

God the Holy Spirit in you is the guarantee of God's promise for the things to come in Christ. He is the seal of God's ownership in you. He is a deposit in you that guarantees your inheritance, which is full Christformation in you. What other inheritance do you need besides full Christformation in you? All things will pass away; only Christ, who is the Word of God, will remain. He is the Tree of Life that you must eat from to live forever. Full redemption is full Christformation in you. Full Christformation is the divine nature of Christ formed in you successfully with the help of God the Holy Spirit through your personal obedience to all that Christ our Lord has commanded.

2 Timothy 1:13–15:

"What you heard from me, keep as the pattern of sound teaching, with faith and love in Christ Jesus. Guard the good deposit that was entrusted to you—guard it with the help of the Holy Spirit who lives in us."

D) The Five-fold Ministry Led by God the Holy Spirit

1 Corinthians 12:27–31:
"Now you are the body of Christ, and each one of you is a part of it. And God has placed in the church first of all apostles, second prophets, third teachers, then miracles, then gifts of healing, of helping, of guidance, and of different kinds of tongues. Are all apostles? Are all prophets? Are all teachers? Do all work miracles? Do all have gifts of healing? Do all speak in tongues? Do all interpret? Now eagerly desire the greater gifts."

This glorious ministry of reconciliation through Christ our Lord is helped by God the Holy Spirit now so that many more of the chosen will answer God's call and be faithful to Him till Christ is fully formed in them. The apostles, prophets, evangelists, pastors, and teachers are given to the body of Christ by the Head of the church, who is the Lord Jesus Christ. God the Holy Spirit enables these chosen men and women of God to preach, teach, warn, admonish, rebuke, correct, and train believers in righteousness. Various gifts are given to different individuals who have been chosen by God. All of them work toward full Christformation in themselves and in other believers placed under their charge.

The greater gifts given by the Lord Jesus Christ is for building the faith of believers in Christ. What better way to build them than to encourage the believers of Christ toward gaining full Christformation in themselves? The five-fold ministry sows Christ into them by teaching them to obey everything He has commanded, and the believers reap full Christformation in themselves by obeying everything Christ has commanded them. The five-fold ministry, through the power of God the Holy Spirit, exhorts believers toward obedience to Christ. Let us read the passage below to learn more about the five-fold ministry in relation to Christformation in you.

Ephesians 4:11–16:
"So Christ himself gave the apostles, the prophets, the evangelists, the pastors and teachers, to equip his people for works of service, so that the body of Christ may be built up until we all reach unity in the faith

and in the knowledge of the Son of God and become mature, attaining to the whole measure of the fullness of Christ. Then we will no longer be infants, tossed back and forth by the waves, and blown here and there by every wind of teaching and by the cunning and craftiness of people in their deceitful scheming. Instead, speaking the truth in love, we will grow to become in every respect the mature body of him who is the head, that is, Christ. From him the whole body, joined and held together by every supporting ligament, grows and builds itself up in love, as each part does its work."

There is a danger of remaining as infants in the faith without Christformation growth in you. Teachings and the ways of the Lord can be muddied by cunning, crafty people who have deceitful schemes up their sleeves. Without Christformation in you, you will be tossed back and forth by the waves of false teachings. One of the temptations of the Devil that comes your way when you first believe in the Lord is to take shortcuts to your destination. There will be many alternative routes suggested and if you are not careful you will be blown here and there by every wind of teaching. As a result, you will remain an infant in the faith with no growth in Christformation.

These five types of ministers of the Lord are important servants for equipping you with Christformation. When there is full Christformation in every believer of Christ, there will be obvious maturity and unity of purpose to do God's will on earth as the body of Christ. We will never be confused or easily influenced to conform to the standards of this world by obeying the sinful nature of the Devil. All truth is in Christ our Lord. He is the way, the truth, and the life of the heavenly Father. The heavenly Father loves His only begotten Son, so He made peace with us through Him. He did this because He loves us too.

All believers go through testing of their faith like gold tried in a furnace of fire, so that the misdeeds that originate from the sinful nature are burnt away. However, the five-fold ministers of Christ go through much more testing as compared to the rest. As mentioned in Luke 12:47-48, much will be required from the one who has been entrusted with the gift of ministering to others. Then, more of Christ will be formed in

175

them. As Christ is increasingly formed in them, their testimony of Christ grows. If they lack the testimony of Christ, they may have been disobedient to the leading and guidance of God the Holy Spirit for Christformation in them.

Delighting yourself in wickedness is one thing, and loving the truth is another. The former reflects disobedience, and the latter reflects obedience to the Lord regarding Christformation in you. In order to build full Christformation in you, you must willfully and fully destroy the sinful nature of the Devil in you first. You cannot have both growing in you together. If both could grow together, God would have allowed Adam and Eve to remain in the garden of Eden and would not have locked them out with a pair of cherubim guarding it. They would have been free to move around in the garden of Eden if they did not have the sinful nature of the Devil in them.

There is no freedom from condemnation when sin is present in our lives. However, as indicated in 1 John 3:21-22, we have confidence to receive from God, whatever we ask of Him if we are free from the condemnation of sin. Likewise, even those blessed with the gift of the five-fold ministry, like Peter, John, James, and Paul, had to deal with their sinful nature first, before they could receive Christformation in them. That is why, Luke 17:33-37 emphasizes that whoever loses his life will preserve it. Furthermore, this is substantiated by the reference to Lot's wife in the passage. She was not ready to lose the life she led in sinful Sodom and Gomorrah and as a result of that, she lost her life. Hence, it is necessary for those in the five fold ministry to lose their lives of sin, so that they can attain Christformation (preserve their lives). Let's look at some examples of how they overcame the sinful nature and built full Christformation in themselves and others.

1 Corinthians 3:10–15:
"By the grace God has given me, I laid a foundation as a wise builder, and someone else is building on it. But each one should build with care. For no one can lay any foundation other than the one already laid, which is Jesus Christ. If anyone builds on this foundation using gold, silver, costly stones, wood, hay, or straw, their work will be shown for

what it is, because the Day will bring it to light. It will be revealed with fire, and the fire will test the quality of each person's work. If what has been built survives, the builder will receive a reward. If it is burned up, the builder will suffer loss but yet will be saved—even though only as one escaping through the flames."

The day will come when what you have done after you believed in Christ will be brought to light. How much did you value your salvation in Christ? Did you cooperate with God the Holy Spirit and build Christformation in you? Or were you careless and did not make any effort toward Christformation in your born-again spirit? Did you care to obey all that Christ our Lord has commanded? Did you build upon your belief in Christ with wholehearted obedience to Him? Or did you continue obeying the sinful nature of the Devil in you even though you believed in the Lord Jesus Christ?

All this will be revealed on the day of the Lord. The trials and tribulations of faith that tested the genuineness of your faith will also be revealed. If you did not value your salvation in Christ more than the world's pleasures and passions, that will show too, and this may hinder or abort Christformation in you.

Is it possible to believe and not have Christformation in you? Yes, it is possible. Let us read the parable below to help us understand and heed this truth before it's too late.

Luke 13:6–8:

"Then he told this parable: 'A man had a fig tree growing in his vineyard, and he went to look for fruit on it but did not find any. So he said to the man who took care of the vineyard, "For three years now I've been coming to look for fruit on this fig tree and haven't found any. Cut it down! Why should it use up the soil?" "Sir," the man replied, "leave it alone for one more year, and I'll dig around it and fertilize it." ' "

For three years, the fig tree had no figs. This parable tells us how one can believe in the Lord Jesus Christ and yet have no fruit of repentance, which is a life of obedience toward Christformation in him or her. There is a man who takes care of the garden in this parable. God the Holy Spirit cares for God's garden where Christformation grows. When the owner asks, "Why waste your time and effort on this unfruitful tree?" The man replies, "Give it one more year, I'll dig around it and fertilize it"

God the Holy Spirit counsels us to obey all that Christ has commanded. If you do not build Christformation in you with the help of God the Holy Spirit, suddenly, like the unannounced coming of the thief, you will be caught unprepared for His coming and will face His judgment for being careless about Christformation in you. So allow God the Holy Spirit to "dig around" and "fertilize" the ground where the seed (Word of God) falls deep inside of you and remains to produce obedience, if you have not been obeying Him. Trials and more testing of your faith may come, but this time, be faithful to God.

Let's learn more about the faithfulness of the five-fold ministers recorded in the New Testament.

2 Corinthians 6:3–10:
"We put no stumbling block in anyone's path, so that our ministry will not be discredited. Rather, as servants of God, we commend ourselves in every way: in great endurance; in troubles, hardships and distresses; in beatings, imprisonments and riots; in hard work, sleepless nights and hunger; in purity, understanding, patience and kindness; in the Holy Spirit and in sincere love; in truthful speech and in the power of God; with weapons of righteousness in the right hand and in the left; through glory and dishonor, bad report and good report; genuine, yet regarded as impostors; known, yet regarded as unknown; dying, and yet we live on; beaten, and yet not killed; sorrowful, yet always rejoicing; poor, yet making many rich; having nothing, and yet possessing everything."

More than boasting in his strengths, a five-fold minister should glory in the difficulties he faces in bearing the truth to all. His hardships will remain as an example to the flock of God that Christformation occurs in each believer as they resist pleasing the sinful nature of the Devil in them and obey the leading of God the Holy Spirit toward

Christformation. As apostle Paul said, as servants of God, we commend ourselves not only with the good things that happen to us but the trials of our faith also. With faithfulness to God, we bear the shame of the cross, but share the glory and the power of Christ through His resurrection.

What the apostle Paul says in the passage above truly happens to all five-fold ministers of the Lord Jesus Christ's gospel in one way or another. The testimony of Christ flows through the five-fold ministers through their perseverance, patience, endurance, and faithfulness to God in whatever circumstances God wills for them. These come forth as encouragement for believers to press on toward full Christformation in them. Listen to what Paul says about the five-fold ministers in the passage below.

1 Corinthians 4:9–13:

"For it seems to me that God has put us apostles on display at the end of the procession, like those condemned to die in the arena. We have been made a spectacle to the whole universe, to angels as well as to human beings. We are fools for Christ, but you are so wise in Christ! We are weak, but you are strong! You are honored, we are dishonored! To this very hour, we go hungry and thirsty, we are in rags, we are brutally treated, and we are homeless. We work hard with our own hands. When we are cursed, we bless; when we are persecuted, we endure it; when we are slandered, we answer kindly. We have become the scum of the earth, the garbage of the world—right up to this moment."

The five-fold ministry to the body of Christ is no ordinary task. The ministers reflect the sacrifice of Christ with their own lives, bearing the burden of the cross for the body of Christ as examples for all believers. The five-fold ministers serve without recognition and acceptance in this world. In most parts of this world, they are hated and ill-treated. They are drained of all strength because of their sacrificial ministry in prayer and the Word, which requires much of their time and concentration. This they do so that all believers of Christ will benefit eternally through full Christformation in themselves.

Apostle Paul is a good example of a five-fold minister. Physically, emotionally, socially, and financially, he was deprived of comfort and suffered lack because of time needed to pray and to listen to God on a daily basis. He had to rid himself of worldly pursuits so that he could devote his time and effort to eternal matters that benefited the believers. Sometimes, it didn't seem fair that he had to suffer such shame and dishonor, but he knew the call of his Master. He behaved exactly the way Christ did while He was on earth by representing Him with the divine nature of Christ formed in him. He was truly an example of Christformation in a believer, heading toward full Christformation in himself and others who believed in the Lord Jesus Christ.

Besides the ministers, the angels of God assist us with Christformation.

E) The Angels of God

Hebrews 1:14:
"Are not all angels ministering spirits sent to serve those who will inherit salvation?"

How do angels serve those who will inherit salvation? Are angels still around? What kind of assistance do they bring? How do we benefit from their assistance? Do they assist us when we truly need them? How do we know that they are around?

Angels have always been around those who believe in Christ and, at times, around those who would eventually believe in Him. They serve those who will inherit salvation in Christ. Angels are waiting on the sidelines to bring assistance whenever we need. There are situations that will be out of our reach, and the angels will be of assistance if we ask God in prayer. Situations that cannot be solved with human strength or ability can be solved with the assistance of angels at our disposal. During impossible situations for us, God sends angels to assist us. Angels assist young believers to aged ones when and as God orders them.

When Christ is being formed in us, we will go through various tests of our faith that may require the help of angels. Let us learn what kind of situations the angels assisted other believers in Christ in the passage below.

Hebrews 1:6–7:

"And again, when God brings his firstborn into the world, he says, "Let all God's angels worship him." In speaking of the angels he says, "He makes his angels spirits, and his servants flames of fire." "

To bring about something new on earth, God sends His angels to inaugurate, setting the stage for God to do His new thing at His command. They serve all of God's purposes for men who are being saved on earth. They are created as spirits and can be anywhere at any time at God's command. They will do anything that God commands. They serve God in war against the fallen angels and assist believers of Christ when they are warring with demons. God sends assistance to fight the demons directed by the Lord through the power of the Spirit of God.

The angels assist God the Holy Spirit in helping us fight our battles whenever necessary. We, the authors of this book, are affirming this truth because we have seen them at work, time and time again. This assistance has helped us with successful Christformation in us and in those around us under our charge. When we know what is at our disposal, we call for assistance so that Christformation may not be hindered. As indicated in Hebrews 1:7, the ministers of God ought to be like flames of fire that send the burning desire into believers of Christ our Lord to turn to ashes all the misdeeds that originate from the sinful nature of the Devil in them. For Isaiah 55:11 says that His word will not return void unto Him but accomplish what He wills. That is why His word is at times like a hammer and at other times, like fire when the need warrants it as stated in Jeremiah 23:29. God the Holy Spirit burns up the Devil's chaff, or the misdeeds of the Devil's sinful nature in them, as they choose to obey all that Christ has commanded upon conviction.

The book of Revelation has the most reference to the ministry of angels in regards to Christformation in you. Let's read more about them here.

Revelation 7:1:
"After this I saw four angels standing at the four corners of the earth, holding back the four winds of the earth to prevent any wind from blowing on the land or on the sea or on any tree."

Angels are ministering spirits who have a very important place among believers of Christ when it comes to Christformation in them. They work hand in hand with God the Holy Spirit. In many daily life situations, believers are left on their own to fend for themselves in very trying conditions of this world. They are faced with many trials of their faith from opposing demons, evil systems, and corruptions of this world on a daily basis. The angels come to their rescue and assist them to be overcomers. God the Holy Spirit directs the believers in such situations from within while the angels protect them from the onslaughts of the Evil One and the demons on the outside.

We know that the seven churches in the book of Revelation were faced with many troubles, internally and externally. They were attacked by the Enemy so that Christformation was hindered or aborted in them. In the entire book of Revelation, the Enemy was after Christformation in believers, and the angels came to their rescue because the believers of Christ had to deal with fallen angels, which was not easy for them as they were merely humans. Angels are spirits that are able to fight or match the demons who are spirits too. One such example is in the passage below.

Revelation 12:1–9:
"A great sign appeared in heaven: a woman clothed with the sun, with the moon under her feet, and a crown of twelve stars on her head. She was pregnant and cried out in pain as she was about to give birth. Then another sign appeared in heaven: an enormous red dragon with seven heads and ten horns and seven crowns on its heads. Its tail swept a third of the stars out of the sky and flung them to the earth. The dragon stood in front of the woman who was about to give birth so that it might

devour her child the moment he was born. She gave birth to a son, a male child, who will rule all the nations with an iron sceptre. And her child was snatched up to God and to his throne. The woman fled into the wilderness to a place prepared for her by God, where she might be taken care of for 1,260 days. Then war broke out in heaven. Michael and his angels fought against the dragon, and the dragon and his angels fought back. But he was not strong enough, and they lost their place in heaven. The great dragon was hurled down—that ancient serpent called the devil, or Satan, who leads the whole world astray. He was hurled to the earth, and his angels with him."

This is another vision in parable form about Christformation in you. The woman represents the New Jerusalem. The twelve stars represent the twelve tribes in the Old Testament and the twelve apostles in the New Testament, represented here by the twelve angels, which speaks of God's complete and eternal government consisting of the old and the new covenants made complete through Christformation. Her newborn is Christ, who is formed in all those who believe and obey Him. "He will rule with an iron sceptre" means that He is the One who will bring an end to the kingdom of darkness on earth.

When Christ is formed in a believer, the sinful nature of the Devil is put to death in him or her. The Devil, who is the great dragon, desires to devour the child born to the woman, meaning that way before the child was born, the Devil was after him. The dragon desires to end the pregnancy by aborting the child, as the Devil plans with his evil schemes to hinder, abort, or destroy completely Christformation in those who are part of the New Jerusalem. Our Christ-conformed, imperishable bodies are being built in the presence of Christ at God's right hand. It will not be easy for the great dragon, or the Devil, to pluck believers from God's hands unless they start turning to the pleasures and passions of the sinful nature of the Devil in them again.

The angels in this vision come to the rescue once the body of Christ is separated and protected by God. At this point, war breaks out in heaven between the angels of God, led by Michael, and the fallen angels, led by the Devil. The fallen angels fight back but lose their place in heaven and are thrown to the earth.

Christformation in all believers is well protected by God, His Christ, and His angels. Here on earth, God the Holy Spirit helps us war with the fallen angels who were hurled to this earth. Let us read the passage below to see how believers are assisted by angels sent by God.

James 4:6–8:
"But he gives us more grace. That is why Scripture says: 'God opposes the proud but shows favor to the humble.' Submit yourselves, then, to God. Resist the devil, and he will flee from you. Come near to God and he will come near to you. Wash your hands, you sinners, and purify your hearts, you double-minded."

When you submit yourself humbly to God the Holy Spirit, He leads you toward full Christformation. God gives you His grace through His beloved Son because you are meant to be an object of His mercy. But you must cooperate with God the Holy Spirit by resisting the sinful nature of the Devil in you. When you keep resisting and refraining from pleasing the sinful nature of the Devil in you, the Devil will flee from you. When the Lord Jesus Christ was tempted in the wilderness after his forty-day fast, we see how He had resisted the Devil, which made the Devil flee from Him.

If you do not resist him but keep obeying the sinful nature of the Devil in you, he will find an excuse to remain in you. Once you have resisted pleasing the sinful nature of the Devil in you, you must quickly draw closer to God and not be double-minded and doubt Christformation in you. You must keep putting to death all the misdeeds of the sinful nature of the Devil in you with the help of God the Holy Spirit while the angels keep the demons away from you, making continual war with them on your behalf.

Christformation in you will continue to occur as long as you resist the Devil and his demons with God's help. You must know that you are engaged in a war, but always bear in mind that the assistance of the angels are at your disposal any time you need them.

F) THE OLD TESTAMENT WITNESSES

Hebrews 12:1:
"Therefore, since we are surrounded by such a great cloud of witnesses, let's throw off everything that hinders and the sin that so easily entangles. And let us run with perseverance the race marked out for us."

Matthew 27:51–53:
"At that moment, the curtain of the temple was torn in two from top to bottom. The earth shook, the rocks split and the tombs broke open. The bodies of many holy people who had died were raised to life. They came out of the tombs after Jesus' resurrection and went into the holy city and appeared to many people."

The great cloud of witnesses who surround us represent the obedient Old Testament patriarchs, prophets, priests and other people of God who had been raised to life, including God's angels. They are watching to see if we will obey the leading of God the Holy Spirit to put to death all the misdeeds of the sinful nature of the Devil in us like Christ our Lord did. We can be so easily entangled with the sinful nature of the Devil again and again if we do not obey the leading of God the Holy Spirit to put to death the misdeeds of this wretched nature.

The race toward full Christformation has already been marked out for us. If we obey the leading of God the Holy Spirit with perseverance, we will press on toward the goal, which is full Christformation in us. Let us read the following words of encouragement from another passage in the Bible.

Philippians 3:13–14:
"Brothers, I do not consider myself yet to have taken hold of it. But one thing I do: Forgetting what is behind and straining towards what is ahead, I press on towards the goal to win the prize for which God has called me heavenwards in Christ Jesus."

In the past, you may have succumbed to the evil desires of the Devil's sinful nature in you. But now, you must not let it hinder you from gaining full Christformation in you. You must overcome the guilt by confessing and forsaking your past sins with the help of God the Holy Spirit and pledging to never return to seeking their pleasures and passions. You may find this to be a hard-fought battle, but you must press on and never give up or return to pleasing the sinful nature of the Devil in you. If you do so, you may abort Christformation in you. No matter how tough the race gets, you must run to win, which means gaining full Christformation in you. You must persevere because the cloud of witnesses are cheering you on to win the race with full Christformation in you. The Bible passage below tells us more about the people of God in this cloud of witnesses.

Hebrews 11:39–40:
"These were all commended for their faith, yet none of them received what had been promised. God had planned something better for us so that only together with us would they be made perfect."

These people of God, who were obedient servants of His will and purpose, walked by their faith and unshakeable trust in God despite the many trials they endured. They knew that they hadn't reached their ultimate destination in their journey of faith, or full Christformation in them. But "God had planned something better for us so that only together with us would they be made perfect" through full Christformation in all of us. This "something better" is full Christformation in you, which is the fulfillment of the Old Testament promise that the patriarchs were looking forward to. Even though at that time they could not fathom what that promise meant, they faithfully obeyed the commandments of God in the hope of seeing this promise come to pass one day.

Until Christ came, this promise to the patriarchs was not fulfilled. But today, when the 'cloud of witnesses' witness full Christformation in you and me through the completed work of Christ, their faith is perfected and God's promise to them is fulfilled. So watch it! Be mindful of the way you live, and examine yourself to see if you are truly obeying Him.

Although Canaan was promised as the land of milk and honey, it was just a physical journey toward a physical land. We can see that the milk and honey come from a living being, such as a cow or a bee. In the New Testament, we do not have a physical journey to complete but a spiritual one. We partake instead of the bread and cup, which originate as seeds from wheat and grape from the vine that represent Christ's body that was broken for us and the blood of the Lord Jesus Christ that was shed for our sins on the cross at Calvary.

In John 12:23–25, the seed must die in order to produce Christformation in all those who believe. The faithful partaking of the bread and the cup symbolizes your obedience to God for Christformation in you. Just as the seed sprouts into a stalk and then into a head and finally into a kernel of wheat (Mark 4:27–29), Christformation in you occurs in stages until you reach full Christformation. Inevitably, as the wheat faces various challenges to its growth, you too will face many spiritual battles in your journey toward Christformation.

With the Holy Spirit's indispensable help, you can overcome the sinful nature of the Devil in you, but only if you continue to obey His leading toward full Christformation in you. You will need to count the cost and make up your mind who you will follow: Christ or the Devil? The former leads to life in all its fullness eternally while the other leads to eternal destruction.

Completely obeying God the Holy Spirit will lead you to be made perfect in God's eyes through full Christformation in you. When this occurs within all of God's chosen people in Christ, God's promises to the Old Testament people of God are fulfilled. The physical journey of Egypt to Canaan in the Old Testament was a symbolic promise which will be fulfilled through the spiritual Christformation journey in all obedient believers of Christ. God's will is always preceded by a promise from Him that He later honors. Let's read the verses below to understand this point clearly.

1 Corinthians 15:44–50:
"It is sown a natural body, it is raised a spiritual body. If there is a natural body, there is also a spiritual body. So it is written: The first man Adam became a living being; the last Adam, a life-giving spirit. The spiritual

did not come first, but the natural, and after that the spiritual. The first man was of the dust of the earth, the second man from heaven. As was the earthly man, so are those who are of the earth; and as is the man from heaven, so also are those who are of heaven. And just as we have borne the likeness of the earthly man, so shall we bear the likeness of the man from heaven. I declare to you, brothers, that flesh and blood cannot inherit the kingdom of God, nor does the perishable inherit the imperishable. The Old Testament began with creation, especially the creation of the first man whereas the New Testament begins with new creation through the second man, the Lord Jesus Christ who is the last Adam. The natural was created from the dust of the earth whereas the spiritual, from heaven. The natural was revealed first so that the spiritual could follow. The one from the earth came first, and then the One from heaven came later at God's appointed time. The one from the earth failed first, and then came the victor from heaven."

The amazing thing to note is that the One from heaven lowered Himself to take the form of the earthly one but was found without any sin. Even the earth couldn't hold Him for more than three days. He came alive from death. This is the difference between the two. The earthly one brought death to mankind, but the heavenly one conquered death for all who believe in Him. The first Adam was just a living being walking about with a death sentence, but the last Adam was a life-giving spirit that ended the death sentence for those who believe in Him.

Those who refuse to believe in the heavenly one will continue to be like the earthly man, obeying the sinful nature of the Devil in them to their eternal destruction. The others who believe in the heavenly one will put to death the sinful nature of the Devil in them with the help of God the Holy Spirit. Christ's divine nature will be formed in them, and they will live eternally with God once their faithfulness has been proven. A living being with an inherent death sentence cannot live eternally. Likewise, only a life-giving spirit can make others live eternally, but this life-giving spirit must be formed in them first. So, "just as we have borne the likeness of the earthly man, so shall we bear the likeness of the man from heaven."

Let's read to understand the divine nature of Christ that is to be formed in us in the following passage.

Philippians 2:1–11:
"If you have any encouragement from being united with Christ, if any comfort from his love, if any fellowship with the Spirit, if any tenderness and compassion, then make my joy complete by being like-minded, having the same love, being one in spirit and purpose. Do nothing out of selfish ambition or vain conceit, but in humility consider others better than you. Each of you should look not only to your own interests, but also to the interests of others. Your attitude should be the same as that of Christ Jesus: Who, being in very nature God, did not consider equality with God something to be grasped, but made himself nothing, taking the very nature of a servant, being made in human likeness. And being found in appearance as a man, he humbled himself and became obedient to death—even death on a cross! Therefore God exalted him to the highest place and gave him the name that is above every name, that at the name of Jesus every knee should bow, in heaven and on earth and under the earth, and every tongue confess that Jesus Christ is Lord, to the glory of God the Father."

Christformation in you leads you to be united with Christ and will transform your mind into the mind of Christ. As a believer of Christ, the motives of your heart, your attitude, and your actions should spring from Christformation in your born-again spirit. If there is no Christformation in you, how can one expect the divine nature of Christ to flow out of you? When Christ's divine nature is formed in every believer, only then can we be one in spirit, mind, and purpose to do God's will in this life and the next.

The Son of God humbled himself and took the form of a man and was obedient to the heavenly Father even at death on the cross. This obedience must be formed in you if you seek to please the heavenly Father as Jesus our Lord did. You will be with Him for eternity and the triune God will dwell and make their home with you when this complete obedience of Christ is formed within you. Christ will be the King of kings and the Lord of lords over all His children who obey Him.

G) You and Your Decision

Luke 9:23–24:
"Then he said to them all: 'If anyone would come after me, he must deny himself and take up his cross daily and follow me. For whoever wants to save his life will lose it, but whoever loses his life for me will save it.' "

There is no place for carelessness when you have decided to follow Jesus Christ your Lord toward full Christformation in you. You must deny the sinful nature of the Devil in you, and be ready for Christformation in you daily, as this is not an occasional, weekly, fortnightly, monthly, or yearly affair. You must be alert and awake daily and know that Christ is being formed in you. You cannot afford to be asleep, waking up next year, and expect Christ to be formed in you. This will never happen.

Christformation in you is a matter of day-to-day survival as in a war. If you are a soldier, in order to save your country from the enemy, you must be willing to lose your life. But if you count your life more precious, you will compromise with the enemy and surrender the sovereignty of your country when you are cornered. The apostle Paul warns us as he echoes in the following passage what the Lord Jesus said.

2 Timothy 2:3–4:
"Endure hardships with us like a good soldier of Christ Jesus. No one serving as a soldier gets involved in civilian affairs—he wants to please his commanding officer."

When you decide to deny yourself the pleasing of the sinful nature of the Devil in you and follow Christ for full Christformation in you, let me warn that you will go through many hardships. The world around you will be enjoying the short-lived pleasures and passions of the sinful nature of the Devil in them while you will be ridiculed. But who becomes the laughingstock of the world in the end is a well-known conclusion. When you obey the sinful nature of the Devil in you, although you may enjoy it for a moment, it is a sure pathway to your destruction.

On the other hand, when you obey all that Christ has commanded, you will suffer persecution and many hardships, but you will gain Christformation in you, which is your eternal treasure. Let us remind you that it is through many hardships and tribulations that Christ's divine nature is formed within you. Both of us cannot imagine someone living in the comfort and pleasures of this world, and yet, have Christ's divine nature formed within him or her.

You have to be a soldier for Christ to be able to war with the sinful nature of the Devil in you. You will have to endure the hardship of living a sinless life amongst sinful people. That may be the hardest thing to do when you live or work under the same roof with such people. Spiritual battles will be a daily occurrence, and the more you resist the sinful nature of the Devil in you in such situations, the tougher the battle gets. That's why you would need the power of God the Holy Spirit in you to become an overcomer.

As in any war, the hardest thing to do is obey orders from the commander, but you will have to please the Spirit of God and obey all that Christ commands. Many stop fighting the sinful nature of the Devil in them because they find obeying all that Christ our Lord commands too difficult. How then will Christ's divine nature be formed in you if you do not obey all that He commands?

If you please God, the rewards for seeking Christ wholeheartedly are the many crowns promised in the Bible. What exactly are these crowns? They are the divine nature of Christ formed in your born-again spirit that has successfully transformed your mind into the mind of Christ by the power of God the Holy Spirit through your obedience to His leading. Let us look at the verses below to learn about the transformation of our minds into the mind of Christ.

Romans 8:5–8:
"Those who live according to the sinful nature have their minds set on what that nature desires; but those who live in accordance with the Spirit have their minds set on what the Spirit desires. The mind of sinful man is death, but the mind controlled by the Spirit is life and peace; the sinful mind is hostile to God. It does not submit to God's law, nor can it do so. Those controlled by the sinful nature cannot please God."

Your soul, or mind, needs to be transformed. But transformation of your mind cannot happen until there is Christformation in your born-again spirit. Obedience to all that Christ has commanded will bring about Christformation in your spirit. When Christ's divine nature is successfully formed in your spirit, your mind will be transformed into the mind of Christ. How does this happen?

When there is Christformation in your new spirit within you, you will be led by the Spirit of God, which will cause you to live in accordance to the Spirit and set your mind on what the Spirit of God desires. God the Holy Spirit controls your mind so that your mind follows the divine nature of Christ formed within you when you act accordingly. He testifies that you are now a child of God, and you can draw strength to act in any situation on earth from Him, as He leads and guides you so that you do not act contrary to the divine nature of Christ that is formed within you through your obedience to all that Christ has commanded. He reminds you of the life of Christ on earth and gives you the peace of Christ in whatever you do or say when you follow His leading. Do you see the importance of being closely led by God the Holy Spirit?

Now let us see how the hostile, or sinful, mind works. The hostile mind has its roots from the sinful nature of the Devil in you. If you are a person who believes in the Lord Jesus Christ but continues to obey the sinful nature of the Devil in you, there will be no transformation of your mind into the mind of Christ because your mind is hostile to God and His ways. The hostile mind can never submit to what Christ commands. Even the Spirit of God cannot help you here because you have never submitted yourself to obeying His leading in your life but instead have chosen to keep obeying the sinful nature of the Devil in you.

"Those controlled by the sinful nature cannot please God." It is impossible to please God if you keep obeying the sinful nature of the Devil in you. You please God the Father with Christformation in you, which can only happen through the power of God the Holy Spirit in you. How can you please the heavenly Father when you don't obey God the Holy Spirit whom He sent for Christformation in you?

Is it possible for someone to claim that he or she believes in Christ and yet be hostile towards the things of God? If so, why? Let's look at the Bible passage below for the answer to these questions.

James 1:21–25:
"Therefore, get rid of all moral filth and the evil that is so prevalent, and humbly accept the word planted in you, which can save you. Do not merely listen to the word, and so deceive yourselves. Do what it says. Anyone who listens to the word but does not do what it says is like a man who looks at his face in a mirror and, after looking at himself, goes away and immediately forgets what he looks like. But the man who looks intently into the perfect law that gives freedom, and continues to do this, not forgetting what he has heard, but doing it— he will be blessed in what he does."

You may hear God's Word, day after day, week after week, year after year, but if you do not humbly accept it, even though you understand its meaning clearly, the salvation of your soul or the transformation of your mind into the mind of Christ will still not be within your reach. Why must you humbly accept the Word that is planted in you? You need to be humble enough to accept that you have sinned against God, admit it, and repent. You must confess to God that you have a soft spot for a particular sin or temptation. You must be humble enough to hate your own sinful ways and correct them through God's Word planted in you.

The only way you can come to God is by humbling yourself before Him. You must tell Him that you are terribly sorry, and do not take Him for granted when He speaks or convicts you of your sin. You have to be humble enough to not find ways to justify your actions by paying penance with money or offering favors to cover up your sin. You have to be completely humble to accept that He has already paid the penalty for all your sins on the cross. In this way, Christ will be formed in you. You must continue trusting and humbly accepting God's Word that He will lead, guide, and protect you from the Evil One.

Your decision to follow Christ means that you have counted the cost of following Him till the end and have committed your life to Him for full Christformation in you. Do not let anything or anyone hinder your achieving that. Let go of your disobedience and stubbornness in obeying the sinful nature of the Devil in you. Not only will you benefit eternally from this but others around you will benefit from your change also. With Christformation occurring within you, Psalm 23 will be more meaningful as you are led toward full Christformation. He is the Good Shepherd of God's flock and as mentioned in John 10:14-16, "His sheep will listen to His voice and follow Him."

For a long time, both of us weren't too sure about what Psalm 23 meant in our lives. But after faithful seeking and searching, everything is clear to us now. Psalm 23 actually puts into perspective, the leading of our Good Shepherd in our lives, as we journey towards full Christformation. Let's meditate on this beautiful promise of God.

Psalm 23:1–6:
"The LORD is my shepherd; I shall not be in want. He makes me lie down in green pastures, he leads me beside quiet waters, he restores my soul. He guides me in paths of righteousness for his name's sake. Even though I walk through the valley of the shadow of death, I will fear no evil, for you are with me; your rod and your staff, they comfort me. You prepare a table before me in the presence of my enemies. You anoint my head with oil; my cup overflows. Surely goodness and love will follow me all the days of my life, and I will dwell in the house of the LORD forever."

SUMMARY: CHAPTER SIX

God the Father, Christ Jesus, and God the Holy Spirit are all involved with your Christformation; each with different roles. God the Father promised Christformation through the Old Testament, while The Lord Jesus Christ fulfilled the Father's promises and gave the five-fold ministries to His body. God the Holy Spirit instead, helps build full Christformation in each believer of Christ personally. He also enables those involved in the five-fold ministry as they labor toward full Christformation amongst the Lord's flock. Furthermore, the angels of God assist as ministering spirits so that Christformation occurs without any hindrance in these believers. Also, we should be constantly mindful that the obedient Old Testament believers are witnessing the successful Christformation in each New Testament believer.

Finally, it is your decision to obey all that Christ has commanded that leads you to Christformation.

Who is involved?	What is His/their role(s)?
a) God the Father	Christformation was first initiated by God the Father. He predestined Christformation in all those who believe and love His Son. If you obey the Son, the Father will come and dwell in you.
b) God the Son	Christ is the firstborn of God and all those who believe and love Him will have His divine nature formed in them. He is interceding for them that this eternal will of the Father will happen in them.
c) God the Holy Spirit	God the Holy Spirit is the promised Helper for your born again experience and Christformation in you. They who are led by God the Holy Spirit will have Christformation in them.
d) The Five–fold ministers through the Holy Spirit	Christ our Lord gave these ministers to the body of Christ of which He is the head. The five-fold ministers are led of God the Holy Spirit to preach, teach, and demonstrate the power of Christformation in each believer of Christ.
e) The Angels of God.	The angels of God are ministering spirits who assist believers with successful Christformation in them. God sends assistance whenever we need them.
f) The Old Testament Witnesses	The Old Testament faithful servants of God who have risen from the dead are witnessing, cheering and urging on the New Testament believers in Christ who love God to finish the race as they did, but this time with Full Christformation in them.
g) You and Your Decision	Your decision to obey Christ will bring Christformation in you. If you fully obey all that Christ had commanded, then you will have full Christformation in you. You must press on till the end of the race with the help of God the Holy Spirit and win the prize of full Christformation in you.

Diagram 6(a)

CHRISTFORMATION
IS THE WHITE STONE PEARL
IN YOU

REVELATION 2: 17

Chapter Seven:
Full Christformation in You:
When Does it Occur?

A) An Explanation from the Parable of the True Vine

John 15:1–10:
" "I am the true vine, and my Father is the gardener. He cuts off every branch in me that bears no fruit, while every branch that does bear fruit he prunes so that it will be even more fruitful. You are already clean because of the word I have spoken to you. Remain in me, and I will remain in you. No branch can bear fruit by itself; it must remain in the vine. Neither can you bear fruit unless you remain in me. I am the vine; you are the branches. If a man remains in me and I in him, he will bear much fruit; apart from me you can do nothing. If anyone does not remain in me, he is like a branch that is thrown away and withers; such branches are picked up, thrown into the fire and burned. If you remain in me and my words remain in you, ask whatever you wish, and it will be given you. This is to my Father's glory, that you bear much fruit, showing yourselves to be my disciples. As the Father has loved me, so have I loved you. Now remain in my love. If you obey my commands, you will remain in my love, just as I have obeyed my Father's commands and remain in his love."

The mark or outcome of a true disciple of Christ is full Christformation in you. The less Christformation in you, the less you have obeyed Him. On the other hand, the heavenly Father will be glorified when Christformation increases in you. The source of Christformation in you is Christ. The fruit of repentance, evident when you start putting to death the sinful nature of the Devil in you, is Christformation in you. When the Lord Jesus Christ said, "Remain in me," He meant turning away from the sinful nature of the Devil along with putting it to death in total obedience to Him, which is a permanent act. Remaining in Christ is not giving the Devil room to control you. Christformation will be hindered or aborted by your pleasing the sinful nature of the Devil in you.

Christformation will not just appear from thin air. Without obedience to Christ, there will be no fruit of Christformation in you. The more you obey, the more Christformation (fruit) in you, as Christformation in you is the result of a love relationship with God. If the love of God is formed in you, you will remain in Christ and obey Him toward full Christformation in you. If that love of God is not formed in you through Christ, you will not see the importance of Christformation in you. The Lord Jesus Christ set the perfect example of love to God, which creates wholehearted obedience to Him. In this way, Christformation in you will not be hindered, stunted, or aborted. If you believe in Christ but do not have Christformation in you, you, like the unfruitful branch on the vine, will be cut off from Christ when the time comes.

"You did not remain in me", as mentioned in John 15: 6, would mean that you did not obey Him. If there is Christformation in you, He will prune you; that is, lead you to put to death the sinful nature of the Devil in you completely so that full Christformation can occur in you. God's ultimate purpose for every believer in Christ is full Christformation in them. What you believe will show through Christformation in you.

B) Through the Act of Sowing and Reaping

Galatians 6:7–8:

"Do not be deceived: God cannot be mocked. A man reaps what he sows. The one who sows to please his sinful nature, from that nature will reap destruction; the one who sows to please the Spirit, from the Spirit will reap eternal life."

We can be easily deceived in this world. God knows the Devil is a deceiver, and He knows how much we can be deceived by him. A believer of Christ cannot claim that he or she has been deceived by the Devil if Christformation did not develop within him or her. This is because there has been ample warning given through the parables of the Lord about the consequence of ignoring this call towards Christformation. Adam and Eve blamed the Devil for their deception without claiming their own responsibility. However, the Lord judged and punished all three parties fairly.

God has given all things to each believer through God the Holy Spirit to remind them that they are co-heirs with Christ of every inheritance in Him. Only obedience to His leading is required. You need to please Him instead of pleasing the sinful nature of the Devil in you, which you have been doing before you came to Christ. Continuing to do so after God the Holy Spirit has come into you amounts to disobedience to God, which is why the above verses say that you deserve destruction. A man (or woman) reaps what he (or she) sows. When you sow disobedience, you will surely reap destruction, but if you sow obedience to God the Holy Spirit, you will reap Christformation in you.

What about when you sow complete obedience to God the Holy Spirit? Will you also reap full Christformation in you? Yes, you certainly will. God has promised full Christformation in those who truly believe and obey Him. However, this promise could go unfulfilled in your life if you are careless about filling your born-again spirit with Christ. Let's read the following passage and take serious heed of the warning that comes with it so that you are not careless about sowing Christformation in you.

Matthew 12:43–45:
" "When an evil spirit comes out of a man, it goes through arid places seeking rest and does not find it. Then it says, 'I will return to the house I left.' When it arrives, it finds the house unoccupied, swept clean, and put in order. Then it goes and takes with it seven other spirits more wicked than itself, and they go in and live there. And the final condition of that man is worse than the first. That is how it will be with this wicked generation." "

When you believe in the Lord Jesus Christ and are born again, you must make every effort to fill your born-again spirit with full Christformation in you. What is the purpose of having a born-again spirit when you do not fill it with full Christformation in you? Christ is the King and must fill your whole new being through full Christformation in you. In these verses, the Lord warns that you should not be careless after your "house" has been cleansed by the precious blood of Christ Jesus and put in order by God the Holy Spirit. If you do not make every effort to make the Lord the rightful owner of your house through full Christformation in you, the Enemy will occupy it again and, this time, make your life worse than before, as he will bring seven more wicked spirits with him. Many, we are afraid, live like this!

This parable of the Lord has very deep truths in it. There are evil spirits on this earth because they are imprisoned here. This world is their temporary prison until they are thrown into the lake of fire upon the return of the Lord Jesus Christ to earth. But the Lord Jesus Christ has given authority to every believer in Him over these evil spirits. We can overcome all the power of the Devil and the demons because the Lord Jesus has destroyed them through His completed work on the cross and triumphant resurrection. Now the keys to death and hades are in the hands of the Lord and no more with the Devil. He alone has the authority to cast away the demons and the Devil himself into the abyss until they are thrown into the lake of fire eternally reserved for them.

We too can render every demon powerless because we are stronger with the authority given to us by the Lord Jesus; they cannot deceive mankind when we exercise this given authority over them. Demons are restless spirits. If not bound and subdued, they create havoc on earth. Unfortunately, many believers do not know that they have been given the authority to bind and subdue these restless demons, which is why there is so much confusion and sin in this world.

Demons appear in many forms, which the Bible describes in detail. They cause spiritual damage wherever they go. They can't keep still for a moment without causing others to sin. Human beings who are filled with them behave in the same manner. Read the passage below, and be warned.

Proverbs 4:14–17:
"Do not set foot on the path of the wicked or walk in the way of evil men. Avoid it, do not travel on it; turn from it and go on your way. For they cannot sleep till they do evil; they are robbed of slumber till they make someone fall. They eat the bread of wickedness and drink the wine of violence."

As mentioned in the previous chapters, there are only two trees you can eat from. One is the Tree of Life, and the other the tree of death. You can either obey God the Holy Spirit and fill yourself with full Christformation or obey the sinful nature of the Devil in you and be fully occupied by the seven wicked spirits that will bring eternal destruction to your whole being. The Lord cautions us:

Luke 13:23–25:
"Someone asked him, 'Lord, are only a few people going to be saved?' He said to them, 'Make every effort to enter through the narrow door, because many, I tell you, will try to enter and will not be able to. Once the owner of the house gets up and closes the door, you will stand outside, knocking and pleading, "Sir, open the door for us." But he will answer, "I don't know you or where you come from." ' "

Entering through the narrow door is making every effort toward full Christformation in you. Many will look for shortcuts so that they do not have to go through the narrow, difficult door toward full Christformation because they have found obeying God the Holy Spirit difficult. Obeying the sinful nature of the Devil in them, living a carefree life, was easier. But it was not a care*free* life but a care*less* one they led, which they will find out when the narrow door is shut as the door to Noah's ark was shut when the floods came.

Even though you have come to Christ, you might not have made every effort to fill yourself with Christformation because you do not want to give up pleasing the sinful nature of the Devil in you. "A man [or woman] reaps what he sows," so isn't that what he or she deserves? If there is going to be an imperishable, fully Christ-conformed body clothing you on the last day, you must diligently sow full Christformation in your born-again spirit, which will fully transform your once sinful mind into the mind of Christ with the help of God the Holy Spirit through your obedience. The sinful nature of the Devil must be fully destroyed in you by then. If not, you will deserve what you had sown with many tears. But if you obey God the Holy Spirit, all your tears will be wiped away forever in God's presence.

Just hearing the Word of God doesn't fill you with Christ. Only when you do as the Word says is Christ's divine nature formed in you. Judas Iscariot did not have Christformation in him even though he was always with the Lord Jesus and heard Him speak God's truths. The beatitudes reflect the divine nature of Christ that is to be formed in every believer of Christ. Judas heard those words of life, but they did not produce the life of Christ in Him because he did not obey them. Christ was not formed in him because he wasn't a believer. Even though he may have believed initially, he had succumbed fully to the temptation of greed and selfishness. He did not even hesitate to handover Christ to His enemies, just to please the evil desires within him. As a result, he forfeited any eternal reward that was due to him. Will he inherit eternal life? No, certainly not! Because of his disobedience, Judas betrayed Christ. This disqualified him of an eternal relationship with Christ our Lord. Your obedience to Christ makes the difference. If you do not obey Him, He will certainly say, "I do not know you or where you come from" because His sheep hear His voice and follow Him wherever He goes. Judas heard His voice, but did not follow Christ till the end. Let this be a reminder to all of us, always.

Have you been hearing His voice, following Him, and doing whatever He has commanded you thus far? Have you at least made up your mind to do so? If you have, there will be Christformation in you. But if you haven't, there will be no Christformation in you. It's unimaginable to think what will happen after the Lord Jesus says to you, "I do not know you or where you come from." Let us read another passage in the Bible that tells us the Lord's reason for saying this to you.

Matthew 7:21–23:

" "Not everyone who says to me, 'Lord, Lord,' will enter the kingdom of heaven, but only he who does the will of my Father who is in heaven. Many will say to me on that day, 'Lord, Lord, did we not prophesy in your name and in your name drive out demons and perform many miracles?' Then I will tell them plainly, 'I never knew you. Away from me, you evildoers!' "

The reason the Lord would say "I never knew you" is because you continued living according to the pleasures and passions of the sinful nature of the Devil in you, even after claiming that you believe in the Lord Jesus Christ. This would tragically mean that you had never come to Him in the first place. You knew that He is your Lord, but you chose not to obey whatever he had commanded you. You will find out that you have believed in vain in the end. So, He didn't know you then, and He does not know you now.

Evildoers are those who never gave up pleasing the sinful nature of the Devil in them and had delighted in wickedness even after they had been warned of its serious consequences. They are mockers who take the things of God very lightly, especially doing God's will on earth. They go about doing their own will, or indirectly the will of the Devil, for acting out of self-will is actually obeying the sinful nature of the Devil in you. Let's read more verses to clearly understand this point

1 John 2:15–17:

"Do not love the world or anything in the world. If anyone loves the world, the love of the Father is not in him. For everything in the world—the cravings of sinful man, the lust of his eyes, and the boasting of what he has and does—comes not from the Father but from the world. The world and its desires pass away, but the man who does the will of God lives forever."

What does "the love of the Father is not in him" really mean? The love of the Father is His beloved Son. God the heavenly Father's love was in His only beloved Son, but many did not see or understand this love that God the Father had shared with us. Since the love of the Father is

Christ our Lord and that love is not found in the person who loves the world, the love of God is not formed in that person. In other words, Christ, or Christformation, was not formed in that person.

Remember, the love of God the Father is an aspect of the divine nature of Christ that needs to be formed in the believer of Christ. This love of God the Father in Christ our Lord caused Him to faithfully obey the Father while on earth, and this same love compels us to obey everything Christ has commanded us to do. This is the will of the Father for us.

But how can we obey when this same love from the Father is not formed in us through Christformation? It is the will of the Father that His love should be formed in us through Christ His firstborn so that we will obey God the Holy Spirit in us instead of the sinful nature of the Devil. However, the sinful nature of the Devil will remain in us until we choose to put all its misdeeds to death with the help of God the Holy Spirit. Remember, only those who do the will of God the Father through His love will have Christformation in them.

C) Circumcision of the Sinful Nature by Christ through His Spirit

Colossians 2:10–11:
"And you have been given fullness in Christ, who is the Head over every power and authority. In him you were also circumcised, in the putting off of the sinful nature, not with a circumcision done by the hands of men but with the circumcision done by Christ."

Once you have been successfully circumcised from the sinful nature of the Devil through the power of God the Holy Spirit; you will be filled with Christ through full Christformation in you. This circumcision cannot be done by the hands of men but rather by the hands of Christ our Lord because, the sinful nature is hidden deep inside of the spirit of man and only God the Holy Spirit can circumcise the believer as he or she obeys what Christ has commanded. This circumcision of the sinful nature is necessary if Christ is to be formed in your born again spirit. This is because; both the sinful nature and Christ's divine nature cannot grow together at the same time. One will die and the other will grow. Your complete obedience to Christ will ensure the death of the sinful nature, and the formation of the whole divine nature of Christ within you. The fullness of Christ comes into a believer as he or she obeys all that Christ has commanded. "Circumcision done by Christ" means that as you obey His commands, circumcision occurs in your spirit with the help of God the Holy Spirit. "Putting off" and "putting to death" the misdeeds of the sinful nature of the Devil is the same action; without obedience to His commands, there will be no spirit-led circumcision of the Devil's sinful nature in you.

Let's read another passage regarding circumcision of the sinful nature of the Devil.

Romans 2:28–29:
"One is not a Jew if he is only one outwardly, nor is circumcision merely outward and physical. No, a man is a Jew if he is one inwardly; and circumcision is circumcision of the heart, by the Spirit, not by the written code. Such a man's praise is not from men, but from God."

Successful circumcision of the sinful nature of the Devil in you will bring praise to God because, with the help of God the Holy Spirit, full Christformation will occur in you. We cannot impress God with our physical, outer circumcision or any other rituals because the reason why Christ came into this world was to wash away our sins, which is an inner action. Men cannot take glory for that because only Christ died for our sins on the cross to make Christformation in us possible. If there is no circumcision of our heart, there will be no Christformation in us because we will continue pleasing the sinful nature of the Devil in us and not God the Holy Spirit. God commanded Abraham to circumcise, but it is Christ our Lord who fulfilled the law of circumcision by not obeying the sinful nature of the Devil. By doing so, He circumcised away the sinful nature of the flesh. Now for those who believe and obey Him, their sinful nature will be circumcised off them like Christ through the power of the Holy Spirit. Abraham was not able to put to death the sinful nature of the Devil within himself or anyone else. Otherwise, Christ would not need to come to earth and take the form of flesh to redeem us from the bondage of the sinful nature of the Devil. Hence, Abraham was commanded to circumcise all the male inhabitants of his household through faith and obedience to God. This was done to signify that Christ would come from his lineage in the future, to set us free from the sinful nature, if we have faith and obedience to Christ as had been displayed by Abraham.

Galatians 6:14–15:
"May I never boast except in the cross of our Lord Jesus Christ, through which the world has been crucified to me, and I to the world. Neither circumcision nor uncircumcision means anything; what counts is a new creation."

Circumcision was the putting to death of the misdeeds of the sinful nature of the Devil in everyone who obeys God through Christ so that a new creation comes through Christformation in their born-again spirits. Christformation cannot be formed in the old sinful spirit. That spirit must be born again through the power of God the Holy Spirit.

If you were to ask the both of us what the greatest demonstration of God's power within us is, we would say, it is being born again in the spirit. This is so because, without being born again in the spirit, there can be no Christformation in us. In order to come to that, there must be a genuine conviction of guilt by God the Holy Spirit. Only then, does the true desire to put to death the misdeeds of the sinful nature of the Devil follow. This should continue until there is full Christformation in that new creation. The new creation of God through Christ His Son is full Christformation in you. The old creation is our flesh, our sinful mind, and our spirit before it was born again. If we still live according to the old creation, we haven't come to Christ yet.

Here is a warning from the apostle Paul.

Philippians 3:2–4:
"Watch out for those dogs, those men who do evil, those mutilators of the flesh. For it is we who are the circumcision, we who worship by the Spirit of God, who glory in Christ Jesus, and who put no confidence in the flesh—though I myself have reasons for such confidence. If anyone else thinks he has reasons to put confidence in the flesh, I have more."

Sorry for the word *dogs* here which refers to men who do not know how to appreciate truth. As stated in Matthew 7:6, the Lord had commanded us not to throw what is sacred to dogs, for they are those who are not able to discern the truth. These are men whom Paul refers to as false teachers; who teach believers to put their confidence in their flesh instead of in God the Holy Spirit. Circumcision is not about confidence in our flesh, but in the Spirit of the Lord who gives us victory over the sinful nature when we obey him. The Spirit of the Lord has only one purpose in us: to bring maximum glory to the Lord Jesus Christ who will raise that glory to the heavenly Father. Apostle Paul warns us that nothing of our flesh should steal the glory of the power of God the Holy Spirit in us. Christformation in you is not possible if you have confidence in the old creation.

Everything that God the Holy Spirit manifests in and through you is for the glory of God the heavenly Father. That's how the Lord Jesus lived when He walked on this earth. For Himself, He prayed that if God the Father wished to glorify Him, He could do so. Through full Christformation in you, assisted by God the Holy Spirit, full glory goes to the Lord Jesus Christ. The Lord Jesus then brings that glory to God the Father for all eternity.

Colossians 2:13–14:
"When you were dead in your sins and were not circumcised of your sinful nature yet, God made you alive with Christ. He forgave us all our sins, having cancelled the written code, with its regulations, that was against us and that stood opposed to us; he took it away, nailing it to the cross."

What is left for us to do now? Even when we weren't yet circumcised of the sinful nature of the Devil in us, we were made alive in Christ by His grace and mercy toward us. He nailed every sin of ours on that cross at Calvary so that we will be free from the sinful nature of the Devil completely and be filled with Christformation. But is that happening in you now? It should.

D) THE RACE OF CHRISTFORMATION TOWARD FULL CHRISTFORMATION IN YOU

1 Corinthians 9:24–25:
"Do you not know that in a race all the runners run, but only one gets the prize? Run in such a way as to get the prize. Everyone who competes in the games goes into strict training. They do it to get a crown that will not last; but we do it to get a crown that will last forever."

The prize you will get for running the race of Christformation in you is the crown of full Christformation in you, but only if you compete with determination to win God's full approval on your life in Christ till the end. For this to happen, you must go into strict training, which requires your total obedience to all that Christ has commanded. You will have the promised help of God the Holy Spirit throughout your training in the righteousness of Christ. He will lead you to overcome all hindrances in running this race of life to the path of victory in Christ. He guides you into all truth about full Christformation in you so that you will know, obey, live, and love the truth all the days of your life.

Christformation in you is for eternity because Christ our Lord is the way, the truth, and the life. When He is fully formed in you, you will be accepted in the presence of God the Father forever. This will be your eternal crown: full Christformation in you.

Hebrews 12:1–2:
"Therefore, since we are surrounded by such a great cloud of witnesses, let us throw off everything that hinders and the sin that so easily entangles, and let us run with perseverance the race marked out for us.

Let us fix our eyes on Jesus, the author and perfecter of our faith, who for the joy set before him endured the cross, scorning its shame, and sat down at the right hand of the throne of God."

The race of full Christformation in us has already been marked out for us. Like a disciplined athlete, we need to run the race with perseverance. Since the Lord Jesus Christ is the author and perfecter of Christformation in us, our eyes must be fixed on Him as an athlete's eyes are fixed on the finishing line. We need to fix our eyes on Him because He is our perfect example of obedience to God the heavenly Father. Even a cruel and unjust death on the cross did not deter Him from doing God's will till the end. He endured every shame of temporary defeat at the hands of sinful men until He showed true victory over sin, death, and the Devil. He is interceding for us at God's right hand in heaven so that we too might obey God as He did and overcome the sinful nature of the Devil in us so that the divine nature of Christ is formed in us (full Christformation in us). We escape the corruption of this world when the divine nature of Christ is formed in us. Let's read the passage below about this.

2 Peter 1:3–11:
"His divine power has given us everything we need for life and godliness through our knowledge of him who called us by his own glory and goodness. Through these he has given us his very great and precious promises, so that through them you may participate in the divine nature and escape the corruption in the world caused by evil desires. For this very reason, make every effort to add to your faith goodness; and to goodness, knowledge; and to knowledge, self-control; and to self-control, perseverance; and to perseverance, godliness; and to godliness, brotherly kindness; and to brotherly kindness, love. For if you possess these qualities in increasing measure, they will keep you from being ineffective and unproductive in your knowledge of our Lord Jesus Christ. But if anyone does not have them, he is short-sighted and blind, and has forgotten that he has been cleansed from his past sins. Therefore, my brothers, be all the more eager to make your calling and election sure. For if you do these things, you will never fall, and you will receive a rich welcome into the eternal kingdom of our Lord and Savior Jesus Christ."

The message about Christformation in you in the passage above is thorough. Double-mindedness will not produce Christformation in you. God the Holy Spirit is God's divine power in all who believe in the Lord Jesus Christ and obey Him till the end. We who have been called by Him have been given the promise of God the Holy Spirit to help us with full Christformation in us. While we make every effort toward it, He helps us with our weaknesses and teaches us how to overcome the sinful nature of the Devil in us, the same way the Lord Jesus Christ had overcome the Evil One.

Evil desires cause corruption in the world, proceeding from the sinful nature of the Devil in you if you haven't practiced putting to death its misdeeds. You must do this at once if you haven't already put to death the misdeeds of the sinful nature of the Devil in you so that the Devil does not have his grip on you any longer.

All you need to be victorious is God the Holy Spirit. If He dwells in you, He will lead and guide you to full Christformation when you obey Him fully. But if you continue to obey the sinful nature of the Devil in you with all its pleasures and passions, you are choosing to disobey God the Holy Spirit in you. As a result, there will be no Christformation in you.

God the heavenly Father predestined us to be conformed to the image of His only Son. But we cannot be if His divine nature is not formed within us. The born-again spirit must be conformed to the divine nature of Christ first before the mind can be transformed into the mind of Christ. Only then will we have an imperishable, eternal body like Christ's. This requires our running along the path of obedience until the end.

For this reason, you must make every effort to develop the divine nature of Christ in you by obeying everything Christ has commanded. If you start with the faith that comes from believing in Christ, you must not stop there. You must add the goodness of Christ. Faith alone is not enough; Christ's goodness must also be found in you. Will His goodness be found in you if you keep obeying the sinful nature of the Devil in you? You cannot mature if you keep obeying the sinful nature of the Devil in you, for Christ's divine nature will be stunted in you. Instead of being conformed to the image of Christ, you will be conformed into the image of the Devil, who will be destroyed in the lake of fire.

After goodness, you must add knowledge. Full knowledge of God and His will can only be found in Christ our Lord. If Christ is formed in us, we will no longer live in darkness about God and His ways.

In this same manner, we must add, one by one, all the aspects of the divine nature of Christ mentioned in 2 Peter 1:3–11. In fact, there are more aspects of the nature of Christ in the Bible. We must diligently seek them and obey Christ so that these aspects of His nature are eternally formed in us.

These aspects of the divine nature of Christ do not fill us all at once, but rather continue to fill us with increasing measure until the fullness of Christ is found in us. The apostle Peter says that we are to possess these aspects, or qualities, permanently. The reason for this is so that we will be effective and productive in telling and showing others that we truly know God and Christ. The apostle John, another disciple of Christ, explains this same truth in the passage below.

1 John 2:3–6:
"We know that we have come to know him if we obey his commands. The man who says, 'I know him,' but does not do what he commands is a liar, and the truth is not in him. But if anyone obeys his word, God's love is truly made complete in him. This is how we know we are in him: whoever claims to live in him must walk as Jesus did."

"But if anyone does not have them, he is short-sighted and blind, and has forgotten that he has been cleansed from his past sins" as it is stated in 2 Peter 1:9. You should never forget that you have been cleansed from your past sins, even when you have matured with all the aspects of the divine nature of Christ formed in you. In fact, until you have these aspects in you in increasing manner, you will remain blind to the truths about God and His will for you in Christ even though you assume to have seen some things relating to God or His Christ. But actually, you see vaguely because it could be assumptions based just on head knowledge alone. You will remain blind to these truths forever without the experience of Christformation in you, which could only come through your obedience to Him.

If you obey Christ after believing in Him, you must not stop there; you must "be all the more eager to make your calling and election sure" through full Christformation in you, "for if you do these things, you will never fall, and you will receive a rich welcome into the eternal kingdom of our Lord and Savior Jesus Christ", as said in 2 Peter 1: 10. The phrase "you will never fall" means you will never fall into the trap of pleasing the sinful nature of the Devil in you again if you have the divine nature of Christ formed in you. You must press on for this to become true in your life. Obey Christ when you hear His voice through God the Holy Spirit in you today. You will then eternally please the heavenly Father with full Christformation in you.

Finish the race of Christformation with your eyes on the author and finisher of Christformation in you. Christ our Lord started it with His completed work on the cross and will complete Christformation in you if you fully obey all that He has commanded. But you can forfeit this wonderful experience through your own negligence. Let's read the following passage to find out more about negligence toward Christformation in you.

E) An Explanation from the Parable of the Talents

Matthew 25:14–30:
" "Again, it will be like a man going on a journey and who called his servants and entrusted his wealth to them. To one he gave five bags of gold, to another two bags, and to another one bag, each according to his ability. Then he went on his journey. The man who had received five bags of gold went at once and put his money to work and gained five bags more. So also, the one with two bags of gold gained two more. But the man who had received one bag went off, dug a hole in the ground, and hid his master's money. After a long time, the master

of those servants returned and settled accounts with them. The man who had received five bags of gold brought the other five. "Master," he said, "you entrusted me with five bags of gold. See, I have gained five more." His master replied, "Well done, good and faithful servant! You have been faithful with a few things; I will put you in charge of many things. Come and share your master's happiness!" The man with two bags of gold also came. "Master," he said, "you entrusted me with two bags of gold; see, I have gained two more." His master replied, "Well done, good and faithful servant! You have been faithful with a few things; I will put you in charge of many things. Come and share your master's happiness!" Then the man who had received one bag of gold came. "Master," he said, "I knew that you are a hard man, harvesting where you have not sown and gathering where you have not scattered seed. So I was afraid and went out and hid your gold in the ground. See, here is what belongs to you." His master replied, "You wicked, lazy servant! So you knew that I harvest where I have not sown and gather where I have not scattered seed? Well then, you should have put my money on deposit with the bankers so that when I returned I would have received it back with interest. So take the bag of gold from him and give it to the one who has ten bags. For whoever has will be given more, and they will have abundance. Whoever does not have, even what they have will be taken from them. And throw that worthless servant outside, into the darkness, where there will be weeping and gnashing of teeth." "

One of the messages of this parable is the wickedness, laziness, and ignorance of one of the three servants. The warning is: What you have in the end will show how you valued what was given to you. Actually, what has God given you when you first believed in Christ? He gave you a new, born-again spirit and a helper, God the Holy Spirit, along with it. Why did He give you the born-again spirit in the first place? Is it just for you to feel good about yourself? Absolutely not! You were given the new, born-again spirit for you to make every effort to fill it with full Christformation in you through the powerful help of God the Holy Spirit.

If you are wicked, you will continue pleasing the sinful nature of the Devil in you and not please God the Holy Spirit. You will disobey His leading toward full Christformation in you. If you are lazy, you will make no effort and will neglect Christformation in you. If you are ignorant of God's will for you through Christformation in you, you will have the wrong knowledge of God, which will hinder your Christformation. On the other hand, if you are obedient, diligent, and wise, you will work out your own salvation through full Christformation in you with fear and trembling for God with reverence for His Word in you. You will become that good and faithful servant who knows the Master's will.

"For whoever has will be given more, and they will have abundance. Whoever does not have, even what they have will be taken from them." This means that if you have a hunger and thirst to fill yourself with Christ's divine nature and are obedient to all that Christ has commanded, you will be filled with Christformation in you. But if you have been given the new, born-again spirit but are disobedient, lazy, or deliberately ignorant that Christformation should occur within you, the born-again spirit in you, which is void of Christformation, will be taken away from you, even though at one time you were saved and repented of all your sins. What good did that repentance do if it did not produce the fruit of that repentance, which is Christformation in you?

This meaning of this parable is similar to the parable of the true vine, where the owner of the vineyard will cut off the branches that do not produce the fruit of Christformation and throw them into the eternal fire. In this parable of the talents, the wicked, lazy, unwise, and ignorant believer will be thrown outside into the darkness, where there will be weeping and gnashing of teeth.

Of course, some of us have been given more faith than others. The degree to which Christ is formed in our born-again spirit is in proportion to the faith given to us and reveals the measure of our obedience to God. The more faith given to you, the more Christformation will be required of you. Ending up with less Christformation would reveal your disobedience to Him.

God cannot be fooled or mocked. We cannot blame Him or others for our disobedience. This parable is about receiving and producing. Like a plant that produces fruit in proportion to water and light it receives, we must produce Christformation in us to the proportion of faith given to us by Christ our Lord. If we have been given even the smallest portion of faith, but no Christformation has occurred in us, it is because we have not obeyed Christ at all. Let us read the passage below to understand this truth further.

James 2:17–26:

"In the same way, faith by itself, if it is not accompanied by action, is dead. But someone will say, "You have faith; I have deeds." Show me your faith without deeds, and I will show you my faith by my deeds. You believe that there is one God. Good! Even the demons believe that—and shudder. You foolish person, do you want evidence that faith without deeds is useless? Was not our father Abraham considered righteous for what he did when he offered his son Isaac on the altar? You see that his faith and his actions were working together, and his faith was made complete by what he did. And the scripture was fulfilled that says, "Abraham believed God, and it was credited to him as righteousness," and he was called God's friend. You see that a person is considered righteous by what they do and not by faith alone. In the same way, was not even Rahab the prostitute considered righteous for what she did when she gave lodging to the spies and sent them off in a different direction? As the body without the spirit is dead, so faith without deeds is dead."

It is true that you should believe in the works of Christ on the cross and repent by turning away from your sins, but what should follow next? Your obedience to all that Christ has commanded. Abraham believed in and obeyed God even when He was told to offer his precious only son Isaac on the altar. And that was not the only incident where Abraham obeyed God. In the book of Genesis, Abraham obeyed God from the beginning to the end of his days on earth. You should do the same because this will result in Christformation in you.

Anything you do out of obedience to God's will, shall result in Christformation in you as in the case of the Samaritan woman whom the Lord Jesus had met at Jacob's well, in John 4:4-26. Even though she had a questionable past, the Lord knew about it and offered her to drink the living water for eternal life. It is this same living water that will form His divine nature in you which will become a spring of water welling up to eternal life as stated in John 4:14. Likewise, in Hebrews 11:31, Rahab the prostitute was listed among all the other Old Testament faithful servants of the Lord, in recognition of her faith that had saved her from the destruction of the disobedient. We won't be surprised if she is found as one of them in the 'great cloud of witnesses' as mentioned in Hebrews 12:1. Faith and obedience work together to produce Christformation in you.

Our deeds should always follow our faith in God. These deeds must be done out of obedience to all that Christ has commanded. Faith in Christ alone will not produce Christformation in you, but obedience to all that Christ has commanded will. Your faith in the works of Christ on the cross will be made complete by a successful Christformation in you. Better still, if you have been found with full Christformation in you on the day of Christ's return, this will show God that you fully obeyed whatever Christ had commanded you with the help of God the Holy Spirit.

With more Christformation in you, you will be entrusted with all the other heavenly treasures until you are Christlike, as stated in "So take the bag of gold from him and give it to the one who has ten bags." With more Christformation in you, you will be a greater vessel of honor in God the Father's eyes because His only Son's divine nature has been successfully formed in you. The Son's divine nature is God the Father's nature, which He chose to reveal through His Son. Whoever chooses to obey His Son will have the divine nature of God Himself formed in him, as obeying the Son is the same as obeying the Father. Your faith and obedience to Christ will result in full Christformation which will show in the end as your deeds. "As the body without the spirit is dead, so faith without deeds is dead."

F) Word became Flesh; Obedient Flesh becomes Word

John 1:14:
"The Word became flesh and made his dwelling among us. We have seen his glory, the glory of the one and only Son, who came from the Father, full of grace and truth."

In the book of John, the Lord Jesus Christ is introduced as the Word. This Word took the form of flesh and lived like one of us. The Lord came from heaven, sent by the heavenly Father to us, and revealed the Father to us. The divine nature of the heavenly Father was found in Him; He was the exact representation of the Father on earth.

The Father's grace and truth was found fully in Him. He showed us how He and the Father loved each other and how He learned obedience to the Father out of this eternal relationship. God the Father was revealed to us not as an authoritarian figure, but rather one who loves. He disciplines, but this is purely out of love for us. Christ's death on the cross was not a punishment for His sins but for ours, as He had no sin in Himself. God needed to punish us for our sins because He is a sinless God, and He set aside His only begotten Son to be our scapegoat to receive the punishment that we deserved.

Because of man's disobedience, the Word had to become flesh; because of Christ's obedience, flesh will become Word through Christformation in those who obey God. Flesh will become Word through the renewed mind and the Christ-formed born-again spirit, which will be clothed by the imperishable Christ-conformed body.

The Lord Jesus Christ lowered Himself to take the form of a man because Adam and Eve disobeyed God and were responsible for the permanent embedding of the sinful nature of the Devil in all mankind. They disobeyed God's command and allowed the Devil to take control of them. Their disobedience to God made it necessary for the Lord Jesus Christ to take the form of a man to show us obedience to the heavenly Father. Now through His obedience to the Father, we can learn from Him how to obey the Father in the same way. When

Christ is formed in us, His Word is formed in us because Christ is that Word of God. Let's read another portion of Scripture to better understand this truth.

Revelation 19:12–14:
"His eyes are like blazing fire, and on his head are many crowns. He has a name written on him that no one knows but he himself knows. He is dressed in a robe dipped in blood, and his name is the Word of God. The armies of heaven are following him, riding on white horses and dressed in fine linen, white and clean."

The Lord Jesus Christ is the Word of God. The armies of heaven that He was leading were those who were washed and made clean by Him through His Word. In the above passage, He is leading all those who had full Christformation in them for they had obeyed all that He had commanded them. The Word of God requires obedience to Him. He only leads those who are obedient to Him. His army will be one that has proven its obedience to the Word of God and has become like the Word of God Himself with His divine nature formed in it permanently. Let us be reminded of this verse below to know where we stand as a result of our faith in the Lord.

Matthew 24:35:
"Heaven and earth will pass away, but my words will never pass away."

When His divine nature is formed in you, you will never pass away because eternal life, which is only found in Him, will be found in you now and forever. Eternal life has been formed in you. No one can remove you from Him because His divine nature, which is eternal, has been formed in you. Word became flesh so that all obedient flesh to Him could become Word. Those who obey Him on earth will be those who are with Him as an army to defeat the Enemy.

No one can separate you from the Word when the Word Himself has been formed in you for eternity. Because He first loved you, you obey Him. Now that He is formed in you through your obedience to Him, who can separate you from the love of Christ? Let us read the following passage in the book of Romans and apply it to our lives.

Romans 8:35–39:

"Who shall separate us from the love of Christ? Shall trouble or hardship or persecution or famine or nakedness or danger or sword? As it is written: "For your sake we face death all day long; we are considered as sheep to be slaughtered." No, in all these things we are more than conquerors through him who loved us. For I am convinced that neither death nor life, neither angels nor demons, not even the present nor the future, nor any powers, neither height nor depth, nor anything else in all creation, will be able to separate us from the love of God that is in Christ Jesus our Lord."

If it is the love of Christ that causes you to obey Him, no one can stop full Christformation in you. Any other reason will hinder Christformation in you! Nothing can fail the love of Christ in you. We become more than conquerors when the love of Christ compels us to obey all that He has commanded. We will overcome the sinful nature of the Devil in us fully when we are compelled by the love of Christ to obey Him in all situations.

The seed that fell on good soil produced good fruit. The good soil is the heart that is filled with the love of Christ, compelling the believer to do as God's Word says. With more love of Christ in you, you will be more obedient to God. Total obedience to Christ will produce full Christformation in you. The parable below explains this truth to us.

Luke 7:46–47:

"You did not put oil on my head, but she has poured perfume on my feet. Therefore, I tell you, her many sins have been forgiven—as her great love has shown. But whoever has been forgiven little loves little."

This is how you will know the love of Christ has filled your heart: When you truly have the assurance that you have been forgiven, you will be compelled to obey the Lord. It is the love of Christ that will compel you to obey whatever Christ has commanded. When you do only what God says and not what the sinful nature of the Devil urges you to do, you will have Christformation in you. You will only obey Him when you are assured that He has forgiven you. It will be difficult to obey His word when you still doubt whether He has forgiven you.

He was called the Word of God because only He can produce obedience in you. God the Holy Spirit reminds you of all that Christ has commanded so that you will obey Him. Obedience comes from the Word of God, and He is the Word of God because He is the perfect example of obedience to the heavenly Father. Calling Him the Word of God is the same as referring to Him as Obedience.

The Word of God is spoken by God so that there will be obedience. When He speaks, all things – the sun, the moon, the seas, the animals, the trees, the mountains, all dominion and so forth obey Him as stated in Ephesians 1:21. So should we, so that there will be Christformation in us.

G) WE WILL BECOME THE DWELLING OF THE FATHER, SON, AND HOLY SPIRIT

John 14:23:
"Jesus replied, 'Anyone who loves me will obey my teaching. My Father will love them, and we will come to them and make our home with them.' "

You would not be able to obey all that Christ our Lord has commanded without the help of God the Holy Spirit in you, who reminds you of everything the Lord Jesus had spoken while He was on earth. He takes everything that belongs to Christ and makes it known to us.

We become the temple of the Holy Spirit before we can become the tabernacle or the dwelling of the Father and the Son for eternity. We are filled with God Holy Spirit first before the Father fills us through His Son. At our salvation experience, we are born of the Spirit. And thereafter will come another experience of the infilling of God the Holy Spirit's power as promised in Acts 1:8. With this infilling of God's power, we will be fully prepared to war against the sinful nature of the Devil in us. This will enable us to overcome it little by little and put all its misdeeds to death in us. Through full Christformation in us, God the Father and His Son dwell together with God the Holy Spirit within us. Full Christformation also means being filled with the Father, because the Father and the Son are one.

God the Father will love those who obey the teaching of Christ, and because they obey the teaching of Christ, there will be Christformation in them. When this occurs, God the Father will come and fill them. He who has the Son has the Father also. Then God will make His tabernacle among men, which has been prophesied in the book of Revelation.

Revelation 21:2–3:
"I saw the Holy City, the New Jerusalem, coming down out of heaven from God, prepared as a bride beautifully dressed for her husband. And I heard a loud voice from the throne saying, 'Look! God's dwelling place is now among the people, and he will dwell with them. They will be his people, and God himself will be with them and be their God.' "

Through Christformation in you, God's dwelling will be among men forever and ever. All the promises of God in His Son will come to pass when this happens. When Adam and Eve fell into sin, God promised that He would set us free from the sinful nature of the Devil in us and make His home in us through full Christformation, as we will be given the right to eat from the Tree of Life in His garden and live forever without sin.

The Feast of Tabernacles concluded the seven appointed feasts of the Lord in the Old Testament, which represented the celebration of God dwelling among men. But this only happened after six other feasts had been celebrated first, which represent feasting or feeding on the divine nature of Christ until it is formed in us. The feasting starts with the invitation to come and rest from being a slave to the sinful nature of the Devil. This is represented by the feasts of the Sabbath that signifies true rest which comes from feasting on Christ. The series of feasts reach their pinnacle at the Feast of Tabernacles, which signifies the indwelling of the Holy Trinity within you. This is when you experience true rest from bondage to the sinful nature of the Devil. Christformation in you is the richest of fare, which is mentioned in the following verses. Although salvation is free through the completed work of Christ on the cross, you still need to buy (pay with a price) Christformation in you with your obedience to all that Christ has commanded (the price you need to pay).

Let's read the two verses below that foretold full Christformation in you, which was prophesied in the Old Testament.

Isaiah 55:1–2:
"Come, all you who are thirsty, come to the waters; and you who have no money, come, buy and eat! Come; buy wine and milk without money and without cost. Why spend money on what is not bread, and your labor on what does not satisfy? Listen, listen to me, and eat what is good and your soul will delight in the richest of fare."

Psalm 81:16:
"But you would be fed with the finest of wheat; with honey from the rock I would satisfy you."

By the seventh feast, the divine nature of Christ would have been fully formed in us if we have faithfully obeyed whatever He had commanded us. Did you notice the four kinds of food we are to feed on throughout our Christformation journey from the book of Genesis to Revelation in the two verses above? We are to feed on milk, honey, bread, and wine. Do you see the big picture of Christformation in you here? All these represent us feasting on Christ for full Christformation in us. The milk and the honey symbolized God's promise of fullness and abundance in the Old Testament. There weren't actual milk and honey flowing in Canaan Land. It was just another parable of full Christformation in those who fully obeyed God. Whereas each time the bread and the wine is partaken, the Lord's Supper will remind us that His body, sacrificed for our sins on the cross, is the Bread of Life. Also, the wine represents His blood shed for us; which makes it possible for us to come to God in the first place through the remission of sins. When we continually partake of these two emblems, it reminds us that Christ is being filled in us as we "eat and drink" Him. We are reminded of the ongoing full Christformation in us, so that we continually obey Him. That is why apostle Paul warned us not to take part in the Lord's Supper if we do not obey His commandments. It will be of no use to the partaker and in fact, God's judgment could befall anyone who takes the commandments of the Lord lightly by not obeying them.

At the end of the Feast of Tabernacles, we would have fed on the full divine nature of Christ. In the book of Zechariah, it was meant as a lasting prophecy that anyone who did not go up to celebrate the Feast of Tabernacles would be punished by the Lord. This is so because; the Feast of the Tabernacles is the concluding Feast of the Lord which signifies the Father, Son and Holy Spirit will dwell eternally with us through full Christformation. It is true that anyone found not worthy to be in the eternal dwelling of God will be thrown into the lake of fire. Anyone who does not have Christformation in Him will be thrown into the lake of fire after the great white throne judgment.

You would not be able to celebrate the Feast of Tabernacles if you had not celebrated the six prior feasts, which represented feasting or feeding on Christ fully. If you haven't done that, there will be no Christformation in you. Let's read the warning about this eternal sin of omission in the following passage from the book of Zechariah.

Zechariah 14:18–19:
"If the Egyptian people do not go up and take part, they will have no rain. The LORD will bring on them the plague he inflicts on the nations that do not go up to celebrate the Festival of Tabernacles. This will be the punishment of Egypt and the punishment of all the nations that do not go up to celebrate the Festival of Tabernacles."

Christformation is the shelter of the Most High in you. If you do not have this shelter, how will you be protected from the Evil One, who prowls around looking for whom he may attack and devour? Now, we see a clearer picture of what the Enemy will come to steal, kill, and destroy. He will come to steal our obedience, kill our perseverance, and destroy Christformation in us altogether. The Enemy will want us to obey his embedded sinful nature in us if we haven't put to death all its misdeeds by the power of God's Spirit.

We must be alert and watchful of the Enemy, his evil schemes, and traps. He will try to trick and deceive us like he did Adam and Eve. We must, from the start of the journey to the finish, be obedient to all that Christ has commanded. The apostle Paul warns us that the same cunning serpent is waiting to defile our devotion to Christ and defeat us by making us return to pleasing the sinful nature of the Devil in us. We need to be awake and in the light always by deciding to never return to the way of darkness. There must be no part of us trapped in darkness. We must have full Christformation in us. Let us follow this exhortation of the Lord below.

Luke 11:35–36:
"See to it, then, that the light within you is not darkness. Therefore, if your whole body is full of light, and no part of it dark, it will be just as full of light as when a lamp shines its light on you." "

Let the light of Christ be fully formed in you and not in only some parts of your being. Let the light of Christ fill your born-again spirit, your mind (soul), and your body so that you do not surrender to any of the works of darkness that would hinder or abort Christformation in you. The apostle Paul encourages the believers of Christ with these words:

1 Thessalonians 5:23–24:
"May God himself, the God of peace, sanctify you through and through. May your whole spirit, soul, and body be kept blameless at the coming of our Lord Jesus Christ! The one who calls you is faithful, and he will do it."

The passage above reminds us that we must be found with:

1) Full Christformation in our born-again spirit.

2) Full transformation of our mind into the mind of Christ.

3) Readiness to be clothed with the fully imperishable, Christ-conformed body that is being built at God's right hand today.

In this way, we will be a testimony to the faithfulness of the One who has called us out of this corrupt world to be His people. The apostle Peter encourages us with these words below:

1 Peter 2:9–10:
"But you are a chosen people, a royal priesthood, a holy nation, God's special possession, that you may declare the praises of him who called you out of darkness into his wonderful light. Once you were not a people, but now you are the people of God; once you had not received mercy, but now you have received mercy."

With full Christformation in you, you will not be objects of His wrath to be destroyed by the eternal fire reserved for all those who have not obeyed Him. With full Christformation in you, you have proven with your complete obedience to be the called, chosen, and faithful of God through the power of God the Holy Spirit demonstrated within you. You are his chosen people now and can serve the King of kings and the Great High Priest after the order of Melchizedek for all eternity; a powerful nation that cannot be compared to any on earth or in heaven. With you will be formed the new heaven and the new earth, with the old order of things destroyed, about which Isaiah, the prophet of God, prophesied:

Isaiah 66:1–2:
"This is what the LORD says: 'Heaven is my throne, and the earth is my footstool. Where is the house you will build for me? Where will my resting place be? Has not my hand made all these things, and so they came into being?' declares the LORD. 'This is the one I esteem: he who is humble and contrite in spirit, and trembles at my word.' "

God was never looking for a structure to live in because the vastness of the universe existed even before He created heaven and earth. Can we ever build a house that could hold His vastness? No. He was looking for those people who would make Him their dwelling, and this has happened through His beloved Son with Christformation in you. Christformation is the testimony of Christ in you, where the Father, Son, and Holy Spirit dwell within you and you in them according to God's eternal plan. The Word became flesh so that all obedient flesh would fully become Word and live eternally with Him.

SUMMARY: CHAPTER SEVEN

Section A	The Parable of the True Vine explains how there could be full Christformation, when you remain in Christ by being completely obedient to Him. You should be willing to be disciplined (pruned) by God each time you turn to please the sinful nature. And If you desire full Christformation, you should press on and not give up after you have been disciplined by God.
Section B	If you sow Christformation faithfully with the help of God the Holy Spirit and overcome the urges and desires of the sinful nature completely, then you will reap full Christformation.
Section C	The circumcision or putting to death of the sinful nature can only happen through your complete obedience to all that Christ had commanded. You must fill your born again spirit with full Christformation with the help of God the Holy Spirit.
Section D	You have to be trained in righteousness to run the race of Christformation until you reach the finishing line faithfully; full Christformation in you. This training comes through your obedience to God's word.
Section E	In the Parable of the Talents we learn that you must sow your entire life towards full Christformation with unreserved diligence. You must make every effort to fill yourself with the entire divine nature of Christ. He, who has this, will be found faithful.
Section G	The reason Christ was revealed as the Word of God by the heavenly Father is for you to obey Him. You will become like Him with His divine nature fully formed in you when you do as He says.
Section F	When the Triune God finally makes His home in you through full Christformation, your redemption and salvation has been made complete through Christ.

Diagram 7(a)

Full Christformation will occur when there is total obedience to all that Christ had commanded. We might need disciplining from the Lord for this to occur. We need to count the cost of being Christ's disciple by accepting the disciplining that would come from the Lord. These many forms of disciplining from the Lord would be necessary for the putting to death of the misdeeds of the sinful nature. If the sinful nature is fully put to death and circumcised by Christ our Lord, then, there will be no hindrance for the sowing of full Christformation in you. What you sow is what you will reap in the end. If you diligently sow towards Christformation in your born again spirit through your obedience to the Lord, then you will reap full Christformation in you, if you continue sowing till the end of that harvest. But, if you choose to sow to your sinful nature instead, by satisfying its desires and passions, then you will deservedly reap the destruction of your soul and spirit. There will be no incorruptible body clothing you because you had sowed corruption into your spirit and soul. You had been negligent like the foolish 'virgins'. You must remain in Christ by obeying Him towards full Christformation in you. Full Christformation is also likened to an athlete who runs the race with perseverance till the end of that race. He must not be disqualified or quit the race for he had counted the cost of following Christ towards putting to death the misdeeds of the sinful nature from the start of that race.

CONCLUSION:
THE BIG PICTURE OF
CHRISTFORMATION IN YOU

We have discussed extensively on what, why and how Christformation occurs in those who have been called, chosen and are found to be faithful to Christ. These are the objects of his mercies and God is totally involved with their Christformation. What is left for us to do is to reciprocate with our total obedience to Him so that full Christformation occurs in us. This will be raised as *Doxa* (glory) and as incense to God the father. God's pleasure is for us to be filled with His Son in every way.

Christformation in you is the *Doxa* (glory) of God, the promised, demonstrative work of God the Holy Spirit within the believer. In Christian terminology, according to the Hebrew-Greek Key Word Dictionary, *Doxa* means honor and distinction with the approval of God. It refers to something that is favorable to God. Theologically, with reference to believers, it signifies their exalted position as the objects of divine approbation and blessedness.

The *Doxa* glory of God is a state in which the believer is accorded the fullest admiration and honor of God as an object of His highest regard and praise (mercy) when there is:

1) Full Christformation in the born-again spirit.

2) Full transformation of the mind (soul) into the mind of Christ.

3) The complete clothing of both the spirit and soul with the imperishable, Christ-conformed body.

Doxa is God's way of expressing to the believer of Christ that he or she is bestowed with the right to be exalted to His right hand as a co-heir with Christ. This is exemplified by the inheritance of His kingdom, resurrection, and the enjoyment of fullness, satisfaction, joy, righteousness, and eternal life in Christ. Although, this divine glory has not been revealed yet, it will become reality through full Christformation in you at the end of all things. However, the believer presently possesses this glory in his or her spirit with the presence of God the Holy Spirit within him or her.

The expression "the Spirit of glory" in 1 Peter 4:14 means that the Spirit even now imparts glory spiritually, invisibly, and secretly to the soul of believers as a foretaste and promise of full Christformation. While believers suffer public shame and ignominy in the eyes of men, the Holy Spirit inwardly testifies through the encouragement of the Word of God that in His eyes they are honored and that one day in the eyes of all men. especially their persecutors, God will honor them openly. All of this is granted solely through Jesus Christ who, by His perfect obedience, sacrificial death, and triumphant resurrection, secured so great a salvation for God's elect.

Christ, in His state of glory and exaltation at the Father's right hand, is interceding for us that we, like Him, will eventually shine with the magnificence of His obedience and submission to God's will. Beauty, brilliance, and the eminence of full Christformation before the heavenly Father will manifest through this demonstrative work of God's eternal power in you. It is that form, aspect, or appearance that will be pleasing in the sight of the Father in heaven.

Doxa means beauty or elegance and also includes vastness, depth and intensity which in this context refer to the fullness of Christ's unblemished and radiant divine nature successfully formed in the believer as described in Ephesians 5:27. Although more precisely, *Doxa* means the object of one's admiration, it also means honor, distinction, or ornament—for example, 1 Corinthians 11:7-12 states that man is the crowning jewel of creation and woman is of man. Likewise, the inner greatness and moral eminence of Christformation in you is the crowning jewel of the new creation in God's eyes.

Christformation in you is the *Doxa* of Christ's divine nature in you, which will please the heavenly Father with eternal pleasure. When this occurs, you have become the true bride of the Lamb in God the Father's eyes. Let us see how this will be fulfilled in the verses below.

Revelation 21:9–27:

"One of the seven angels who had the seven bowls full of the seven last plagues came and said to me, "Come, I will show you the bride, the wife of the Lamb." And he carried me away in the Spirit to a mountain great and high, and showed me the Holy City, Jerusalem, coming down out of heaven from God. It shone with the glory of God, and its brilliance was like that of a very precious jewel, like jasper, clear as crystal. It had a great, high wall with twelve gates and with twelve angels at the gates. On the gates were written the names of the twelve tribes of Israel. There were three gates on the east, three on the north, three on the south and three on the west. The wall of the city had twelve foundations, and on them were the names of the twelve apostles of the Lamb. The angel who talked with me had a measuring rod of gold to measure the city, its gates and its walls. The city was laid out like a square, as long as it was wide. He measured the city with the rod and found it to be 12,000 stadia in length, and as wide and high as it is long. He measured its wall and it was 144 cubits thick, by man's measurement, which the angel was using. The wall was made of jasper, and the city of pure gold, as pure as glass. The foundations of the city walls were decorated with every kind of precious stone. The first foundation was jasper, the second sapphire, the third chalcedony, the fourth emerald, the fifth sardonyx, the sixth carnelian, the seventh chrysolite, the eighth beryl, the ninth topaz, the tenth chrysoprase, the eleventh jacinth, and the twelfth amethyst. The twelve gates were twelve pearls, each gate made of a single pearl. The great street of the city was of pure gold, like transparent glass. I did not see a temple in the city, because the Lord God Almighty and the Lamb is its temple. The city does not need the sun or the moon to shine on it, for the glory of God gives it light, and the Lamb is its lamp. The nations will walk by its light, and the kings of the earth will bring their splendor into it. On no day will its gates ever be shut, for there will be no night there.

The glory and honor of the nations will be brought into it. Nothing impure will ever enter it, nor will anyone who does what is shameful or deceitful, but only those whose names are written in the Lamb's book of life."

The reason the previous passage was included is to remind you that the exact measurements of the city translate into obedience as the prerequisite for full Christformation in you. What God requires of you must be obeyed to the strictest accuracy and fervency. The precious stones that beautify the walls and the flooring represent the divine nature of Christ that will be formed in you. This vision was to forewarn you that, without obedience to all that Christ has commanded, there will be no Christformation in you. If you fully obey Christ, you will gain full Christformation in you.

Now, for a moment, picture the city incomplete without some of the precious stones or the flooring. That's how you will look in God's presence if your obedience to Christ is incomplete. Are you making every effort to build upon your obedience to Christ, with His divine nature successfully formed in you? For this is what God requires of you with the grace and mercy showered upon you through Christ our Lord.

To recapitulate what we have discussed throughout *Christformation In You: From Genesis to Revelation*, here is a diagrammatic conclusion for your reference.

Chapter	What you should know	What you should do
Chapter 1: **What is Christformation in you?**	There are only two kinds of choices: Christ or the Devil	Choose to belong to Christ
Chapter 2: **Why is Christformation in you necessary?**	God has predestined, promised and given examples of how Christformation should occur in you through the Old Testament.	Believe, accept and follow Christ
Chapter 3: **Where else is Christformation mentioned in the Bible?**	Christformation is spoken about from Genesis to Revelation	Search the scriptures
Chapter 4: **How does Christformation occur in you?**	Your measure of obedience to Christ determines the measure of Christformation in you	Obey all that Christ had commanded
Chapter 5: **Who will have Christformation?**	Only the objects of God's mercy will have Christformation	Pursue Christformation with all your heart`
Chapter 6: **Who is involved with your Christformation?**	The Holy Trinity, the fivefold ministers, the angels of God and the old testament witnesses are involved in your Christformation	Allow their involvement in your Christformation
Chapter 7: **Full Christformation in you: when does it occur?**	You need to fully overcome the sinful nature of the devil in you whilst fully sowing Christformation into your born again spirit. When you do so, your mind (soul) will be transformed fully into the mind of Christ accordingly. Simultaneously, your imperishable body is being built at God's right hand now. This will clothe your Christformed spirit and transformed mind (soul) on the last day	Earnestly seek full Christformation for your new body, soul and spirit for this fully forms the Doxa Glory of God when He finally dwells among us in the new heaven and earth

Finally, we earnestly pray that the Lord has opened "the eyes of your understanding" to all the truths of Christformation in you, as stated in Ephesians 1:18 (NKJV). From here on, we also pray that you will enjoy a very close, deep relationship with God the Father, the Son, and the Holy Spirit. Our desire is that you may fully dwell in them as they fully dwell in you and make their home in you for eternity. God be with you always.

A Personal Testimony of Christformation in You
By Christinal Pillai

God ploughs the ground before He sows the Seed

I must say that I have been a Christian from birth as I was born into a God-fearing, Christian family that attended a mainline church in my neighborhood. My parents were school teachers and disciplining the five of us was not a problem for them. Firstly, I learnt that being born into a Christian family does not guarantee your being a Christian. One cannot be a Christian through physical birth alone but you must have that born-again experience in your spirit to be called a Christian. Until that experience occurs, you are only being prepared by God, just as a farmer prepares the ground by plowing the land before he sows the seed. My parents were given the God-commissioned task to prepare the ground, and they did their duty well, I should say. I would not be where I am without their pointing me and my siblings to Christ our Lord faithfully.

Secondly, the born-again experience is a unique one. It cannot be compared to any other experience in life for me. It's a very special moment of birth into a new realm. For the first time, you will be introduced to a new person, God the Holy Spirit. You will even hear His guiding whispers from within if you listen carefully. He comes into you because you have responded to the gospel of the Lord Jesus Christ. I was convicted that there was something that had gone terribly wrong between me and God, who created me. I realized that I needed help and knew it was beyond me. I knew that it was not in my strength to make things right with God. So I searched for answers and found the sinful nature of the Devil in me to be the cause for this broken relationship between me and my Creator and rightful Master. I was like a sheep that had gone astray far from my shepherd. But, finally, I was convicted of my sins that had separated me from my God and I sincerely wanted to return to Him.

Psalm 103:1–3:
"Praise the LORD, my soul;
all my inmost being, praise his holy name.

Praise the LORD, my soul,
and forget not all his benefits—
who forgives all your sins
and heals all your diseases."

I want to thank the Lord for giving me the opportunity to share with you how real the Lord is through all the miracles He has done in my life. I believe that the Lord has saved me from three life-threatening incidences so that I can be part of this message to you. As I share my testimonies and life experiences, I am sure that the Lord will speak to you. You might be going through a tough time. You may be wondering if the Lord is hearing your prayers. But let me assure you that He is there for you, even though you may feel He is not!

As I grew up with my parents, I observed that when their students were in need, my parents willingly helped them. They loved and feared God and accepted many servants of the Lord who came in His name to have a home meeting and share God's Word with us. They blessed them with a love offering or with homegrown fruits, vegetables, and even poultry (times were tough then) for ministering God's Word to us.

Like any other family, we had our problems. Squabbles, quarrels, fights, and even domestic violence occurred. Furthermore, my mother suffered sudden schizophrenic attacks whenever she felt depressed. During these times, I felt very sad and would find a quiet place to pour my heart out in prayer to God secretly. My dad subscribed to *Reader's Digest* magazine; while reading one of the monthly issues when I was about twelve years old, I came across an advertisement for Pastor Oral Roberts' book, *Seed Faith*. The advertisement was so appealing that I wrote to him, shared my problems, and requested prayer and the book. He replied and encouraged me in the Lord, even though I was located on the other end of the globe. This encouraged me to bring all my problems and burdens to God in prayer. Pastor Roberts also sent me two plaques with the words "Expect a miracle" and "Something good is going to happen" inscribed on them. These acted as reminders whenever I felt down from my troubles.

At times, I have wondered why I am that special in the sight of God for Him to show mercy toward me and save me from death on three different occasions. At the age of fourteen, I was diagnosed with Rheumatic Chorea by a general practitioner who advised my father to rush me to the nearest hospital immediately. I experienced rapid involuntary movements of my limbs, tongue and facial muscles due to a very high fever. On the way to the ward, I became paralyzed from the waist down. During my hospitalization, I became critically ill. The doctors gave up hope and told my parents that I would not survive this illness. Upon hearing the bad news, my dad, who loved me very much, cried out to God to spare my life, vowing me for God's work if I returned home alive.

My family members and friends took turns providing care for me at the hospital. One night, when I became seriously ill with a temperature that rose dangerously to 105 degrees Fahrenheit (40.5 Celsius), I saw two Christian brothers and a sister dressed in white at the end of my bed, praying for me. I found out after I had recovered that they were from the Pentecostal missions and were not angels as I had first thought. The next morning, the elderly woman who had taken care of me told my parents that I got better after the three visitors in white had prayed for me. She was of a different faith than mine, but what a testimony it was to her! And I praise the Lord for this wonderful testimony among those who have not known the power of our God.

As the days passed, I got better, but I had to learn to walk and talk all over again as the illness had affected my speech and legs. I was discharged after three weeks of hospitalization. The Lord chose to be merciful to me by sparing and healing me.

Romans 9:15–16:

"For the Lord had said to Moses, 'I will have mercy on whom I have mercy, compassion on whom I have compassion. It does not, therefore, depend on human desire or effort, but on God's mercy.' "

God did this great miracle in my life so that I can share this healing as a testimony of God's mercy and His mighty power.

At the age of twenty, after being on medication for five long years, I fully recovered from Rheumatic (Sydenham) Chorea. I then went overseas to pursue my nursing career in the United Kingdom. I chose this field because when I was hospitalized, one of the nurses there had treated me unkindly. I told myself that I too would become a nurse one day, but, unlike her, I would really care for my patients. During my stay and training at Romford, in the county of Essex, I knew that the Lord was with me and was watching over me even though I was in a land far away from home. I also knew that God was watching as to how I conducted my life in a foreign land and that I was accountable to Him for my actions. I thank the Lord for enabling me to achieve my goal of becoming a nurse. I also attained my certification in theatre nursing (a specialized field of nursing) before I returned to Malaysia after my memorable five-year stay in the UK.

I then joined a private nursing home, and worked as a theatre nurse for a short duration. During this time, I got emotionally involved with an unbeliever. It was a prearranged relationship by family members. However, the relationship didn't materialize into marriage because it wasn't God's will for me to be unequally yoked with an unbeliever. Nevertheless, it was difficult for me to do God's will at this juncture, as I was in a state of limbo. But, I made a stand for my God who had never failed me in any way. Nevertheless, I had initially obliged to my family's wishes and there was a price to pay for it. It was a painful experience for me. I didn't foresee what was yet to come.

I was disappointed with myself because I became entangled in such a situation. I felt that I didn't deserve to be in such a predicament. Worse still, there was a great sense of uncertainty in my life because I was not sure of what to do after this. Constant thoughts of this situation made me depressed. I did not know what to do. I couldn't concentrate on my job either. I became fearful of even being in the operation theatre in case I made mistakes at the operation table. I had loved and enjoyed my nursing profession at one time, but I had also lost interest in it because of this emotional uncertainty that I was going through. At times, I even thought that I was losing my sanity. I knew what it was like to lose one's sanity because my mother was a psychiatric patient herself. For many years, she suffered from schizophrenia whenever she was unable to cope with circumstances that depressed her. She had many sleepless nights. I grew up with witnessing her being occasionally hospitalized in a mental health center. I was always the one caring for her during these episodes.

I had great expectations for how my life should be. That's why I couldn't bear what I was going through at this point in time. I felt useless, and thus decided that I didn't want to live life this way. Furthermore, I felt that I was burdensome to my family. So, I contemplated suicide. I informed my mother that I was going out for awhile and left for town in a taxi. I intended to jump off one of the tallest buildings in town and end my life there. As I was about to do so, suddenly fear engulfed me, and I began to reason. What if I jumped off the building and, instead of dying, permanently injured myself? Wouldn't I become a greater burden to my family then? That thought really scared me, and I made a conscious decision to turn around and go home. When I went home, I found my mother crying bitterly because I had been unusually missing for many hours. I was told that she went around town looking for me frantically. My family enquired about my absence. That is when I told my family that I felt useless. I explained to them that I was depressed and felt like I was losing my mind. I needed spiritual help.

I believe that I was going through all this because it was time for the Lord to claim the vow that my dad made at the age of fourteen when I was dying. This Bible verse below teaches how seriously God views our vows to Him.

Numbers 30:2:

"When a man makes a vow to the LORD or takes an oath to obligate himself by a pledge, he must not break his word but must do everything he said."

My family members urgently took me to pastors, whom we all knew, and shared my problems with them. After listening to my problem, they took me to a Bible Institute run by the one of the pastor's son-in-law. I was left there so that they could counsel, pray for, and involve me in whatever ministry they were doing. During my temporary stay, I observed that the students were enjoying what they were doing for the Lord. There was peace evident in them. They were from simple backgrounds, but I was attracted to what they were experiencing and wanted to know what it was. The answer was Jesus, as John 14:27 says: "Peace I leave with you; my peace I give you. I do not give to you as the world gives. Do not let your hearts be troubled and do not be afraid."

Full Christformation in me is like experiencing the pains of childbirth

John 16:21–22 (NKJV):

"A woman, when she is in labor, has sorrow because her hour has come; but as soon as she has given birth to the child, she no longer remembers the anguish, for joy that a human being has been born into the world. Therefore you now have sorrow; but I will see you again and your heart will rejoice, and your joy no one will take from you."

As long as we are still on this earth, we will experience many trials and tests of our faith. With much tribulation, we will enter into the kingdom of God. Just like a woman who is in labor pains, we will experience much pain and anguish to see full Christformation in us occur. Only a woman who has endured the suffering of labor pains knows the extent of this pain. Furthermore, every pregnancy is a unique experience for the mother. I have two sons, and both pregnancies and deliveries were different. Likewise, every one of us who belong to Christ will have Christformation with difficulties and troubles of our own. But the Lord Jesus Christ has assured us that this pain and anguish will turn into joy once we see the fruit of full Christformation in us at His return; like a woman who has given birth experiences the joy of seeing her child being born. Let me continue with my testimony here, where you will see the difficulties and joyful moments I have been through.

The students at the Bible Institute were friendly, kind, and willing to share their testimonies to strengthen me. They volunteered to fast and pray for me. I was very touched by their Christlike gestures. The pastor shared with me the good news once again and asked me to accept the Lord Jesus as my personal savior. After that prayer, such peace filled my heart, and over the weeks, I got better with their love and prayer support.

When I had recovered fully, the principal of the Bible Institute gave me a form to sign up as a full-time student. I hesitated, and told him that I came there to be prayed for so that I could get healed and return to my nursing profession with a clear mind. He gave me the weekend off to seek the Lord in prayer and to come back with a decision. I was so troubled and indecisive. I sought the Lord in prayer and asked for His will to be done in my life. The Lord spoke to me through a Tamil chorus that resounded, "I laid down my life for you, but what have you done for me in return?" ("unakaga naan marithayneh, yenakaga nee yennaseithai?"). These lyrics were part of a hymn from the hymnal book we used in the Bible Institute, during devotion time

Then I surrendered my life and will to the Lord so that I could serve Him in full-time ministry. At last, my parents' vow was fulfilled, and such peace filled my heart when I decided to serve the Lord.

During the two-year course, the Lord led me to meet my future husband, who was already a student at the Bible Institute. At first, I wasn't prepared for another relationship and turned down his advances. But he was a prayerful man and didn't give up easily, pursuing me persistently. Finally, I told him that I would seek the Lord to help me forget my past and give me love for him. The Lord showed me through a dream that I would be married to Ron and have two children born to us: a toddler of about three years old while I was about six months pregnant with the second child. I shared this with my family members, but they weren't too keen because I would be married to a pastor and life would be tough. But I wanted to get married with their approval and blessings, so I went into fasting and prayer. After the Lord intervened, we got engaged with our families' blessing. Six months later, on November 11, 1982, we tied the nuptial knot.

We started our ministry among the poor rural folks. It was tough, and we faced a lot of challenges during our ministry. We started with the children's, home, and prayer ministry. Later, when our congregation grew in number, we moved into a two-story shop-lot. The Lord not only blessed us with our ministry, but also with two healthy, handsome boys. During the early years of our married life, Ron suffered from severe gastritis that turned into stomach ulcer. He had to avoid spicy dishes and had to drink a lot of milk. He was on medication too. He was prayed for, but the actual healing took place one night in our bedroom when he felt the healing touch of the Lord while he was sound asleep. Today, he consumes spicier food than I do with no medication whatsoever. Praise the Lord for his mighty healing power.

Our ministry was amongst gangsters, drug addicts, victims of domestic violence, staunch idolaters, people dabbling in witchcraft, practitioners of sorcery, and those with all kinds of chronic illnesses and diseases. The Lord placed the compassion for these people in our hearts, and we pioneered and labored in His field. The Lord was with us, for He helped us and caused His work to grow and multiply. The Lord used individuals and family members to support our ministry in prayer and with financial help whenever there was a pressing need.

Joshua, our eldest son, was born to us two years after our marriage in February 1984. I had a miscarriage prior to conceiving him and was told by the doctor that I had retroversion of the uterus (uterus tilted backward). I had to be very careful to avoid further miscarriages. We were very troubled and shared this issue with a brother in Christ. He laid his hands on me and prayed for my healing. I was healed and gave birth to Joshua, a healthy baby boy, weighing seven pounds five ounces. This the Lord spoke to me through a dream, and it came to pass on the dot. I had complications during labor. The doctors told me that the baby had passed its excrement into the water bag and this would be harmful for it. They would give me an hour to have strong labor pains, but if I failed to, they would have to do a caesarean delivery of the baby. I cried out to the Lord to give me a normal delivery. Praise the Lord, another miracle happened there. We carried on with the Lord's work, sowing with tears, but reaping with joy. The ministry grew along with signs and miracles as mentioned in Mark 16:15–18:

"He said to them, 'Go into the entire world and preach the gospel to all creation. Whoever believes and is baptized will be saved, but whoever does not believe will be condemned. And these signs will accompany those who believe: In my name they will drive out demons; they will speak in new tongues; they will pick up snakes with their hands; and when they drink deadly poison, it will not hurt them at all; they will place their hands on sick people, and they will get well.' "

The miraculous birth of Jeremy, our second child in January 1987, was the third time God had saved me from death. During my pregnancy, I had a number of complications and had to get special medical attention. During the later stages of my pregnancy, Jeremy was found to be a breech baby, and the attending physician told us that it would be a caesarean delivery. I was also found to be hypertensive and had to be extra careful at birth. The due date was January 3, 1987. My prenatal checkups were at a private clinic. On January 1, I had strong labor pains and felt giddy too. I was admitted to the clinic; my blood pressure read 180/120. The doctor panicked as he was understaffed and unable to deal with the situation. He immediately gave us a referral letter to the general hospital, and a nurse accompanied us to the hospital.

I was admitted and treated to bring down and stabilize my blood pressure so that I could have a normal delivery. Ron was with me during the evening visit, and I was having strong labor pains. I started to cough and told Ron that I couldn't breathe. That was the last I spoke to him, as I had collapsed. According to Ron, the buzzers were going off, and the medical team was all over the place. Immediate attention was given, and they waited for the attending consultant for further specialized treatment. I was unconscious for a number of hours.

All this occurred between the evening of January 2 and the early hours of January 3. Finally, I was revived to life! My husband was in agony while they were trying to revive me. Our senior pastors and friends were there to support us in prayer and cried out to the Lord to save me. Indeed the Lord was merciful to us, and we recognized that I am an object of His mercy for His glory and honor!

For the moment, I was out of the "collapsed stage," but my condition was still serious, and I hadn't delivered yet. The consultant physician explained my condition to my husband and asked him to sign the "high risk" consent form, stating that only one could be saved—either the mother or the baby. I also faced the risk of ending up as a paraplegic, or in layman's terms, a "vegetable." He had to sign the form to state that he would not hold the medical staff responsible should any of the above occur. Imagine the trauma that Ron had to go through. I was conscious, and I remember being wheeled into the operating theatre not knowing if I would return alive. Worst of all, the baby was in danger. They continued to pray for us while I was being operated on. A great miracle took place! Both of us came out alive from the operation theatre and were placed in the intensive care unit for a couple of days for further observation, medical care, and treatment.

We are indeed God's objects of mercy, as both Jeremy and I came out alive from such a life-threatening, impossible stage. We give Him all the glory and honor. We can attest that the verse below is real in our lives.

Romans 9:22–24:
"What if God, although choosing to show his wrath and make his power known, bore with great patience the objects of his wrath—prepared for destruction? What if he did this to make the riches of his glory known to the objects of his mercy, whom he prepared in advance for glory—even us, whom he also called, not only from the Jews but also from the Gentiles?"

I was famously called the "collapse case," or "the one who had come back to life" amongst the hospital staff. One of the attending nurses (a woman of a different religion) even commented that, "It was your God that had saved you." What a living testimony unto the Lord! She also said that there were people praying for me outside the operating theatre.

The next day, the consultant (whom I didn't recognize) visited me on his ward rounds. He claimed that he had "brought me back to life." He also said that I was very fortunate because about two years earlier, a woman with a similar situation died on the operating table. Jeremy was discharged five days later while I went home nine days after I had delivered. Whenever I recollect this great miracle, I am reminded that God is indeed merciful and compassionate towards us.

It didn't end there. Because of my preeclampsia, the attending physician said that I had to escort Jeremy for regular postnatal checkups until he was a year old. Due to my collapsed state (lack of oxygen to the brain), they wanted to make sure that Jeremy was growing normally, physically and mentally.

At the end of one year, the doctors discharged him and certified that he was growing normally like any other child. Praise the Lord! Today, he is a twenty-four-year-old web and graphic designer, pursuing his degree in multimedia. He is also involved in the layout and graphics of this book, *Christformation in You*. In our eyes, he is a multimedia genius. He always somehow solves all our computer problems in the family.

Our lives went on as usual, and our ministry grew. I helped Ron in the ministry with the ladies' fellowship and children's ministry. As in most churches and ministries, we went through a phase where we felt it was time to move on. We had sowed our lives and souls into this ministry, and it was time to be led into the harder ground of prison ministry. After much prayer and consideration, we decided to hand the church we had pioneered back to the mother church. We were there for ten years. This transition took place between 1992 and 1993.

Life wasn't a bed of roses after this, as we had to start all over again. We suffered a great deal spiritually for a while. We wondered if we had made the right decision. But after this, you will see how our lives were beautified through these sufferings.

Christformation is the beauty of the Lord in me.

1 Peter 3:3–5 (NKJV):

"Do not let your adornment be *merely* outward—arranging the hair, wearing gold, or putting on *fine* apparel—rather *let it be* the hidden person of the heart, with the incorruptible *beauty* of a gentle and quiet spirit, which is very precious in the sight of God. For in this manner, in former times, the holy women who trusted in God also adorned themselves, being submissive to their own husbands."

Every trial and testing of our faith works for the good of those who love Christ and obey everything He has commanded. All these trials are like gold tried in fire that brings the beauty and the shine of full Christformation in you before God the Father. Christformation in you is the inner beauty that is very precious in the sight of God. Full Christformation in you is the eternal beauty of the Lord in you. We were tested and tried in many ways, but we knew that obeying His Word at all costs would fill us with the beauty of the Lord in us. The divine nature of Christ is formed in us when we obey all that He has commanded us. Let me continue with my testimony.

We were tested in the area of accepting others as they are. We were tested to see if we would be faithful to the Lord even if we have to give up what we had treasured and had worked hard to achieve. After much prayer, the Lord directed us to let go of what we had held onto. We decided to take on a new, challenging full-time work and ministry among prisoners while continuing with the ministry of God's Word. We saw it as another ministry to the outcasts, the broken, the forsaken, and those despised by the society. We treasured the counsel of God in the passage below.

Matthew 25:34–36:

"Then the King will say to those on his right, 'Come, you who are blessed by my Father; take your inheritance, the kingdom prepared for you since the creation of the world. For I was hungry and you gave me something to eat, I was thirsty and you gave me something to drink, I was a stranger and you invited me in, I needed clothes and you clothed me, I was sick and you looked after me, I was in prison and you came to visit me."

This wasn't an easy ministry because Ron had to undergo a four-month intensive training to equip him for the job. This was entirely a different field compared to his pastoral ministry. He had to deal with hardcore drug addicts and convicts. They were there to serve their prison sentences as well as get rehabilitated to fit into society again. He struggled to cope and needed much prayer support. It was during this period that we bought many Christian books on intercessory prayer. They were great books that challenged us to get into intercessory prayer, especially me. Both of us spent a lot of time in prayer and stood on the promises of God. These inmates were from broken families, and under the influence of drug addiction, hooliganism, and other related crimes. They needed to know that there is a God who cares for them, loves them, and wants to show His compassion to them.

The Lord spoke to us through this verse:

Jeremiah 1:10:
"See, today I appoint you over nations and kingdoms to uproot and tear down, to destroy and overthrow, to build and to plant."

We started tearing down the forces of the Evil One, who was keeping these prisoners in bondage to sin and evil vices, and rebuilding them through kindness, love, compassion, and, of course, a lot of prayer. We fasted and prayed for many days, especially when Ron faced opposition due to evil forces at work in the prisons and ministry. Praise the Lord! We had the victory because the Lord was interceding for us and the inmates.

Ron served as a prison officer for about twelve years. During this service, the Lord taught him truths and revealed secrets about Christformation. All these revelations have materialized into this book only this year, 2011, seven years after leaving the prison work. Through many trials, tests of the faith, impossible moments, and after much perseverance and God's mercy and faithfulness to His calling, this book is finally written.

1 Thessalonians 5:24:
"The one who calls you is faithful, and he will do it."

It was also during this period that the Lord revealed through many dreams and visions of the things that would take place. The Lord continued to sustain us through prayer, His mercy, and His compassion. In 2004, Ron suffered a mild stroke (TIA) due to job stress, which affected his performance and fitness as a whole. We spent many days fasting and in prayer, seeking the Lord's will in regard to Ron's next move.

Putting our children through college and our move to Kuala Lumpur, the capital city of Malaysia, was the next step led by the Lord. We had lived in Johor Bahru for about twenty-five years; totally uprooting and resettling in another state is not as easy as it may seem. Once we got clear direction from the Lord, Ron tendered his resignation and left the prison service at the end of 2004. We did mention to the Lord in our prayer that we were willing to go through anything as long as His presence was with us. Only after we had left Johor Bahru for Kuala Lumpur did we realize that we had bitten off more than we could chew! We never imagined that we would go through the "valley of the shadow of death" for the next five years.

Ron received a gratuity sum when he left his job, and with that money, we paid our existing bills and enrolled Joshua and Jeremy in college. This took a great toll on us financially, and we wondered what we were going to do from here on. So, with Ron's past experience in running a food stall, that is what we decided to do. However, this was something new for the boys and me. We wanted to support ourselves through the stall business and do the Lord's work. Unfortunately, it failed twice due to lack of manpower and resources. We not only had problems fending for ourselves, putting our children through college seemed impossible. In spite of this, we faithfully pressed on with our ministry of the Word and prayer and intercession for the nations.

We moved to a smaller town in August 2005 and practically lived out of boxes in a tiny, rented apartment for eight months. It was really tough. Joshua took a weekend job, and Ron started working for a Christian friend. We were doing fine for a while and tried to lead a normal life. I cried out to the Lord, asking that since He was the One who brought us here, if He wouldn't care for us, who would? I also told the Lord that we were not going to ask anyone for help, as He would not fail in feeding and caring for us. Praise the Lord! He never failed us, not a single day! Jeremy even received a scholarship to pursue his studies in multimedia and computing when it seemed impossible for us to pay for his tertiary education.

God brought new friends to help us through. On April 21, 2006, a Christian couple gave us a beautiful, clean, newly painted, and fully furnished single-story terrace house to live in. They said that we are the servants of the Lord and could stay there as long as we wanted to. In fact, we only started paying rent to this couple once our situation improved. At one point in time, we were tested to the utmost whereby even making ends meet was a challenge. But thereafter, we saw God's miraculous provision through various ways.

We pressed on day to day, and the Lord was there for us. Ron couldn't concentrate on his teaching job (which he was newly trained for) because there is a higher calling upon his life towards a ministry of prayer, intercession and the writing of *Christformation in You*. He shared with a couple of people regarding his burden to write, but there was no support from anyone at that time. Nevertheless, the Lord reminded me of our prayer before we left Johor Bahru for Kuala Lumpur, and He spoke through the following verse

Romans 12:12:
"Be joyful in hope, patient in affliction, faithful in prayer."

Let me tell you, it wasn't easy doing God's will. Nonetheless, we continued with our fasting and prayer for countless days whenever the Lord burdened our hearts to pray for the nations and the situations around us. With these verses—Jeremiah 1:10; Luke 10:19; Ephesians 6:10–18; and Jeremiah 1:17–19, we continued battling against the forces of the Evil One.

As the years passed, the Lord began to restore us slowly to our former situation while strengthening our faith more and more. We decided to concentrate fully on prayer and writing *Christformation in You*. God didn't want any man to steal His glory, which is why we had to wait for His provision through Ron's Provident Fund to pay for the initial payment of publishing this book. Now it is God's time, and He will make all things beautiful in His time! Praise the Lord! As I look back, I am really thankful and grateful to the LORD for all the testing, trials, impossible moments, and situations that we endured. Through it all, we came out victoriously. We have yet to overcome some hurdles, but we surely will in His time. I am sure the Lord will be there to help us as promised in Psalm 121.

Psalm 121:1–2:

"I lift up my eyes to the mountains—where does my help come from? My help comes from the LORD, the Maker of heaven and earth."

Running the race of Christformation toward full Christformation in me.

Fellow brothers and sisters in the Lord, we are living in the last days! As I have shared my experiences and my walk with the Lord, we are reminded to walk on earth as the Lord Jesus did. If we love Him, we will choose to obey and live for Him and bring glory and honor to the heavenly Father through our lives on this earth.

Luke 9:23–26:

"Then he said to them all: 'Whoever wants to be my disciple must deny themselves and take up their cross daily and follow me. For whoever wants to save their life will lose it, but whoever loses their life for me will save it. What good is it for someone to gain the whole world, and yet lose or forfeit their very self? Whoever is ashamed of me and my words, the Son of Man will be ashamed of them when he comes in his glory and in the glory of the Father and of the holy angels.' "

A reminder to those of us who come from Christian families! You do not become a Christian just because you were born into a Christian family. You need to have that personal acceptance of the Lord Jesus Christ as your Lord and Savior, your born-again experience, and, most importantly, the hunger and thirst for the righteousness of Christ so that the divine nature of Christ will be formed in you permanently.

It isn't easy to live a life that pleases the Lord because we are living in the last days, and Satan is like a roaring lion, waiting to devour us and our faith in the Lord.

2 Timothy 3:1–5:
"But mark this: There will be terrible times in the last days. People will be lovers of themselves, lovers of money, boastful, proud, abusive, disobedient to their parents, ungrateful, unholy, without love, unforgiving, slanderous, without self-control, brutal, not lovers of the good, treacherous, rash, conceited, lovers of pleasure rather than lovers of God—having a form of godliness but denying its power. Have nothing to do with such people."

You have to decide whether you really want Christ to be fully formed in you, because the Lord Jesus doesn't force anyone. He gives you a choice!

Revelation 3:19–22:
"Those whom I love I rebuke and discipline. So be earnest and repent. Here I am! I stand at the door and knock. If anyone hears my voice and opens the door, I will come in and eat with that person, and they with me. To the one who is victorious, I will give the right to sit with me on my throne, just as I was victorious and sat down with my Father on his throne. Whoever has ears, let them hear what the Spirit says to the churches."

Let us not be bogged down by our bitter past, bad experiences, failures, rejections, broken relationships, and whatever else that might cause us to take our eyes off our Lord and Savior, Jesus Christ. I am sure you know that when we stop desiring the pleasures of this world and divert our desires toward the things of God, we are on the right track toward Christformation in us. We have a great race to run and need to fix our eyes on the author and perfecter of our faith and finish the race within the grace period He has given us on this earth.

Hebrews 12:1–3:

"Therefore, since we are surrounded by such a great cloud of witnesses, let us throw off everything that hinders and the sin that so easily entangles. And let us run with perseverance the race marked out for us, fixing our eyes on Jesus, the pioneer and perfecter of faith. For the joy set before him he endured the cross, scorning its shame, and sat down at the right hand of the throne of God. Consider him who endured such opposition from sinners, so that you will not grow weary and lose heart."

Let us encourage one another to grow in the Lord by praying for one another, giving a helping hand to the needy, and walking carefully in our faith in the Lord. The Bible reminds us that "the eyes of the LORD are on the righteous and his ears are attentive to their cry" (Psalm 34:15; 1 Peter 3:12).

Jesus the Great High Priest

Hebrews 4:14–16:

"Therefore, since we have a great high priest who has ascended into heaven, Jesus the Son of God, let us hold firmly to the faith we profess. For we do not have a high priest who is unable to empathize with our weaknesses, but we have one who has been tempted in every way, just as we are—yet he did not sin. Let us then approach God's throne of grace with confidence, so that we may receive mercy and find grace to help us in our time of need."

Beloved brothers and sisters, I hope that my testimony will be a great source of encouragement and a timely reminder that we belong to a loving and living Savior, who is the same yesterday, today, and forever. He will not fail you nor forsake you. My sincere, earnest desire and prayer is that all of us hunger and thirst for Christ to be fully formed in us. May the Good Lord bless and keep you and reveal Himself to you so that Christ will be formed in you fully as you choose to obey him.

Lastly, let me leave you with these words of encouragement from the book of James to all of God's beloved on this earth:

James 1:2–4:
"Consider it pure joy, my brothers, whenever you face trials of many kinds, because you know that the testing of your faith develops perseverance. Perseverance must finish its work so that you may be mature and complete, not lacking anything."

ABOUT THE AUTHORS

Ronald and Christinal Pillai are the writers of *Christformation in You* and speakers for Christformation in You Ministries International. Their written works on Christformation in you have been featured on blogs, websites, and literature. Many have benefited from their ministry worldwide. They are ordained ministers and have jointly ministered in South East Asia for the last thirty-four years since October 1977.

They have planted churches and trained capable and tested leaders to lead God's flock. God's work has multiplied tremendously ever since. Ronald has served as a prison officer while Christinal is a trained medical professional. They have two adult sons, Joshua and Jeremy. Currently, they serve as the editors of Christformation in You Ministries International. They are also involved with the intercessory prayer arm of Christformation ministries, known as International Intercessory Intervention.